ENGLISH H

Highlight 4

Ausgabe B

Cornelsen

ENGLISH H
HIGHLIGHT
BAND 4   AUSGABE B

Im Auftrage des Verlages herausgegeben von

Roderick Cox, Aachen ▪ Raymond Williams, York

Erarbeitet von

David W. Bygott, Oxford ▪ Sydney Thorne, York

Verlagsredaktion

Frank Donoghue (Projektleitung)
Marie Keenoy (verantwortliche Redakteurin)
Sandhya Gupta, Barbara Jung, Murdo MacPhail, Jutta Seuren
und Birgit Herrmann, Aachen (Außenredaktion)

Beratende Mitwirkung

Hans Bebermeier, Bielefeld ▪ Johannes Berning, Münster ▪ Roderick Cox, Aachen
Prof. Dr. Liesel Hermes, Karlsruhe/Koblenz ▪ Ingrid-Barbara Hoffmann, Böblingen
Prof. Dr. Peter W. Kahl, Hamburg ▪ Wolfgang Klingenfeld, Lörrach ▪ Hermann Mohr, Sinsheim
Ingrid Springer, Koblenz ▪ Raymond Williams, York

Grafik

Donald Gott, London
Sue Tewkesbury, Penton Mewsey
Roy Schofield, Cheam
Skip G. Langkafel, Berlin

Umschlaggestaltung

Knut Waisznor

Gestaltung und technische Umsetzung

Heike Freund, Berlin

Bildquellen

s. Verzeichnis auf Seite 160

Zusatzmaterialien zum vorliegenden Schülerbuch

Workbook (Best.-Nr. 78132)
Workbook Lehrerfassung (Best.-Nr. 78140)
Extra Workbook (Best.-Nr. 83543)
Extra Workbook Lehrerfassung (Best.-Nr. 83535)
1 Cassette zum Schülerbuch (Best.-Nr. 78167)
1 CD zum Schülerbuch (Best.-Nr. 78221)
Arbeitsfolien (Best.-Nr. 78175)
Auf weitere Bestandteile wird im Handbuch für den Unterricht (Best.-Nr. 78159) verwiesen.

---

1. Auflage ✔   Druck 5 4 3 2   Jahr 01 2000 99 98

Alle Drucke dieser Auflage können im Unterricht nebeneinander verwendet werden.

© 1997 Cornelsen Verlag, Berlin
Das Werk und seine Teile sind urheberrechtlich geschützt. Jede Verwertung in anderen als den gesetzlich zugelassenen Fällen bedarf deshalb der vorherigen schriftlichen Einwilligung des Verlages.

Druck: Universitätsdruckerei H. Stürtz AG, Würzburg

ISBN 3-464-07812-4

Bestellnummer 78124

gedruckt auf säurefreiem Papier, umweltschonend hergestellt aus chlorfrei gebleichten Faserstoffen

INHALT

Welcome ... **to the club**	Vier Jugendliche aus Sheffield treffen sich in einem Jugendclub	6
UNIT 1 Free time	Über Jugendclubs und Aktivitäten sprechen Vorlieben und Abneigungen formulieren Über Freizeitjobs reden Verabredungen treffen	8

I like playing table-tennis.
Are you good at skiing?
Skiing is an expensive sport.
[It's a good one.]

STORY	Fun at the fair	12
ACTIVE ENGLISH	**ACTIONS** Going out	14
* OPTIONS	**CONTEXTS** At a fair	16
	POEM At the fair	17
	ACTIVITY Make a chart.	
	ACTION CARDS Going out	
PRACTICE PAGES	Structures ▪ Situations ▪ Wordpower ▪ Dictionary	18
	READING From a shopping centre guide	20
	LISTENING An interview	21
SUMMARY	*ing*-Form	22
	[one/ones]	23
* Look Around 1	The Caribbean	24
UNIT 2 Friends	Über Freundschaften sprechen Freizeitaktivitäten mit Freunden planen Sagen, was man (nicht) selbst tun kann Jemanden aufmuntern und Probleme ansprechen	26

We enjoyed ourselves.
They taught themselves inline-skating.
[He's nice, isn't he?]

STORY	A day at Sheffield Ski Village	30
ACTIVE ENGLISH	**ACTIONS** Being a good friend	32
* OPTIONS	**CONTEXTS** Presents for friends	34
	POEMS Good friends	35
	ACTIVITY A message in code	
	ACTION CARDS Being a good friend	
PRACTICE PAGES	Structures ▪ Situations ▪ Wordpower ▪ Dictionary	36
	READING From a magazine for teenagers	38
	LISTENING Best friends	39
SUMMARY	myself, yourself, themselves ...	40
	[... isn't it? / ... aren't they?]	41
* Look Around 2	Australia	42

[ ] Rezeptiv
   (Strukturen, die nur verstanden werden sollen)
 * Fakultativ
   (wahlfreie Bestandteile)

UNIT 3 Young and old	Über das Zusammenleben verschiedener Generationen sprechen	44	*You should be here before 11 pm.*
	Verpflichtungen und Erwartungen ausdrücken		*She shouldn't sing.*
	Über Konflikte sprechen		*[Daniel only thought about*
	Meinungen äußern		*the girl he liked.]*
STORY	The mistake	48	
ACTIVE ENGLISH	**ACTIONS** Talking about TV	50	
* OPTIONS	**CONTEXTS** Film posters	52	
	SONG I want to be free	53	
	ACTIVITY Rules for a happy home		
	ACTION CARDS Talking about TV		
PRACTICE PAGES	Structures ▪ Situations ▪ Wordpower ▪ Dictionary	54	
	READING From a book about a star	56	
	LISTENING When I was young …	57	
SUMMARY	*should*	58	
	[Relativsatz ohne Pronomen]	59	
* Look Around 3	India	60	
UNIT 4 A city project	Über Umweltprobleme und deren Lösungen sprechen	62	*They started making plans.*
	Sagen, wem etwas gehört		*Can I have yours?*
	Einen Standpunkt vertreten		*[The factories were closed.]*
	Auskünfte einholen		
STORY	The demonstration	66	
ACTIVE ENGLISH	**ACTIONS** Getting information	68	
* OPTIONS	**CONTEXTS** Recycling and the environment	70	
	SONG Where do the children play?	71	
	ACTIVITY Do a class survey.		
	ACTION CARDS Getting information		
PRACTICE PAGES	Structures ▪ Situations ▪ Wordpower ▪ Dictionary	72	
	READING From a brochure	74	
	LISTENING A programme about a competition	75	
SUMMARY	*ing*-Form	76	
	Possessivpronomen: mine, yours, …		
	[Das Passiv]	77	
* Look Around 4	Canada	78	

UNIT 5 Choosing a job	Über Berufe und Zukunftspläne sprechen	80	*I'm interested in learning*
	Über Berufspraktika und Arbeitsabläufe reden		*I'm looking forward to*
	Sich um eine Stelle bewerben		*working there.*
			although
STORY	The Coffee Pot	84	*[After she had made the*
ACTIVE ENGLISH	**ACTIONS** Talking about work	86	*coffee, …]*
* OPTIONS	**CONTEXTS** Different jobs	88	
	LIMERICKS Work	89	
	ACTIVITY Job poster		
	ACTION CARDS Talking about work		
PRACTICE PAGES	Structures ▪ Situations ▪ Wordpower ▪ Dictionary	90	
	READING Applying for a job	92	
	LISTENING An interview for work experience	93	
SUMMARY	*ing*-Form	94	
	although		
	[The past perfect]	95	
* Look Around 5	Living abroad	96	
* EXTRA UNIT 1	Joining a club	98	*able to*
	At the swimming-pool	99	*allowed to*
	A group holiday	100	
	The Outdoor Centre	101	
* EXTRA UNIT 2	Dangerous dogs	102	*If we don't ban these dogs,*
	Dogs for people with disabilities	103	*the streets won't be safe.*
	Two newspaper stories	104	
* EXTRA UNIT 3	An alternative lifestyle	106	*We needn't pay for*
	The streets of London	107	*accommodation.*
	A social project	108	
	Letters about *Wheels*	109	
* EXTRA UNIT 4	A new start	110	*They speak very politely.*
	A year later	111	*A modem is used for sending*
	Feeling lonely	112	*e-mail.*
	An inventions quiz	113	
* EXTRA UNIT 5	Times have changed … and jobs too!	114	
	Old jobs, new jobs	115	
	Mobile phones	116	
	Phoning and driving	117	
Anhang	▪ The English alphabet / English sounds	118	
	VOCABULARY	119	
	DICTIONARY	140	
	▪ List of names	156	
	▪ Irregular verbs	158	
	▪ Quellen	160	

Differenzierungshinweis

☐ Leichtere Übung
■■ Schwierigere Übung

Welcome ...

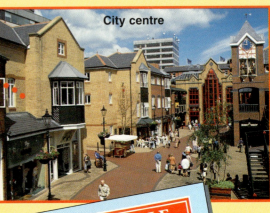

City centre

Sheffield

ABBEYDALE YOUTH CLUB

ABBEYDALE YOUTH CLUB wants new members between 14 and 18.

We meet at 6.30 pm on Tuesdays and Thursdays.

You can do lots of different activities – and every month we organise a trip.

Become a member this week!

 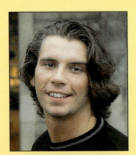  

Marian Kennedy (14)   Alex Barker (16)   Daniel Green (14)   Shellina Akbar (14)

Tip: You can find new words in the *Dictionary* (page 140).

Are you a member of a youth club or another club? Do you like clubs? Say why/why not.

... to the club!

"Hi! It's my first evening at the youth club. I'm new in Sheffield. My name is Alex Barker. What's the club like?"

"Oh, it's fun. You'll like it, Alex. I come here every week. I've made some good friends here. I'm Marian Kennedy."

"Hallo. I'm Daniel Green. I haven't seen you here before. I play the guitar in our rock group. Can you play the guitar? Or can you sing?"

"Yes, I can sing a little. But I'm more interested in computers. That's why I've come to the club. Oh, my name is Shellina Akbar."

Where can you go if you want to make some new friends?
Where did you meet your friends?
Do you play the guitar or can you sing well?
Are you interested in computers? Do you have a computer?

UNIT ONE
Free time

 CLUBS FOR YOUNG PEOPLE

- British schools often have clubs for their students (for example, computer and photography clubs). Members usually meet after lunch or after school.
- There are school sports clubs too – hockey, football, tennis, rugby. School teams play against teams from other schools on Saturday mornings.
- Clubs for young people who are interested in animals or the environment and its problems are very popular. People make friends at clubs.
- Most towns have a youth club. Big cities like Sheffield have lots of youth clubs. Some clubs have a coffee bar and can use a sports hall. Other clubs meet in church halls. They often have discos for members.
- All youth clubs have the same problem: they never have enough money. They usually get money from local councils or from churches.

- What clubs are there for young people in your town or village?

W 1, 1*

A In Abbeydale Youth Club the new members went on a tour with Marian and Daniel. They started in the coffee bar.
"You can buy snacks here," said Daniel. "And tea and coffee, of course."
Next to the coffee bar there was a room for small groups. "We have a computer group," said Marian. "And a group that's interested in photography."
Then they went into the sports hall behind the youth club. "We use the hall for indoor football," explained Marian.

Upstairs they saw the room for fitness training. There were a lot of people in the room, but Shellina wasn't very interested.
"Can we play table-tennis?" she asked.
"Yes, in that room over there you can play darts, snooker and table-tennis," said Daniel. "What about a game of table-tennis later, Shellina?"

EXERCISE 1 ■ **What can you do at the youth club? Work with a partner.**
1 What activities can you do at Abbeydale Youth Club?
2 What rooms are there at the club?

W 1, 2-3

* Die blau gedruckten Verweise bezeichnen den frühestmöglichen Einsatzort der Übungen im Workbook.
W 1, 1 = Workbook Seite 1, Übung 1

B After the tour Daniel and Shellina played table-tennis.
"Hey, you're really good," said Daniel.
"Thanks," said Shellina. "I play in a club at our school.
I like playing table-tennis."
Shellina won the game, 21 to 19.
"Thanks, Shellina," said Daniel. "That was a good game."
"What other sports do you like, Daniel?" asked Shellina.
"Not many. I don't like doing outdoor sports," answered
Daniel. "But I like watching football on TV."

EXERCISE 2 ■ What sports do they like doing?

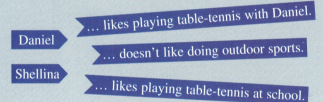

Daniel — ... likes playing table-tennis with Daniel. — ... likes watching football on TV.
      — ... doesn't like doing outdoor sports.
Shellina — ... likes playing table-tennis at school.

What sports do you like doing?
What sports do you like watching?

C

Do you enjoy ...
ice-skating?   tenpin bowling?   skiing?
   inline-skating?   canoeing?

You can do all these activities with the youth club this year!

EXERCISE 3 ■ Do you like these five activities?

I like … ▪ I don't like … ▪ I've never tried …

1 I don't like ice-skating.
2 I …   3 I …   4 I …   5 I …   W 2, 4

✓ **CHECKPOINT**

Sagen, dass du etwas gerne bzw. nicht gerne tust:
I like inline-skating.   Susan enjoys playing tennis in the summer.
I don't like ice-skating.   Sophie and Jack enjoy dancing.

I like playing table-tennis. **9**

D
MARIAN   There's a trip to Sheffield Ski Village next month. Can you ski, Daniel?
DANIEL   Well, I haven't skied very often. Are you good at skiing, Marian?
MARIAN   Well, we had a winter holiday in Scotland last year, and we skied every day. So I'm not bad at skiing.
DANIEL   I'm not good at stopping. I fall over.
MARIAN   I can teach you, Daniel, if you're interested.

W 2, 5

> I'm good at …   I'm not bad at …   I'm not good at …   I've never tried …
> ice-skating · running · inline-skating · sailing · skiing · snowboarding · swimming

E   Marian loves skiing. But skiing is an expensive sport. So she wants to earn some money. She needs a job for a few hours a week – a job that pays well. Every week Marian reads the newspaper at the youth club. But finding a job is very difficult. Most jobs don't pay well.

Here are some jobs for young people who go to school:

babysitting   working in a shop   working in a garden centre   delivering newspapers

EXERCISE 4 ■ What do you think?

Babysitting	is boring.
Working in a shop	is fun.
Working in a garden centre	is hard work.
Delivering newspapers	pays well.
	doesn't pay well.
	is the best job.

> Which is the best job for you? Why?

 CHECKPOINT

> Über eine Tätigkeit oder ein Hobby sprechen:
> I'm good at skiing.   My sister isn't bad at playing darts.
> Babysitting is fun.   Hiking is boring.

F Ray works for the local council. He looks after the youth club. This evening Ray has some good news. Abbeydale Youth Club has just got some money for new equipment from Sheffield City Council. Ray is talking to the members about things in the youth club. Some of the equipment is old and broken.

RAY What about a new dartboard? What do you think?
MARIAN Oh no. We have a dartboard. The black one. It's a good one.
DANIEL But let's buy some new darts. The old ones are terrible. Yes, buy some new darts, Ray.
RAY OK. But we really need new cups in the coffee bar. We have only 22 cups.
DANIEL Then buy 10 new ones. That's enough. And a new football.
MARIAN A new football? Why do you want a new one?
DANIEL The old one isn't very good.

EXERCISE 5 ■ **Is the equipment old or new?**

> an old one • a new one
> old ones • new ones

1 RAY Look, this telephone is really old. Let's get ...

2 MARIAN The chairs are OK. We don't need ... this year.

3 DANIEL We bought this table-tennis table last summer. It's new. It isn't ...

4 DANIEL But these balls are terrible. They're ... We can't play with them.

W 2, 6

G
ALEX Are you leaving already, Shellina? It's only 9 o'clock.
SHELLINA Yes, I have to go home. I'm sure my brother is waiting for me outside.
ALEX Bye, Shellina. Don't forget the fair at Endcliffe Park. I'll be there with Marian and Daniel on Friday.
SHELLINA OK, see you there, perhaps. Bye!

DANIEL She's very nice.
MARIAN Stop talking about Shellina. You don't even know her.
DANIEL Oops, sorry, Marian. I've brought you this newspaper. Look at page 9. There are some good jobs.
MARIAN There won't be any good ones in the newspaper.
DANIEL There *is* a good one. Look!

DO YOU LIKE SKIING?
ARE YOU OVER 14?
Work six hours a week at
Sheffield SKI VILLAGE
and you can ski for free!
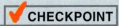
Phone Sheffield Ski Village.

✓ **CHECKPOINT**

one, ones
Which football do you want? – The new one.   Which jeans did you buy? – The black ones.
Is this your snowboard? – Yes, it's a good one.   The old darts are missing. – Use the new ones.

It's a good one.   **11**

STORY

Which members of the youth club will become boyfriend and girlfriend?

Fun at the fair

"Wow!" Daniel shouted. "Ah!" Alex said. They were sitting in a car on the *Voyager*, high above the fair. Like the other people in the cars, they were upside down!

5 Marian was with them. "Are you two feeling OK?" she asked.
Daniel laughed. "Of course. It's great!"
When the *Voyager* stopped, Alex looked ill.
"I didn't like being upside down," he said.
10 "I ate a big hamburger just before we got on."

"Look," Marian said, "over there, near the funny mirrors. There's Shellina."
Suddenly Alex felt better. He liked Shellina.
"Hey, Shellina!" he shouted.
15 "Hi, everybody," Shellina said.
"Let's go in here. OK?" Daniel said.
When Marian saw Shellina in the first mirror, she laughed. "You look so tall!"
When they came to the next mirror, Shellina
20 said, "Oh no! You look so fat, Marian!"

After that, they stopped at the darts stall. "I'm good at playing darts," Marian said. "I'll win a dog for you, Daniel." She paid for some darts and threw them. She wasn't really interested in winning a dog. And she didn't win anything. 25
She wanted to show how clever she was.
"Perhaps *I* can win one," Daniel said.
"Oh, let's go to a different stall. The dogs aren't really that great," Marian said.
"I think they're nice," Shellina said. 30
Daniel threw some darts – and he was lucky. He won a small, soft dog.
"Here you are, Marian," he said. "It's for you."
Marian said, "Oh, I don't really want it. You can have it, Shellina." 35
Daniel was disappointed when he heard this – but Shellina was happy.
Then they came to the ghost train.
"Come on," said Marian to Daniel.
They bought their tickets. 40

Their car started very fast and went through a door. Suddenly it was dark. Marian put her hand on Daniel's arm. A ghost jumped out in front of them. Then they saw a tall pink monster with green teeth and red eyes. Daniel put his hand on Marian's hand, and they kissed …

When the car stopped, they opened their eyes and got out. Their friends were waiting.
"That was exciting!" Daniel said.
"Yes, very exciting," Marian said.
Alex looked at Shellina. "Do you want to go on the ghost train?" Shellina didn't like Alex as much as Daniel, but she said, "Why not?" Alex and Shellina paid for their tickets.

They laughed when they saw all the ghosts and monsters. But there was no kissing. Alex was disappointed.
When they got out of the car, somebody phoned Shellina. It was Iqbal, her brother.
"It's late, Shellina," he said. "I'll meet you in ten minutes. I'll walk home with you."
"It isn't very late," Alex said.
"But my parents think it's late," Shellina explained. "They always worry when I'm not at home."
Marian wanted to go through the *Tunnel of Love* with her new boyfriend. Alex didn't wait for them. He bought a bag of chips and ate them on the way home.

TASK A ■ **Finish the sentences.**
1 When Alex got out of the car, he looked …
2 At the darts stall, Marian wanted to show how …
3 Marian wasn't really so good at …
4 Daniel was lucky and won …
5 Marian didn't really want …
6 On the ghost train, Marian put …
7 After the ghost train, Iqbal …
8 Iqbal wanted to walk …
9 Shellina's parents always worry …
10 Alex ate some …

TASK B ■■ **Why do you think …**
1 … Alex felt better when he saw Shellina?
2 … Marian wanted to throw the darts?
3 … Shellina was happy when Daniel gave her the dog?
4 … Marian and Daniel enjoyed the ghost train?
5 … Shellina didn't really want to go on the ghost train with Alex?
6 … Iqbal phoned Shellina?
7 … Alex went home without his friends?

W 3, 7-9

ACTIVE ENGLISH

ACTIONS Going out

Are Lisa and Imran going to make a date?

LISA   Can we do something together on Saturday morning?
IMRAN On Saturday morning? No, I'm sorry I can't.
LISA   That's a pity. Why not?
IMRAN I have to go to the mosque.
LISA   What about Saturday afternoon?
IMRAN I have to visit my grandmother in hospital.

EXERCISE 1 ■ Make more dialogues about a date.

YOU   Can we do something together on …?
A PARTNER On …? No, I'm sorry. I can't.
YOU   That's a pity. Why not?
A PARTNER I have to …
YOU   What about …?
A PARTNER I have to …

> write a letter ■ babysit
> visit my grandmother
> tidy my room ■ go to church
> work in the garden centre
> play hockey ■ …

What does Ann want to do?

ANN   What are you doing on Saturday evening?
STEVE I haven't made any plans. Why?
ANN   Would you like to go to the cinema with me?
STEVE Yes. That's cool.

EXERCISE 2 ■ Make more dialogues.

YOU   What are you doing on … evening?
A PARTNER On … evening? I haven't made any plans. Why?
YOU   Would you like to … with me?
A PARTNER Yes. That's cool.

> play some computer games
> listen to my new CDs
> go ice-skating ■ go to a disco
> go tenpin bowling ■ …

EXERCISE 3 ■■ Make a dialogue with a friend from Britain.

- Can we do something together on …?
- That's a pity. Why not?
- What are you doing on …?
- Would you like to … with me?

- No, I'm sorry. I can't.
- I have to …
- I haven't made any plans. Why?
- Yes. That's cool.

Where should they meet?

GARY Where should we meet?
JILL Let's meet at the bus station.
GARY OK, at the bus station.
JILL Or should we meet outside the football stadium?
GARY Yes. Let's meet outside the stadium.

EXERCISE 4 ■ Make two dialogues. Ask about a place. Use the words in the boxes.

YOU Where should we meet?
A PARTNER Let's meet at the …
YOU OK, at the …
A PARTNER Or should we meet …?
YOU Yes. Let's meet …

church hall · bus station · cinema
football stadium · town hall

at · outside · in

When are they going to meet?

SUE I have two tickets for the match on Friday. Would you like to come with me?
TIM Yes, great. When does it start?
SUE At 7.30.
TIM When should we meet? At 7 o'clock?
SUE Mm. That's too late. Let's say at 6.30.
TIM That's too early for me. Let's say at 6.45.

EXERCISE 5 ■ Make more dialogues. Ask about a time.

YOU When does the film / the fair start?
A PARTNER At …
YOU When should we meet? At …?
A PARTNER Mm. That's too late. Let's say at …
YOU That's too early for me. Let's say at …

EXERCISE 6 ☐ Make a date with a friend from Britain.

Frage, wo ihr euch treffen sollt.
▼
Schlage vor, dass ihr euch am Kino trefft.
▼
Frage, wann ihr euch treffen sollt.
▼
Schlage vor, dass ihr euch um 18.45 Uhr trefft.

EXERCISE 7 ■■ Make a date with a friend from Britain.

Frage, ob ihr am Freitag etwas unternehmen könnt.
▼
Sage, dass es dir Leid tut. Du musst am Freitag deinen Onkel besuchen. Frage, wie es am Samstag wäre.
▼
Sage, dass du keine Pläne gemacht hast. Frage, ob er/sie ein Basketballspiel sehen möchte.
▼
Sage, dass du das toll findest. Schlage vor, dass ihr euch am Stadion trefft. Frage, wann ihr euch treffen sollt. Schlage 19.30 Uhr vor.
▼
Sage, dass das zu spät ist. Schlage 19.15 Uhr vor.

W 4, 10-11

* ACTIVE ENGLISH OPTIONS

* CONTEXTS At a fair

Here are some stalls and signs at a fair in Sheffield.

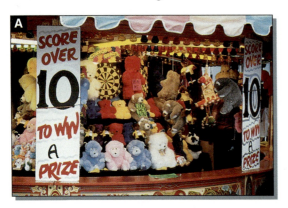

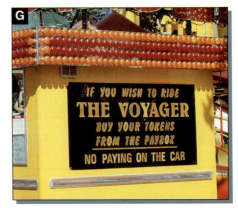

Which sentence belongs to which photo (A-G)?
1. Throw a ring around a toy and you can have it.
2. On Saturday the fair opens at 2 pm.
3. First you must pay. Then you can get into the car.
4. A good game for Robin Hood?
5. If you score 9 here, you can't have a prize.
6. Stop here if you're hungry at the fair.
7. If you throw a ball into a bucket – and if it stays there – you'll win a prize.

16   * Fakultativ

Practice makes perfect!

Cassette/CD zum Lehrbuch
Mit der Cassette bzw. CD zu HIGH-LIGHT 4B kann man das Hörverstehen trainieren. Texte, Dialoge, Lieder, Hörverständnistexte werden von *native speakers* vorgetragen. So lässt sich der Unterrichtsstoff zu Hause in Ruhe wiederholen und festigen.

Extra-Cassette
Zu den fünf Extra-Units im Buch gibt es eine Extra-Cassette mit allen Texten.

English Coach
Das Computerprogramm *English Coach* hilft beim Vokabeltraining: Aufgaben, Übungen und Tests sind abwechslungsreich gestaltet und genau auf HIGH-LIGHT 4B abgestimmt.

Weitere Angebote gibt es auf der Rückseite dieser Karte.

Bestellkarte

Hiermit bestelle ich zur Lieferung durch Nachnahme. Preis zuzüglich Porto (ca. 3,50 DM), Nachnahmegebühr (ca. 5,— DM), Zustellgebühr (ca. 3,— DM).

English H Highlight Band 4B
- ☐ **Cassette** Best.-Nr. 78167 ca. 70 Min. ◇ 29,80 DM
- ☐ **CD** Best.-Nr. 78221 ca. 70 Min. ◇ 39,80 DM
- ☐ **Extra-Cass.** Best.-Nr. 83551 ca. 60 Min. ◇ 29,80 DM
- ☐ **Diskette: English Coach, Vokabeltrainer, zu Band 4B** Für PC 3,5". Best.-Nr. 921662 ◇ 78,— DM

Cornelsen English Grammar, Ausgabe B
- ☐ **Grammar** 144 Seiten Bestellnr. 51471 21,90 DM
- ☐ **Practice Book** 144 Seiten Bestellnr. 52397 19,80 DM

Das Oxford Schulwörterbuch (Cornelsen & Oxford) ca. 768 Seiten.
- ☐ **kartoniert** Best.-Nr. 27686 ca. 21,90 DM
- ☐ **gebunden** Best.-Nr. 27678 ca. 25,— DM

Cornelsen English Library
- ☐ **Roads to Success** Best.-Nr. 53334 8,90 DM
- ☐ **Teenage Detectives** Best.-Nr. 53369 8,90 DM
- ☐ **Lake District Camp** Best.-Nr. 68048 8,90 DM

Gewünschtes bitte in dem entsprechenden Kästchen deutlich ankreuzen. Alle Titel können auch durch den Buchhandel zum Ladenpreis ohne die Postgebühren bezogen werden.
Preisstand 1.1.1998. Änderungen vorbehalten. ◇ = Unverbindliche Preisempfehlung.

**Cornelsen English Grammar –
Ausgabe B mit Practice Book**
Diese zweisprachige Grammatik ist zum Nachschlagen und Wiederholen gut geeignet. Sie stellt anschaulich und leicht verständlich alle wichtigen Strukturen der englischen Grammatik dar.
Das *Practice Book* bietet vielfältige Übungen unterschiedlichen Schwierigkeitsgrades zu allen Grammatikkapiteln. Ein Lösungsheft liegt bei.

Das Oxford Schulwörterbuch
Deutsch-Englisch/Englisch-Deutsch.
Das Wörterbuch berücksichtigt gezielt die Bedürfnisse deutschsprachiger Lernender und präsentiert den Wortschatz klar und übersichtlich. Es bietet:
- ca. 27.000 Stichwörter;
- farbige Hervorhebung von wichtigen Konstruktionen, *Idioms, Phrasal Verbs* und zusammengesetzten Begriffen;
- Beispielsätze für unterschiedliche Bedeutungen eines Wortes;
- 32 farbige Bildseiten, die thematischen Wortschatz präsentieren;
- typografische Hervorhebung von grammatischen Informationen;
- ein Verweissystem für zusammenhängende Begriffe;
- im deutsch-englischen Teil Hinweise auf die englische Aussprache sowie auf unregelmäßige Verben, Adjektive und Substantive.

Cornelsen English Library:

Roads to Success
Zwei lebensnahe Geschichten über die Schwierigkeiten, mit denen Schulabgänger/innen konfrontiert werden, und deren Bemühungen um eine bessere Zukunft.

Teenage Detectives
Zwei Geschichten. Ein Mädchen, Computerfan, gerät in den Verdacht, Schuleigentum beschädigt zu haben. Sie findet die Täter – das Problem wird gemeinsam gelöst. Zwei Jungen decken einen Drogenring auf.

Lake District Camp
Miteinander auskommen, Spaß haben und die Landschaft entdecken sind einige der Herausforderungen für eine Gruppe von Jugendlichen auf einem Abenteuerurlaub im Lake District.

Bitte in Druckschrift ausfüllen

Name / Vorname

Straße / Hausnummer

Postleitzahl / Ort

Ort / Datum

Unterschrift des / der Erziehungsberechtigten

Bitte freimachen

Antwortkarte

Cornelsen

Cornelsen Verlag
Postfach 110167

10831 Berlin

* POEM At the fair

Look in a tall–short mirror,
You won't believe your eyes.
Throw some darts at a board –
Perhaps you'll win a prize.

Ride on modern carousels,
That spin you round and round.
Climb slowly to the sky –
Then fall towards the ground.

Feel happy, ill or frightened,
You'll still know why you're there.
And you'll always come again –
For a day out at the fair.

* ACTIVITY Make a chart.

Work in four groups. Each group asks the students in the class about their activities in their free time. Your group can ask about:
- jobs for students, sports, clubs or favourite activities at the fair.

Collect the information and then make a bar chart or a pie chart.

Tell the class about the information that you've collected. Use your bar chart or pie chart.

* ACTION CARDS Going out

- Make action cards with useful words and phrases from this unit. Your cards can have phrases about:
  Activities ▪ Places ▪ Times
  Saying 'yes'/'no' to a date.

- Write the English word or phrase on one side and the German word or phrase on the other side. Suggestion: Draw a picture on each card.

PRACTICE PAGES

STRUCTURES

EXERCISE 1 ■ What are these activities?

EXERCISE 2 ■ Free time: What other activities do you know?

Playing …   Watching …   Visiting …   Buying …   …

EXERCISE 3 ■ What activities is Daniel good at? (✓ = is good at   ✗ = isn't good at)

1 He's good at playing table-tennis.   2 He isn't …

EXERCISE 4 ☐ Free time: What do you think about these activities?

1 Phoning friends …   4 Going to parties …
2 Going to a fair …   5 Meeting friends in town …
3 Surfing the Internet …   6 Watching sport on TV …

is fun.   *is boring.*   *is expensive.*   *is OK.*

EXERCISE 5 ■■ What does Jenny think of these jobs for young people?

1 Working in a shop is boring but it pays well.   3 …
2 Babysitting is fun and …   4 …

1

SITUATIONS

Anna spricht kein Englisch. Kannst du für sie dolmetschen?

1 Ich fahre sehr gern Ski.
2 Ich kann nicht gut Darts spielen.
3 Ich kümmere mich um den Jugendclub.
4 Eine Stelle zu finden ist sehr schwierig.
5 Das ist zu spät.

1 She loves …
2 She …
3 She …
4 Finding …
5 That's …

Tip: Look again at pages 8-15.

WORDPOWER

WORDPOWER 1 ■ What's the wrong word in the group? Say why.

1 reading, mirror, taking photos, playing darts, singing
2 Belfast, Sheffield, Scotland, Birmingham
3 skiing, teaching, babysitting, delivering newspapers
4 snowboarding, going to the fair, skiing, swimming
5 football stadium, sports hall, youth club, inline-skating

a city ▪ a hobby ▪ a job
a place ▪ a sport

1 mirror: It isn't a hobby.
2 …: It isn't a …

WORDPOWER 2 ■ Write the sports in the right lists.

tennis ▪ football ▪ hiking
ice-skating ▪ mountain-biking
inline-skating ▪ rugby ▪ sailing
skiing ▪ snowboarding ▪ swimming
table-tennis ▪ tenpin bowling

ball sports	outdoor sports	indoor sports
tennis	tennis	tennis
…	…	…

WORDPOWER 3 ■■ Make a word web.

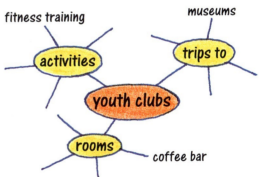

USING A DICTIONARY

DICTIONARY 1 ■ Put these words in alphabetical order.

training ▪ climbing ▪ rescuing ▪ pushing ▪ drowning

1 climbing
2 …

DICTIONARY 2 ■■ Use your dictionary.
Find these verbs in your dictionary:

climb
train ▪ rescue
drown ▪ push

Which words go together?

climbing ▪ training
rescuing ▪ drowning
pushing

Retten ▪ Klettern
Schieben ▪ Dressieren
Ertrinken

PRACTICE PAGES

READING From a shopping centre guide

Tip: You can find new words in the Dictionary (page 140).

WELCOME TO
MEADOWHALL

A GREAT DAY OUT

SHOPS – SHOPS – AND MORE SHOPS

You'll find over 270 shops, from famous, big department stores to small boutiques.

FOOD – DRINKS – FUN

But **Meadowhall** means much more than only shopping. In the **Oasis**, you can eat and drink in a French café, a Greek bar or a Mexican restaurant. Then listen to the musicians in the shopping streets. Finish your day with a visit to the cinema. It shows 11 different films.

BY CAR – BY TRAM

Meadowhall shopping centre is between Sheffield and the M1 motorway.
Travel from the city centre to Meadowhall by **Supertram** – Britain's most modern tram.

OPENING TIMES SHOPS	
Monday – Thursday	9 am – 8 pm
Friday	9 am – 9 pm
Saturday	9 am – 7 pm
Sunday	11 am – 5 pm

A GREAT DAY OUT – 7 DAYS A WEEK

You'll soon understand why over 30 million people come to **Meadowhall** every year. Have a great day out – indoor shopping, eating out, relaxing. And there are lots of games for your children!

EXERCISE 1 ■ Basic reading: What's right?
1 The guide *tells you / doesn't tell you* where *Meadowhall* is.
2 It *tells you / doesn't tell you* when *Meadowhall* is open.
3 It *shows you / doesn't show you* how you find your way from the car park to the shops.

EXERCISE 2 ■ Reading for details: These sentences are wrong. But what's right?
1 *Meadowhall* is in Sheffield city centre.
2 There are only big department stores in *Meadowhall*.
3 You can only eat British food there.
4 The cinema can show six films.
5 Not many people come to *Meadowhall* every year.

EXERCISE 3 ■ Language tasks: Find words for … Tip: All the words are on page 20.
1 having a meal in a restaurant
2 Britain's most modern tram
3 people who play music
4 everybody knows it
5 a small shop for clothes
6 a big road for fast traffic

LISTENING An interview
The *Radio Sheffield Show:* Four teenagers are talking about their weekend jobs.

EXERCISE 1 ■ Find the right job, (A-D).
1 Katy: Job …
2 Matthew: Job …
3 Joanna: Job …
4 Thomas: Job …

A
We are looking for:
Young People
to work
six hours a week.
Ski for free.
Phone: 697 40 02

B
We need a
Shop Assistant
Ask in the shop.

C
DELIVER NEWSPAPERS
(BOY OR GIRL)
ASK IN SHOP

D
BABYSIT FOR 2 CHILDREN AGE SIX AND FOUR
PHONE 454987

EXERCISE 2 ■■ First read the questions. Then listen, and answer them.
1 Does Katy work on Sundays?
   What does Katy sell?
2 Does Matthew like his work?
   Where does Matthew work?
3 Does Joanna earn £1.50 an hour?
   When does Joanna get extra money?
4 Does Thomas do his job after school?
   What does Thomas think of his job?

Weitere Fragen: W 36

SUMMARY

ing-Form

Manchmal willst du über eine Tätigkeit, eine Gewohnheit oder ein Hobby sprechen.

Inline-skating is Tom's hobby. Sophie loves swimming.

Waiting for a bus is boring.   Es ist langweilig auf einen Bus zu warten.
Making new friends is easy at a youth club.   Es ist einfach im Jugendklub neue Freunde zu finden.
Amy's favourite sport is windsurfing.   Windsurfen ist Amys Lieblingssport.
Her parents' hobby is sailing.   Das Hobby ihrer Eltern ist Segeln.

Du gebrauchst die *ing*-Form nach:

> good at
> not bad at
> interested in

Rebecca is good at skiing.   Sam likes old cars.
He's interested in repairing them.

Are you good at drawing?   Kannst du gut zeichnen?
The boys aren't bad at running.   Die Jungen sind nicht schlecht im Laufen.

Die *ing*-Form folgt oft auf:

> like • enjoy
> love • hate
> start • stop
> try

Emma enjoys writing e-mail messages on her computer.   She likes getting e-mail messages from her friends in other towns.

one – ones

Mit *one/ones* kann man Wortwiederholungen vermeiden.

one ersetzt ein Substantiv im Singular.	*ones* ersetzt ein Substantiv im Plural.
Jack's snowboard is old. He wants to buy a new ~~snowboard~~. He wants to buy a new one.	All the table-tennis balls are broken. Jane needs some new ~~table-tennis balls~~. Jane needs some new ones.

Achte auf die deutsche Übersetzung der folgenden englischen Sätze:

Jill has two dogs, an old one and a young one.
   Jill hat zwei Hunde, einen alten und einen jungen.
Which is your bag? – The red one near the door.
   Welches ist deine Tasche? – Die rote neben der Tür.
Which bike belongs to you? – The small one.
   Welches Fahrrad gehört dir? – Das kleine.
Don't buy small bottles. Big ones are cheaper.
   Kaufe keine kleinen Flaschen. Große sind billiger.

IN DIESER UNIT HAST DU GELERNT, ...

… wie du über Hobbys, Gewohnheiten und andere Tätigkeiten sprichst.	➡ *Hiking is fun – in good weather.* *My favourite sport is swimming.*
… wie du über Vorlieben oder Abneigungen sprichst.	➡ *My dad likes cooking.* *He doesn't enjoy washing up.*
… zu sagen, was jemand (nicht) gut kann.	➡ *My youngest sister is good at reading.* *But she isn't good at writing.*
… wie man Wortwiederholungen vermeidet.	➡ *The blue shirt is nicer than the pink one.* *Which are your trainers? – The old ones.*
wie du für ein geplantes Treffen	
… den Treffpunkt vorschlagen kannst.	➡ *Let's meet outside the football stadium.*
… die Uhrzeit verabreden kannst.	➡ *Let's say at 7 o'clock.*

*LOOK AROUND 1
The Caribbean

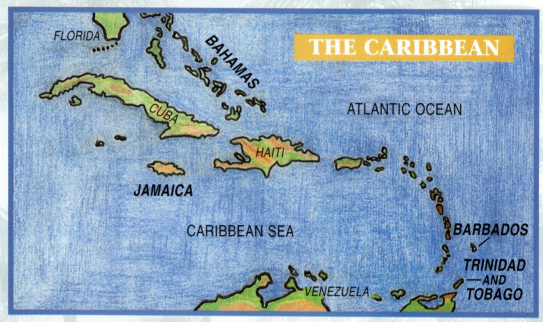

The Caribbean Islands are a group of island states between North and South America. The largest islands where people speak English are Barbados, Jamaica, Trinidad and Tobago and the Bahamas.

The Caribbean Islands are always warm and it rains a lot. Many people from Britain go to the Caribbean on holiday.

The people who live in the Caribbean have to work and go to school in the hottest hours of the day.

More than two million people live on the island of Jamaica. About 85% are Afro-Caribbean.

LINDA I live on the island of Jamaica. We speak English and Creole. At school I speak English. At home I speak Creole.

TREVOR and RAS The food in the Caribbean is special. We have lots of fruit.

Many Afro-Caribbean people went to Britain between 1950 and 1960. Britain needed more people for jobs in some industries.

DONNA My grandfather came to Britain in 1955. He became a bus driver. Other Afro-Caribbean people got jobs that didn't pay well.
Today over 500,000 Afro-Caribbean people live in Britain. Now many of us have better jobs.

NEVILLE In 1966 a group of Afro-Caribbean people from Trinidad and Tobago missed their old homes and families and friends. They wanted to have a Caribbean carnival in London. That's how the Notting Hill Carnival started. Caribbean music is popular in Britain today. My band plays reggae.

UNIT TWO
Friends

At the fountain in the city centre

 GOING OUT IN SHEFFIELD

- You can travel around the city by Supertram or by bus. One Supertram can carry 250 passengers. Children under 16 pay only 30p for a Supertram ticket.
- Sheffield has 5 cinemas. They're all multiscreen. Each cinema shows 5 or 6 films. If you're under 16, a cinema ticket costs £3.
- Some young people in Sheffield spend a lot of time at *Meadowhall* shopping centre. They meet their friends there, have a coffee together or go window-shopping.
- Another popular meeting place for teenagers is the fountain in the city centre.
- There are 19 clubs in Sheffield where people can dance. You must be 18 if you want to go to a club.

- What places are popular with teenagers in your town or village?
- How much do you have to pay for tram/bus/cinema tickets?
- What are the rules in your favourite discos?

W 8, 1

A On Saturday Daniel Green ate his lunch in 10 minutes. Then he took the bus into Sheffield city centre. He hurried past Tudor Square, where he often met his friends.
"I don't want to meet them today," he thought.
"I don't want to be late for my date."

A girl was at the fountain.
"Hi, Daniel," Marian said. "Do you still want to go to the cinema?"
"Yes, of course," said Daniel. "Let's take the Supertram to *Meadowhall*. We can go to the multiscreen cinema there. Then we can go window-shopping later."
"Great," Marian said.

What do you do on Saturday afternoons?
Where do you go if you have a date?

3 After the film Daniel and Marian went window-shopping. Marian saw a cheap hat that she liked. They went into the shop and Marian tried the hat on. Daniel looked at her. "Cool. It looks great," he said. Marian looked at herself in a mirror. "Are you sure?" she asked. "Yes," said Daniel. "Buy it." Marian bought the hat.

W 8, 2

> Do you ask your friends before you buy new clothes?
> Do you and your friends sometimes buy the same clothes?

C Later Marian and Daniel sat in a café. Daniel bought himself a coffee and a cola for Marian.

DANIEL You're good at skiing. Did your mum teach you?
MARIAN No, I taught myself.

DANIEL Wow! I can teach myself songs on the guitar. But skiing?

MARIAN It's easy. I can give you a book. Then you can teach yourself.

> What games/sports/hobbies/songs/… have you taught yourself?

D On the tram back to the city centre, Marian looked out of the window. She saw Sheffield Ski Village. "Look. Over there!" she said to Daniel. "That's where we'll be next Saturday." Daniel looked and thought, "Hmm … I know she'll enjoy herself. She's good at skiing. But what about me?" Daniel didn't want to hurt himself. "What's it like if you fall over on a dry ski slope? Does it hurt?" he asked Marian.
"Oh no. Don't worry. You won't hurt yourself. I'll be there. I can help you," she laughed.

EXERCISE 1 ■ On the Supertram: What's the right word?
1 "Stop looking at (yourself/herself) in the window. Your hat looks cool," Daniel laughed.
2 Marian enjoyed (myself/herself). Her date with Daniel was fun.
3 "I mustn't forget that book. Daniel can teach (yourself/himself) skiing," thought Marian.
4 "Did you teach (myself/yourself) the guitar?" asked Marian.
5 "Yes. First I bought (herself/myself) a book. Then it was easy. But skiing!" he answered.
6 "Stop worrying. You won't hurt (yourself/himself)," Marian laughed.

✓ **CHECKPOINT**

myself, himself, herself, yourself
David looked at himself in the mirror.
Did you enjoy yourself at the club?
Anne bought herself a computer magazine.
I hurt myself on the ski slope last year.

She looked at herself in a mirror. **27**

E Marian and Daniel became good friends. They taught themselves inline-skating. They often talked on their mobile phones. They even earned some money together, when they babysat for neighbours. They sometimes argued. But they usually enjoyed themselves. They almost forgot their other friends.

> People enjoy themselves at the cinema / the fair / …

F Marian and Daniel didn't go to the youth club so often.

SHELLINA Daniel isn't here again. Do you think he's ill?
ALEX No. I'm sure he's with Marian – again. But we can enjoy ourselves without them. We can have a coffee together before the next computer game.
RAY Are you waiting for coffee?
SHELLINA Yes, we are. Two, please.
RAY Here you are. Help yourselves to milk and sugar.
ALEX Thanks.

EXERCISE 2 ■ **Put in the missing word.**

> ourselves ▪ yourselves ▪ themselves

1 Marian and Daniel earned some money.
So they bought … some cheap CDs.
2 Daniel met Alex. "Did you and Shellina enjoy … at the youth club?" he asked.
3 "Yes," Alex said. "But we enjoy … more when you and Marian come to the club."
4 "I hope Marian and Daniel don't hurt … on the slopes," said Marian's mum.
5 "Here's £5. Buy … lunch with this money," said her dad.
6 "Thanks, Dad," said Marian. "Now we'll really enjoy … on Saturday."   W 8, 3

EXERCISE 3 ■ **Write these sentences in the right order.**
1 a mobile phone / bought himself / Mr Akbar
2 to biscuits / can / Everybody / help themselves
3 enjoy ourselves / When / we always / we're in Sheffield
4 Three people / at Sheffield Ski Village / hurt themselves
5 look at yourself / If you / in a funny mirror / want to laugh

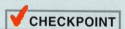 **CHECKPOINT**

> *ourselves, yourselves, themselves*
> Is snooker a difficult game? – No. We taught ourselves snooker in one evening.
> Can we have some ketchup, please? – Here you are. Help yourselves.
> My parents built our garage themselves.

G When Shellina left the youth club, her brother walked home with her. She didn't say much.

EXERCISE 4 ■ **Finish the sentences.**

isn't he? (2x) ■ isn't she?
isn't it? ■ aren't they? (2x)

1 Shellina's youth club is in Sheffield, …?
2 Iqbal is Shellina's brother, …?
3 Shellina is interested in computers, …?
4 Iqbal and Shellina are brother and sister, …?
5 When Daniel and Marian go to the club, their friends are happier, …?
6 Daniel is Marian's boyfriend, …?

H When Shellina got home, her grandmother was waiting for her.

GRANDMA Did you have a nice time, Shellina?
SHELLINA It was OK, Grandma. But Daniel wasn't there again.
GRANDMA You like him, don't you?
SHELLINA Yes, I do. But Daniel is always with Marian.
GRANDMA They spend a lot of time together, don't they?
SHELLINA Yes, they do. And she's organising a youth club trip to Sheffield Ski Village. I'd like to go. But dad always says no, doesn't he? He thinks I'm still a baby.
GRANDMA Perhaps he'll listen to me.

EXERCISE 5 ■ **Make questions.**

Shellina likes Daniel,
Alex goes to the youth club,
Most parents worry too much,
Cinema tickets cost too much,
Marian likes skiing and skating,

doesn't she?
doesn't he?
don't they?

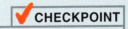

✓ **CHECKPOINT**

Die Frageanhängsel *isn't it? / doesn't he? / don't they?* usw. entsprechen dem deutschen „nicht wahr?", „oder?", „gell?" usw.

It's expensive in this café, isn't it?
Your dad plays the guitar, doesn't he?
Dogs are good pets, aren't they?
English people drink a lot of tea, don't they?

He's nice, isn't he? 29

STORY

Skiing wasn't Daniel's only problem on the ski slopes ...

A day at Sheffield Ski Village

OUR SLOPES:
the blue slope
• easy
the red slope
• more difficult
the black slope
• the most difficult

LIFT PASS PRICES
9.00 am – 10.00 pm
	Adult	Under 16
Two hours	£9.00	£6.00
Four hours	£11.00	£9.00

Free equipment with lift pass.

It was Saturday, the day of the visit to Sheffield Ski Village. Marian was very happy in the youth club minibus. But Daniel was nervous. "Marian is good at skiing, but I'm not good at it. I'll leave this place in an ambulance, I'm sure," he thought.
The teenagers got out of the bus. They put on their ski equipment. Then they waited at the ski-lift. Marian and Daniel went up together.
"Come on, Daniel!" said Marian, when they were at the top. "Let's go down the red slope."
"The red slope is too difficult for me," said Daniel. "I can only ski on the blue one. It's easier, isn't it?"
But Marian didn't hear him. She was already skiing down the red slope.
Then Shellina got off the ski-lift. "I'll come with you down the blue slope, Daniel, if you like," she said. "Thanks, Shellina," said Daniel. "It's silly, I know, but I'm frightened. I prefer to go down with somebody," he said.

Shellina and Daniel went down the blue slope together. "That was great!" said Daniel.
"Let's do it again," said Shellina. She liked being with Daniel.
They waited for the next ski-lift. Marian came towards the ski-lift. "I'll come with you this time, Daniel!" she shouted. But Daniel and Shellina were already going up together on the ski-lift. Marian looked very unhappy.

The youth club members met in the café for lunch. When Marian came in, Shellina and Daniel were sitting together. Marian wanted to sit next to Daniel. "I'm sorry," said Shellina. "There's no room."

Marian looked angry. "Oh, yes there is," she said, and she sat on Daniel's knee.
Daniel wanted to say something nice to Marian. "You ski really well, Marian," he said. "Go down the red slope again after lunch. I'll watch you."
"The red slope is too easy," said Marian. "I can go down the black slope. It's the most difficult one."
"The black one? I bet you can't!" said Shellina.
"I can!" said Marian. "I'll show you!"
After lunch, she went up on the ski-lift. Then she started skiing down the black slope.

She went faster and faster. And then, suddenly, she fell over and hurt herself. "Ow! My leg!" she screamed. An instructor helped Marian. "She has hurt herself!" he shouted. "She'll need an ambulance. I'll phone the hospital."

Daniel and Shellina waited for the ambulance with Marian. "I'm sorry, Marian," said Daniel. "I haven't spent much time with you today. But you know I can't ski well."
"And I wasn't nice to you in the café," said Shellina. "I'm sorry."
"Well, it's my fault too," said Marian. "I was showing off when I tried the black slope."
The ambulance came. Daniel helped Marian into it.
"I'll come with you," said Daniel.
And he thought, "I'm leaving this place in an ambulance. I knew it!"

TASK A ■ **Who did what? Start each sentence with the right name(s): Marian, Shellina, Daniel.**
1 … travelled together in the minibus.
2 … was nervous in the minibus.
3 … went down the red slope.
4 … wanted to go down with somebody.
5 … was sitting next to Daniel in the café.
6 … sat on Daniel's knee.
7 … wanted to show off on the black slope.
8 … hurt herself.
9 … said sorry.

TASK B ■■ **Why?**
1 Daniel wanted to ski with somebody because *he was nervous*.
2 In the café, Marian was angry because …
3 Marian went down the black slope because …
4 Marian needed an ambulance because …
5 Shellina was sorry because …
6 Daniel went with Marian in the ambulance because …

W 10, 6-8

ACTIVE ENGLISH

ACTIONS Being a good friend

Can David cheer Molly up?

DAVID Cheer up, Molly. You look down.
MOLLY I don't feel great.
DAVID What about going to the cinema? That'll cheer you up.
MOLLY No, I'm fed up with going to the cinema.
DAVID I know – let's go to the youth club.
MOLLY OK. That isn't a bad idea.

EXERCISE 1 ■ Make dialogues with a partner.
Cheer him/her up.

YOU Cheer up, *(name)*. You look …

> ill ▪ down ▪ fed up ▪ sad ▪ tired ▪ …

A PARTNER I don't feel …

> great ▪ very happy ▪ very well

YOU What about …?

> going to: my/your/…'s house ▪ the cinema
> the youth club ▪ a match
>
> playing: cards ▪ computer games ▪ football
>
> listening to: CDs ▪ cassettes ▪ the radio
>
> going: ice-skating ▪ swimming ▪ shopping
> inline-skating ▪ dancing

A PARTNER No, I'm fed up with …

YOU I know – let's …

> phone … ▪ surf the Internet ▪ tell jokes
> go for a walk ▪ …

A PARTNER OK. … / Oh no! …

> That's a good/great/bad/boring/silly idea.
> That isn't a bad idea.

ℹ HELP FOR YOUNG PEOPLE WITH PROBLEMS

● Students at British schools can talk to their teachers if they have problems at home or at school.
● Teenagers can write about their problems to magazines like *Just Seventeen*, *Sugar* or *TV Hits*.
● Some young people can't talk about their problems with their parents. Perhaps they even want to leave home. They can phone *Childline* or the *Samaritans* for help – even at night.

● If you have a problem, who can you tell?
● Do you like reading problem pages in magazines?

Has David cheered Molly up?

DAVID How do you feel today, Molly?
MOLLY Much better, thanks, David.
I'm sorry that I was so grumpy yesterday.
DAVID That's OK. We all feel down sometimes.
MOLLY Well, you cheered me up. Thanks again, David.
DAVID That's OK. That's what friends are for.
MOLLY Well, you're a great friend, David.

EXERCISE 2 ■ Make a dialogue between Tom and Diana. Put the sentences in the right order.

- That's what friends are for.
- Yes, much better, thanks, Diana. Sorry I was so grumpy yesterday.
- Thanks, Diana.
- That's OK. I'm sometimes grumpy too.
- Do you feel better today, Tom?
- Well, you cheered me up. You're a great friend, Diana.

EXERCISE 3 ☐ Make a dialogue: Your partner feels fed up. Cheer him/her up.

- Sage ihm/ihr, dass er/sie bedrückt aussieht.
- Sage, dass du dich nicht gut fühlst.
- Schlage vor in den Jugendklub zu gehen.
- Sage, dass du es satt hast in den Jugendklub zu gehen.
- Schlage vor schwimmen zu gehen.
- Sage, dass das eine gute Idee ist.

EXERCISE 4 ■■ Make a dialogue.

- Schlage vor zusammen im Internet zu surfen.
- Lehne den Vorschlag ab.
- Mache einen weiteren Vorschlag auszugehen. *(Wohin? Das kannst du entscheiden.)*
- Lehne diesen Vorschlag auch ab. Füge hinzu, dass es dir Leid tut, dass du so schlechte Laune hast.
- Sage, das macht nichts. Mach einen zweiten Vorschlag auszugehen.
- Nimm den Vorschlag an. Schlage ein Treffen vor. *(Wo? Wann? Das kannst du entscheiden).*

W 11, 9-10

* ACTIVE ENGLISH OPTIONS

* CONTEXTS Presents for friends

A **For your favourite photo**
This photo frame costs £6 at Selfridge's – a small price to pay, and you can look at your favourite star all day!

Furry frame

B **Kickin'**
These orange trainers are cool – and a cool price at £49.99.

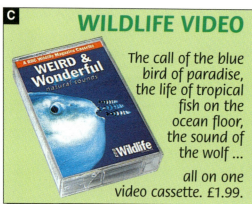

C **WILDLIFE VIDEO**
The call of the blue bird of paradise, the life of tropical fish on the ocean floor, the sound of the wolf ... all on one video cassette. £1.99.

D **Animal Bags**
Buy a present and help homeless people. Buy one of these animal bags. Part of the price will help homeless people in Sheffield. £9.99. Interested?

E *Cheese computer mat and mouse*
A great idea for the Internet surfer. Tesco, £10.

F **Aussie Soap Stars**
The magazine with all the news from your favourite Australian soaps
• Free 10 great posters
• Interviews with top soap stars
• £3.

Choose the best present (A-F) for these people:
1 A friend who's interested in animals.
2 A friend who enjoys watching Australian soaps on TV.
3 A friend who loves sport and likes looking cool.
4 An e-mail partner.
5 A friend who loves collecting photos of his/her favourite stars.
6 A friend who likes helping homeless people.

POEMS Good friends

Don't walk in front of me:
I may not follow.
Don't walk behind me:
I may not lead.
Just walk next to me
And be my friend.

Albert Camus

You can hardly make a friend
In a year;
But you can lose one
In an hour.

Chinese proverb

Make new friends
But keep the old;
Those are silver,
These are gold.

Joseph Parry

A true friend is somebody
who can make us do
what we can.

Ralph Waldo Emerson

ACTIVITY A message in code

Sometimes you want to give a friend a message. It's often a secret message. Here's a useful code:

- First, look at the code.

For example:
friends = ⌐⌐○⌐⊓⎍∨

- What's this message?

⌐⌐⌐∨ ⊃⊓< ⌐∨ ⌐⊓<⌐ ⌐⊓

- Now write your own message.

Write it in English, in code. Give it to a partner. Can he/she write your message in words?

ACTION CARDS Being a good friend

■ Make action cards with useful words and phrases from this unit. Your cards can have phrases about:
Cheering up a friend ■ Making suggestions
Saying you're sorry ■ …

* Fakultativ

PRACTICE PAGES

STRUCTURES

EXERCISE 1 ■ At the hospital

> myself (2x) ▪ yourself ▪ herself ▪ ourselves ▪ themselves

Marian had to wait at the hospital. There were other people in the queue. They all asked the same questions!
"How did you hurt …?" they asked.
"I was skiing at Sheffield Ski Village. I fell, and I hurt …," answered Marian.
"Were you with friends?" was the next question.
"Yes," said Marian. "We were enjoying … Well, my friends were enjoying … I wasn't enjoying … I was grumpy." And Marian said to …, "I'll be happy when I can go home."

EXERCISE 2 ■ Talk to a friend about your family and school.

1 Our teachers are OK, aren't they?
2 My … is …, isn't he?
3 My … is …, isn't she?
4 Your … are …, aren't they?
5 My … are …, aren't they?
6 In our class …'re all …, aren't we?

> brother ▪ aunt ▪ mum ▪ dad ▪ cousins
> parents ▪ sister ▪ uncle ▪ we ▪ teachers

> friendly ▪ nice ▪ silly ▪ unfriendly ▪ boring

EXERCISE 3 ☐ What did Alex do yesterday?

1 He (go) to school. – He *went* …
2 He (arrive) home at four o'clock.
3 He (have) a cup of tea.
4 He (do) his homework.
5 He (take) the Supertram into town.
6 He (meet) Daniel at the fountain.
7 They (see) a film at the *Showroom*.
8 Then they (eat) some fish and chips.

EXERCISE 4 ■■ On Saturday evening: For each picture, write two sentences.

1 Marian/come out/hospital
2 Daniel/meet

3 Daniel/give/Marian/present
4 cassette/her favourite group

5 sit/next to/in *Peace Gardens*
6 talk/a lot

1 Marian came out of hospital on Saturday evening.
2 Daniel met …
3 …

7 6 o'clock/go/Supertram stop
8 where/cassette?

9 Daniel/run/back
10 but/not find/cassette

2

SITUATIONS

Was sagst du auf Englisch in diesen fünf Situationen?
1 Ein Freund probiert etwas an. Du willst ihm sagen, dass es großartig aussieht.
2 Du willst jemanden ermutigen sich etwas selbst beizubringen.
3 Zu Hause willst du Freunden sagen, sie sollten sich selbst Milch und Zucker nehmen.
4 Es gibt auf der Parkbank keinen Platz mehr.
5 Eine Freundin hat sich (gerade) verletzt. Das erzählst du jemand anderem.

Tip: Look again at pages 26-33.

WORDPOWER

WORDPOWER 1 ■ Girlfriends and boyfriends: Find the words and write the sentences.

After their first …, Jamie and Alison wanted to … their free time together. They were very … And when Jamie felt …, Alison … him up. That's what … are for!

WORDPOWER 2 ■ Look at pages 26-33. Find the words.

5 words with -self	5 skiing words	5 places in town
hurt yourself	ski-lift	shops
… yourself	…	…

WORDPOWER 3 ☐ Find the opposites.

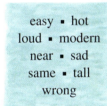

easy ▪ hot
loud ▪ modern
near ▪ sad
same ▪ tall
wrong

cold ▪ different
difficult ▪ far
happy ▪ old
quiet ▪ right
short

WORDPOWER 4 ■■ Make a word web.

USING A DICTIONARY

These exercises will help you to find words in a dictionary.

These are the (first) and (last) words on page 148. All the words on these pages come in alphabetical order between **lie** and **motorway**. For example, you'll find **meal**; you won't find **much**.

DICTIONARY 1 ■ Are they on page 148?
1 library – *no*   3 lorry   5 mountain
2 month   4 language   6 mistake

DICTIONARY 2 ■■ Use your dictionary.
What do these words mean in German?
1 lose   4 medal   7 mine
2 meat   5 life   8 look
3 lonely   6 lorry   forward to

37

PRACTICE PAGES

READING From a magazine for teenagers

Tip: You can find new words in the *Dictionary* (page 140).

ANDY'S QUESTION PAGE

MOST OF YOU have a best friend: a girl or boy at school perhaps or your brother or sister. But what are the most important qualities of a really good friend? That's my question for you today.

I asked some teenagers in Sheffield about this. Here are some of their ideas. Which six ideas are the most important in your opinion?

A best friend is somebody ...

- ... who's always there when you need help.
- ... who spends a lot of free time with you.
- ... who tells you when you're wrong.
- ... who shares your secrets – but only with you.
- ... who likes the same music, hobbies etc.
- ... who you can always trust.
- ... who sends postcards when he's/she's on holiday.
- ... who feeds your pets when you're on holiday.
- ... who lends you money if you need some.
- ... who understands your problems.
- ... who lends you magazines or CDs.
- ... who laughs at your jokes.
- ... who visits you when you're ill.
- ... who never forgets your birthday.

I also talked to two TV stars about their idea of a perfect friend ...

Jill Patrick, the star of the show *West London*, said, "In my opinion, a best friend should live near you and can help you night or day. At the moment my best friend is working far away, in Australia. I miss her."

Dan Collins, who reads the 9 o'clock news, said, "If you ask me, the perfect friend is somebody who knows that you aren't perfect – but still likes you. Your best friend takes you as you are. You can be yourself."

What do YOU think? Write to Andy and tell him. We'll print the best letters in our magazine next month.

2

EXERCISE 1 ■ **Basic reading: What's right?**
1 Andy wants to hear about people's *families / best friends*.
2 The teenagers told Andy how people can *help / hurt you*.
3 Jill Patrick and Dan Collins are *friends / TV stars*.

EXERCISE 2 ■ **Reading for details: Who says this?**

> Andy ▪ a teenager
> Jill Patrick ▪ Dan Collins

1 My best friend is in another country.
2 I talked to some young people in an English city.
3 A best friend lends you things.
4 A perfect friend understands that you aren't perfect.
5 A member of your family can be your best friend.
6 A best friend thinks about you when he's/she's on holiday.

EXERCISE 3 ■ **Language tasks**   Tip: All the words are on page 38.

> animals ▪ CDs ▪ time
> postcards ▪ somebody

1 Which word is wrong here: *spend, tell, send, money*?
2 Make the sentences: You spend …   You send …   You lend …
   You trust …   You feed …
3 Find the missing words: a) You laugh … jokes.   b) Somebody takes you … you are.
   c) A friend shares secrets … you.   d) Please write … Andy.
4 Find five things that you do for *your* best friend.
5 Find seven words for people.

LISTENING 🎧 Best friends

The *Radio Sheffield Show:* Six teenagers are talking about their best friends.

EXERCISE 1 ■ **Find the picture of their best friends.**
1 Katie: Picture …   4 Amy: …
2 Steve: Picture …   5 Barry: …
3 Jack: …   6 Liz: …

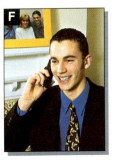

EXERCISE 2 ■■ **Right or wrong?**
1 Katie's best friend is her brother.
2 Steve's best friend doesn't go to school.
3 Jack's girlfriend is 27.
4 Amy's best friend can cook.
5 Barry's best friend is older than him.
6 Mike is Liz's boyfriend.

Weitere Fragen: W 36

SUMMARY

myself, yourself, themselves …

Nach Verben wie *buy, hurt, look at* usw. kannst du *myself, yourself, themselves* usw. hinzufügen. Aber nur, wenn jemand sich (selbst) etwas kauft, sich (selbst) verletzt oder sich (selbst) anschaut usw.

Jack Taylor hurt himself on his old bike.

"What happened to you?" asked his mother. "Look at yourself in the mirror."

Jack earned some money in the holidays.
"Now I can buy myself a new bike," he thought.

I	→	**my**self
you	→	**your**self
he	→	**him**self
she	→	**her**self
we	→	**our**selves
you	→	**your**selves
they	→	**them**selves

The Wilsons enjoyed themselves on holiday.

"Did your friends enjoy themselves at the party?"
　„Haben deine Freunde sich auf der Party amüsiert?"
The boy hurt himself in the sports hall.
　Der Junge hat sich in der Sporthalle verletzt.
　Der Junge verletzte sich in der Sporthalle.
We taught ourselves a very difficult computer game.
　Wir haben uns ein sehr schwieriges Computerspiel beigebracht.
　Wir brachten uns ein sehr schwieriges Computerspiel bei.
"Buy yourselves lunch in town," said Grandfather to Joe and Sam.
　„Kauft euch Mittagessen in der Stadt", sagte Großvater zu Joe und Sam.

Help yourselves!　Nehmt euch!
Enjoy yourself!　Amüsier dich gut! / Viel Spaß!

..., isn't it? – ..., aren't they?

Die Frageanhängsel ..., *isn't he?* ..., *aren't they?* ..., *don't they?* usw., die am Ende eines Satzes stehen, entsprechen dem deutschen „nicht wahr?" „oder?" „gell?"

British people are polite, aren't they?

British pop music is great, isn't it?   Britische Popmusik ist toll, nicht wahr?
Mr Bean is funny, isn't he?   Mr Bean ist lustig, oder?
The Queen lives in London, doesn't she?   Die Königin wohnt in London, gell?

IN DIESER UNIT HAST DU GELERNT ...

... Sätze mit *myself, themselves* usw. zu bilden.	➡ *I taught myself snooker.* *It'll be cheaper if you repair your bike yourself.*
... Sätze mit Frageanhängseln zu verstehen.	➡ *Janet is clever, isn't she?* *You go out together, don't you?*
... Freunde/Freundinnen zu ermuntern.	➡ *Cheer up.*
... dich für deine schlechte Laune zu entschuldigen.	➡ *I'm sorry I was so grumpy yesterday.*

*LOOK AROUND 2
Australia

Australia is a very large country. It takes over 4 days to drive from Perth to Sydney.
18 million people live in Australia – only 2 people for every square kilometre.
Some children live over 60 km from the nearest school.
They talk to their teachers by radio or they have lessons on the Internet.

Most parts of Australia are very sunny.
But the sun can be dangerous. You have to wear a hat and a T-shirt, and use a lot of suncream in Australia.

You can find these animals only in Australia.

kangaroo

kookaburra

platypus

koala

*Fakultativ

The first people from Europe arrived in Australia over 200 years ago. But they weren't the first people in Australia. The Aborigines were there thousands of years before them. Aborigines believe that people should protect plants and animals.

Australians love sport.

 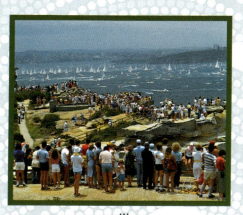 

cricket sailing Australian football

GREG I live on a sheep farm with my parents. The nearest town is 120 km away.
I have lessons on the Internet.
I miss being with other teenagers.

TINA I live in Sydney. My parents came to Australia from Britain 20 years ago. My favourite sport is surfing. When I can't surf, I like lying beside the pool in the garden.

UNIT THREE
Young and old

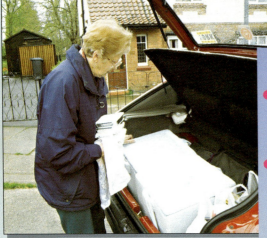

The Meals on Wheels service

LIVING TOGETHER

- Today a lot of old people over 75 live alone in Britain. They look after themselves. They do their own housework and shopping. If they can't cook, the Meals on Wheels service brings a hot meal to their house every day.

- A lot of old people can't look after themselves. Some live with their children and their families. Other old people live in old people's homes. They have their own rooms but they eat their meals together. Usually a nurse looks after them if they're ill.

- Most towns and cities have day centres for old people. Here they can meet their friends or make new friends. Day centres are important places where old people can enjoy themselves. But they still live in their own homes.

- Do your grandparents look after themselves?
- Who looks after them?
- How often do you see your grandparents?
- Do you write to them or phone them?

W 15, 1

 A After tea last Thursday Alex's mother was reading the newspaper. Suddenly she said, "That's terrible! Listen to this!" Alex and his father listened. Mrs Barker read a short article about an old woman:

Police find dead woman

The police found a 76-year-old woman dead in her home on Tuesday. Her neighbours said, "We saw her three months ago."

ALEX Grandma is always alone too. Why did we leave her back in Scotland when we came here?
MOTHER She didn't want to leave her home.
FATHER And she wanted to stay near her friends.
ALEX But they're all old. They can't help her if she's ill.
MOTHER Perhaps I'll phone her tonight.
FATHER Or perhaps Alex can write a letter to her tonight.
ALEX Tonight? Well, perhaps tomorrow. I'd like to go out tonight.

W 15, 2

B

MOTHER Tonight? Where are you going?
ALEX Oh, Mum. It's Thursday. It's youth club this evening.
MOTHER Well, don't come home late. I think you should be here before 11 pm. Oh no, trainers again. They aren't good for your feet. You should wear your shoes sometimes.
FATHER And what about your hair, Alex? It's too long.
ALEX Too long? I like my hair, Dad.
MOTHER It looks untidy. You should comb it before you go out.

EXERCISE 1 ■ What parents often say: Put the right sentences together.

1 Trainers aren't good for your feet.	You should go out more.
2 Your room is very untidy.	You should send her a card.
3 It's very late. You look tired.	You should tidy it.
4 You sit in your room too much.	You should go to bed.
5 It's grandma's birthday next week.	You should eat more.
6 You haven't eaten your potatoes.	You should wear shoes sometimes.

W 16, 3

What do parents often say before teenagers go out? Write 3 sentences with *should*.

C

Shellina was at home with her parents on Thursday evening too. She was very interested in an article about parents and children in her favourite magazine.

> **British teenagers' top 10 rules for parents**
> **A GOOD FATHER OR MOTHER SHOULD …**
> ■ be kind
> ■ always listen to you
> ■ keep promises
> ■ have time for you
> ■ make rules for you
> ■ do things with you
> ■ have a sense of humour
> ■ help with homework
> ■ never hit you
> ■ say when you have to be home or go to bed

Write *your* top 5 rules for parents.

D

Then the phone rang. It was Shellina's brother, Iqbal. "I have to work till 10 pm. I can't walk home with you after youth club," he said.
"Oh, I can walk home alone," Shellina said. But her parents didn't think so …

MOTHER No, no. It isn't safe. Not for a girl.
SHELLINA Oh, Mum! All the other girls who …
FATHER The streets aren't safe late at night.
GRANDMA I have an idea. Perhaps your father can meet you, Shellina.
SHELLINA No, I can come home early. OK?

What do you argue about with your parents?
We argue about …   We don't argue about …
homework ▪ clothes ▪ going out ▪ coming home late ▪ money
my friends ▪ my room ▪ my hair ▪ housework ▪ trainers ▪ …

 CHECKPOINT

Mit *should* sagst du, was jemand tun soll/sollte:
You **should** do your homework. She **should** take the dog for a walk. He **should** phone his parents.

E When Shellina arrived at the youth club, she got a surprise. Daniel was there. He was with Patrick, another member of the club's rock group.

PATRICK Kirsty is ill. So she can't sing with us, Daniel. Her parents say she shouldn't sing if she has a cold.
DANIEL Parents! They always know better: "You shouldn't do this and you shouldn't do that."
SHELLINA Hallo, Daniel. Is Marian here too?
DANIEL Hi, Shellina. No, she has to babysit tonight.
PATRICK Really? Or have you stopped going out together?
DANIEL I hope not. Hey, Shellina! You can sing this evening.

EXERCISE 2 ■ What shouldn't you do? Finish the sentences.
1 If you have a cold, you shouldn't …
2 If you're really ill, you shouldn't …
3 If you're tired, you shouldn't …
4 If you have homework, you shouldn't …
5 If you're in a lesson, you shouldn't …
6 If you have a test at school, you shouldn't …

F It was an exciting evening. Shellina knew the group's favourite songs. And she sang well.
Some other members of the club came into the coffee bar and listened. They liked Shellina's voice. But Shellina had a problem.

SHELLINA I'm sorry. I have to be home early. I should leave now.
DANIEL Oh, you can stay 10 minutes longer, Shellina.
PATRICK Yes, sing one more song. Please.
SHELLINA Well, I shouldn't stay. But it's fun. And 10 minutes shouldn't be a problem. OK. What's the last song?

EXERCISE 3 ■ After the youth club: Put in *should* or *shouldn't*.
1 Patrick said, "You have a great voice, Shellina. You … sing with us every week."
2 Daniel said, "That's right. You … spend so much time in the computer room."
3 Shellina said, "Look, it's 9.30 now. I … stay. I'm sorry, but I … go home."
4 "And I … go home now too," Daniel said. "I haven't done my homework. Really, I … be here."
5 Daniel walked home with Shellina. Shellina said, "I enjoyed singing with the group tonight." Daniel said, "Yes, we … do it again."
6 Shellina got home a few minutes late. "You're safe. Good," her father said. Shellina said, "You … worry so much, Dad. I'm not a baby."

W 16, 4

✓ **CHECKPOINT**

Mit *shouldn't* sagst du, was jemand nicht tun soll/sollte:
I shouldn't eat so much chocolate.

Mit *Should …?* fragst du, was jemand tun soll/sollte:
Should parents make rules for children?

G After school on Friday Daniel phoned Marian.

But Marian didn't phone. Daniel didn't go out on Friday evening or at the weekend. He was unhappy because he didn't hear from her. He stayed in his room and played his music very loud. His parents didn't know why.

EXERCISE 4 ■ Make short dialogues with a partner.

YOU	A PARTNER
Do you tell your parents about your problems?	– Yes, I do. / No, I don't. / Sometimes.
Do your parents ask you about your problems?	– Yes, they do. / No, they don't. / …
Do you stay at home if you're fed up?	– Yes, I do. / No, I don't. / …
Do you play your favourite music very loud?	– Yes, I do. / No, I don't. / …
Do you phone your friends at the weekend?	– Yes, I do / No, I don't. / …

H Daniel only thought about the girl he liked. His parents got on his nerves with the questions they asked. When they asked Daniel what was wrong with him, he said, "Oh, I don't know." Their neighbours, the Skeltons, complained about the loud music from Daniel's room.
"Young people only think of themselves," Mrs Skelton said.

EXERCISE 5 ■ Daniel's weekend: Make sentences.

1 Daniel thought about the girl   Daniel gave them.
2 He hated the questions   Daniel played.
3 His parents didn't like the answers   his parents asked.
4 Their neighbours didn't like the music Daniel had.
5 They didn't know about the problems   he liked.

Daniel only thought about the girl he liked.   **47**

STORY

Is the colour of your hair important?

The mistake

On Sunday evening Alex hurried along the street where Daniel lived. It was snowy.
Then he stopped. There was a red car opposite Daniel's house. Some of the snow under the car was black.
"That must be oil," thought Alex.

At that moment an old man looked out of a window.
"Beth," he said to his wife. "There's a young man outside, near our car. Look at his green hair – and he has an earring. Do you think he's going to steal the radio?"
"Perhaps he's going to steal the car," Mrs Skelton said. "Should we phone the police?"

Alex didn't see Mr and Mrs Skelton.
"The car has lost a lot of oil," he thought. "Perhaps the Greens know who the car belongs to. I think I should tell Daniel about it."

Alex walked up to Daniel's door and rang the bell.
Daniel was on the phone when the bell rang. When he opened the door, he got a surprise. Daniel almost didn't recognize Alex. His hair was *very* green.

"Come in, Alex," he said. "What have you done with your hair?"

"Oh, my dad got on my nerves about my hair," Alex explained. "I decided to spray a different colour on my hair. Do you like it?"

Daniel didn't want to hurt his friend. But he didn't like Alex's new hairstyle.

He said, "Well, it *is* very different. Why should everybody look the same? What did your dad say when he saw your hair?"

Alex smiled, "He didn't like it. But my mum thinks the colour is OK. But listen," said Alex. "Does that red car opposite your house belong to your parents?"

Before Daniel could answer, Alex told him about the oil under the car.

"Don't worry," said Daniel. "That isn't our car. We've just sold our car. The red car belongs to our neighbours, Mr and Mrs Skelton. Let's tell them about the oil."

When Daniel and Alex left the house, they saw a police car in the street. Two police officers were with Mr and Mrs Skelton. Then Daniel heard Mrs Skelton's voice.

"Look!" Mrs Skelton shouted. "That's the young man we saw. The boy with the green hair! He's the boy who tried to steal our car!"

The police officers looked at Alex and Daniel. Daniel explained everything fast.

"I only wanted to help," Alex said.

"I'm sorry, young man, it was all a mistake," Mr Skelton said. "We often have problems with boys in this part of Sheffield. They help themselves to people's cars."

"Well, we know that, Mr Skelton," one of the police officers said. "But, don't forget, people aren't bad because they look different."

TASK A ■ Correct the sentences.
1 A boy with green hair and earrings looked under a car.
2 The Skeltons didn't know that the boy was Daniel's neighbour.
3 Alex knew who the red car belonged to.
4 The Greens phoned the police before they knew who Alex was.
5 The police officers thought people who look different aren't good.

TASK B ■■ Tell the story.
Mrs Skelton recognized Alex's green hair.
→ Alex saw some oil in the snow under a car.
The police officers didn't think people who look different steal cars.
Daniel knew that Alex meant his neighbour's car.
The Skeltons thought Alex wanted to steal their car.
Alex told Daniel about the red car.

W 17, 5-7

ACTIVE ENGLISH

ACTIONS Talking about TV

Linda is Darren's cousin from Australia.
What programme do they want to watch on TV?

LINDA   What's on TV at 7.30?
DARREN Well, there's *Tomorrow's World* on BBC 1.
         It's a documentary.
LINDA   Oh, I think documentaries are boring.
DARREN There's *Coronation Street* on ITV. It's a soap.
LINDA   Oh, I can't stand soaps. Hey, what's that?
DARREN That's *Unplugged* on MTV.
         It's a music programme.
LINDA   OK, let's watch that.

EXERCISE 1 ■ Make dialogues with a partner.
YOU   What's on TV at 7.30?
A PARTNER Well, there's … on … It's a …
YOU   Oh, I think … are boring.
A PARTNER There's … on … It's …
YOU   Oh, I can't stand … Hey, what's that?
A PARTNER That's … on … It's a …
YOU   OK, let's watch that.

BBC 1
Eastenders: a soap

BBC 2
Black Britain: a documentary

ITV
The Bill: a police drama

TV IN BRITAIN

- There are five British TV channels.
- BBC 1 and BBC 2 don't show adverts. BBC gets its money from people who have a TV.
- ITV, Channel 4 and Channel 5 show adverts. They get a lot of their money from adverts.
- With cable or a satellite dish you can get lots of other channels.

- What do you know about TV in Germany?
- How many hours a day do you watch TV?
- Do other members of your family watch more TV?

IN BRITAIN PEOPLE WATCH TV:

age	hours a day
4 – 15	2 hrs 48 mins
16 – 24	2 hrs 37 mins
25 – 34	3 hrs 32 mins
35 – 44	3 hrs 40 mins
45 – 54	3 hrs 55 mins
55 – 64	4 hrs 32 mins
65 +	5 hrs 17 mins

Linda is talking about TV with Darren's family.
Does Linda watch a lot of TV?

MOTHER Do you watch a lot of TV, Linda?
LINDA About two hours a day.
MOTHER And when do you usually watch TV?
LINDA Between 8 and 10 pm.
FATHER And what sort of programmes do you like?
LINDA Oh, I like programmes about music, and I like cartoons. I like the news too. But I don't watch talk shows very often.

a cartoon

a talk show

the news

EXERCISE 2 ■ Make dialogues about watching TV.

YOU Do you watch a lot of TV, …?
A PARTNER Well, about … a day.
YOU When do you usually watch TV?
A PARTNER Between … and …
YOU And what sort of programmes do you like?
A PARTNER Oh, I like … I like … But I don't watch …

> programmes about sport/…
> documentaries ▪ talk shows
> police dramas ▪ soaps
> the news ▪ MTV ▪ cartoons
> …

EXERCISE 3 ☐ You want to watch TV.
Make a dialogue with your partner.

| Frage, was im Fernsehen läuft. |
▼
| Sage, im BBC 1 gibt es *Eastenders*. |
▼
| Sage, du kannst Seifenopern nicht ausstehen. |
▼
| Sage, im BBC 2 gibt es eine Talkshow. |
▼
| Schlag vor die Talkshow anzuschauen. |

EXERCISE 4 ■■ You're talking about TV.
Make a dialogue with your partner.

| Frage, ob er/sie viel fernsieht. |
▼
| Sage, wie viele Stunden du am Tag fernsiehst. |
▼
| Frage, wann er/sie fernsieht. |
▼
| Sage, von wann bis wann du üblicherweise fernsiehst. |
▼
| Frage, was für Sendungen er/sie mag. |
▼
| Sage, was für Sendungen du magst. |

W 18, 8-10

ACTIVE ENGLISH OPTIONS

CONTEXTS Film posters

In Britain there are rules about the films children and teenagers are allowed to see.

> (U) – Everybody can see this film.
> (12) – You have to be 12 if you want to see this film.
> (15) – You have to be 15 if you want to see this film.
> (18) – You have to be 18 if you want to see this film.

A (U)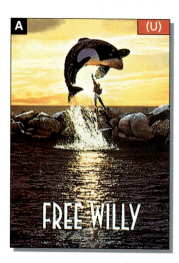

B (12)

C (15)

D (U)

E (18)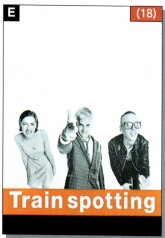

F (U)

Here's some information. Can you find the right film (A-F)?
1 Everybody can laugh at this special film – a basketball star in a cartoon.
2 Young children can see this film about a famous animal.
3 This isn't a film about trains – it's about young people and their drug problems.
4 Children are the stars of this film but you have to be over 12 if you want to see it.
5 If you enjoy watching science fiction films, this is one of the best – for all the family.
6 You have to be fifteen if you want to see this Scottish love story.

* SONG 🎧 I want to be free

I'm bored.
I don't want to go to school.
I don't want to be nobody's fool.
I want to be me, I want to be me.
I don't want to be sweet and neat.
I don't want someone living my life for me,
I want to be free.

I'm going to turn this world
– inside out,
I'm going to turn suburbia
– upside down.
I'm going to walk the streets
– scream and shout,
I'm going to crawl through the alleyways
– be very loud.

I don't want to be told what to wear.
As long as you're warm – who cares?
I want to be me, I want to be me.
So what if I dye my hair?
I've still got a brain up there,
And I'm going to be me,
I'm going to be free.

* ACTIVITY Rules for a happy home

When younger and older people live together in families, they need rules.

- Work in a team. Make a poster about what parents and children should (or shouldn't) do.

- Put your lists of rules on the classroom wall. Do all the teams have the same rules?

- Class activity: Choose the six most important rules. Write these rules for parents and children on the board.

Parents should:
pay pocket-money on time
spend time with their children
…

Parents shouldn't:
shout
…

Children should:
…

Children shouldn't:
…

* ACTION CARDS 📁 Talking about TV

- Make action cards with useful words and phrases from this unit. Your cards can have phrases about:
    - TV programmes you like
    - TV programmes you can't stand
    - different TV programmes
    - different TV channels in Britain

* Fakultativ

PRACTICE PAGES

STRUCTURES

EXERCISE 1 ■ That's a good idea. Put in the right verbs.

should + babysit • phone • cheer • talk • do • tidy

1 If you have to come home late, you … home.
2 If your parents want to go out, you …
3 If your grandparents visit you, you … to them.
4 If your parents are ill, you … more housework.
5 If your mother is fed up, you … her up.
6 If somebody complains about your room, you … it.

EXERCISE 2 ■ Mike's talk show for teenagers on the radio

a Read the things Mike wants to talk about. Ask Mike's questions.

people / eat / animals
1

we / build / more roads
2

parents / help with / homework
3

teachers / give / homework
4

parents / hit / children
5

shops / open / on Sundays
6

1 Mike: Should people eat animals?   2 Mike: Should we …?   3 …

b Now answer Mike's questions. Write what you think.
  1 Should people eat animals? – Yes, they should. / No, they shouldn't.
  2 Should we build … ? – Yes, … / No, …

EXERCISE 3 ☐ That's what Ray thinks. Find the right sentence for the pictures (1-6).

It's the best news I've heard today. • That's the coolest hairstyle I've ever seen.
Sue is the friendliest girl I've ever met. • It's the most expensive present I've ever bought.
He has the best voice I've ever heard. • It's the most boring soap I've ever watched.

1   2   3   4   5   6

EXERCISE 4 ■■ Grandfather's new friends

1 Rebecca is reading a letter | he can't carry home.
2 Her grandfather lives alone in a flat | he has just met.
3 In the letter, he talks about two students | he loves eating.
4 He's helping them with a history project | he bought last year.
5 They visit him and cook meals | they're doing at school.
6 They go to the shops for big things | she has just got from her grandfather.

3

SITUATIONS

Was sagst du in diesen fünf Situationen?

1 Du willst von einem Freund erfahren, ob er nicht mehr mit seiner Freundin geht.
2 Jemand bittet dich zu bleiben, aber du willst sagen, dass du gehen solltest.
3 Du versprichst, dich bei jemandem am Wochenende telefonisch zu melden.
4 Du willst eine Freundin nicht verletzen. Zur neuen Haarfarbe sagst du, sie sei sehr anders.
5 Ein Freund will eine Seifenoper ansehen. Du willst ihm sagen, dass du Seifenopern nicht ausstehen kannst.

Tip: Look again at pages 44-51.

WORDPOWER

WORDPOWER 1 ■ Find the words.

a
```
R A L D E L S E
E P H I N B F O
C E A R R I N G
O H I M Y L U K
G V R S T Y L E
N I Z E S C E X
J G Q A C R W T
M E L B O R P D
```

Jack has a new h… He wears an e… too. When his mum saw him, she almost didn't r… him! "Let's hope your teachers don't have the same …," she said.

b
```
C L B H V H U B
O F A E R U N H
M P L A I N E D
P E W D O T H C
E S T A C H E I
Q K J A D E S S
C O G I Z H F U
R N E R V E S M
```

Liz has a bad h… and she's in bed. But her neighbour is getting on her n… An hour ago Liz phoned and c… about his loud m…

WORDPOWER 2 ■ Make two lists.

> **do or make?**
> shopping ■ sports ■ a cake ■ a date
> homework ■ a mistake ■ housework
> a rule ■ friends ■ a test

WORDPOWER 3 ■■ Make a word web.

USING A DICTIONARY

A dictionary can tell you how to say a word. (The help you need is usually in brackets.)

DICTIONARY 1 ■ Can you say these words?

delicious [dɪˈlɪʃəs] köstlich	**alone** [əˈləʊn] allein
also [ˈɔːlsəʊ] auch	**tough** [tʌf] hart
foreign [ˈfɒrən] aus dem Ausland	**plumber** [ˈplʌmə] Installateur/in

DICTIONARY 2 □ Find the missing words.

1 Is being a [ˈplʌmə] a [tʌf] job?
2 Jim is ill and he's [ˈɔːlsəʊ] [əˈləʊn].
3 [ˈfɒrən] food is often [dɪˈlɪʃəs].

DICTIONARY 3 ■■ Do these words rhyme?

1 should – wood
2 love – move
3 road – abroad
4 snow – grow
5 leaf – deaf
6 again – brain

abroad [əˈbrɔːd] im Ausland	**love** [lʌv] lieben
again [əˈgen] wieder	**move** [muːv] Umzug
brain [breɪn] Gehirn	**road** [rəʊd] Straße
deaf [def] gehörlos	**should** [ʃʊd] sollte(n)
grow [grəʊ] anbauen	**snow** [snəʊ] Schnee
leaf [liːf] Blatt	**wood** [wʊd] Holz

PRACTICE PAGES

READING From a book about a star

Tip: You can find new words in the *Dictionary* (page 140).

Linford Christie

At the Olympic Games in 1992, Linford Christie won the gold medal for Britain in the 100 metres. The great athletics star was born in Jamaica in 1960. When he was two both his parents had jobs in Britain. There weren't many jobs in Jamaica at that time.
"My parents wanted to take me with them, but my grandmother said no. So I lived in Kingston, Jamaica, with my grandmother, my two older sisters and my three cousins."

Linford Christie at the Olympic Games in 1992

"I loved my grandmother very much. She was the greatest. She was strict but fair. I was the youngest, but I had to help at home too. We got pocket-money but we had to earn it. For example, we had to get water every morning before school. The water came from a pipe near our house. I had a very small bucket and, when I arrived home, there was often no water in it. My grandmother didn't complain. She knew I was learning about life."

"Before I went to school, I could read and write. At school the teachers sometimes hit us with a cane, if we made too many mistakes. But I really enjoyed school in Jamaica."

Linford had a younger brother and two sisters who were all born in Britain. He was looking forward to meeting everybody in his family.

His father often visited Jamaica. He decided to bring the family to Britain when Linford was seven. Linford arrived in Britain with his older sisters, his cousins and his grandmother in 1967.

Linford's parents lived in London. His aunt and uncle lived in Nottingham, so his cousins went there. Linford's grandmother went with them. He missed her very much.

"Being with my parents again was difficult. I didn't know them. I thought: why didn't they take me with them to Britain when I was very young? Of course it was difficult for my mum and dad too. They had to work hard in jobs that didn't pay well."

The large Christie family lived in a flat in a big old house.
"We shared a bathroom with other families. I remember that I had a key, because my parents were still at work when I came home from school."

When he was eight a teacher asked him to run a race at school.
Linford Christie won the first race in his long career.

Winning in Munich in 1997

3

EXERCISE 1 ■ Basic reading: What's wrong here?
1 Linford left Britain and went to a new home in Jamaica.
2 Linford came from a small family.
3 Linford started school in Britain.
4 He lived with his grandmother in Jamaica and in Britain.
5 Life in Britain was easy for Linford.
6 Linford Christie is a famous football star.

EXERCISE 2 ■ Reading for details: Who is it?
1 … was born in Britain.
2 … had to help his grandmother in Jamaica.
3 … brought his family together in 1967.
4 … didn't live with him in London.
5 … began his athletics career at school.
6 … didn't earn a lot of money in their jobs.

Linford Christie *Linford's father* *Linford's brother* *Linford's parents* *Linford's grandmother*

EXERCISE 3 ■ Language tasks   Tip: All the words are on page 56.
1 Which word is wrong here:
   nice, strict, kind, friendly, polite?
2 And which word is wrong here:
   swimming, sailing, athletics, windsurfing?
3 You can get this at the Olympic Games, but only if you win.
4 Linford ran a lot of these in his career.
5 What are these three things?

LISTENING When I was young …

The *Radio Sheffield Show:* Vincent runs for the British team.
He's talking about when he was young.

EXERCISE 1 ■ Find the right picture for each sentence.
1 Vincent liked this when he was at school.
2 Vincent didn't enjoy learning this.
3 His mother used this.

EXERCISE 2 ■■ Listen again. What's the missing word?
1 Vincent played … at school.
2 He didn't … with his parents.
3 Vincent's … taught him to cook.
4 His mother made … for all the family.
5 Vincent was a … of the British team.
6 Vincent travelled to … in Germany.

Weitere Fragen: W 37

SUMMARY

should

Mit *should* sagst du, was jemand tun soll/sollte – mit *shouldn't*, was jemand nicht tun soll/sollte.

He should go to bed.   She should hurry. The bus is there.   We shouldn't ride our bikes here.   You shouldn't talk here.

It's late. I should go now.   Es ist spät. Ich sollte jetzt gehen.
David should do more sport.   David sollte mehr Sport treiben.
He shouldn't talk so much.   Er sollte nicht so viel reden.
It isn't funny. They shouldn't laugh.   Es ist nicht komisch. Sie sollten nicht lachen.

AUSSAGEN/VERNEINUNGEN

I / You / He/She/It / We / You / They	should / shouldn't	leave now.

FRAGEN

Should	I / you / he/she/it / we / you / they	come?

Your mum and I think you should stand on your own two feet.

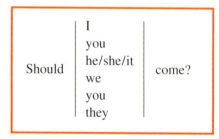

You should make your own way in the world.

You're a big boy now.

3

who/that

Mit *who/that* kannst du weitere Auskünfte über eine Person oder eine Sache geben.

Heike has friends who live in London. Kate has a camera that takes great photos.
Jim is somebody who gets on my nerves. Phil has bought a radio that doesn't work.

Manchmal kann *who* oder *that* auch einfach weggelassen werden:

Steve is the boy (who) Lucy likes. But Mary is the girl (who) Steve likes.

Is that the girl (who) we saw yesterday? Ist das das Mädchen, das wir gestern gesehen haben?
Here's the card (that) I bought. Hier ist die Karte, die ich kaufte / gekauft habe.
Is Chris the boy (who) you visit in Sheffield? Ist Chris der Junge, den du in Sheffield besuchst?
Here's the earring (that) I bought. Hier ist der Ohrring, den ich kaufte / gekauft habe.

IN DIESER UNIT HAST DU GELERNT, ...

… wie du sagst, was jemand tun soll/sollte. ➥ *Bob should write to his grandfather. You should clean your room every week.*

… wie du sagst, was jemand nicht tun soll/sollte. ➥ *You shouldn't ride your bike without lights at night.*

… wie du fragst, was jemand tun soll/sollte. ➥ *Should parents decide everything for you?*

… wie du (ohne *who/that*) weitere Auskünfte über eine Person oder Sache gibst. ➥ *Liz has just met a boy she likes. I don't like the shirt Pat is wearing.*

wie du beim Fernsehen

… deine Meinung sagen kannst. ➥ *I can't stand soaps.*

… sagst, was in welchem Programm läuft. ➥ *There's a documentary on Channel 5.*

*LOOK AROUND 3
India

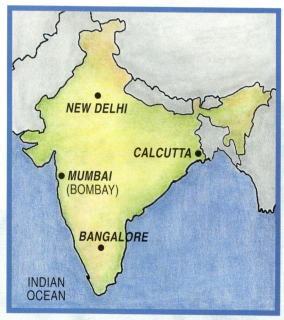

The largest city in India is Bombay. Over 12 million people live there. It's one of the largest cities in the world. The capital of India is New Delhi.

Over 900 million people live in India. Hindi is the official language. English is also an important language in India. About 45 million people speak English in India – almost as many as in Britain.

About 70% of Indians live in the country. Indian farmers grow sugar-cane, rice, wheat and tea. People have to work very hard.

Many Indians are very poor. Parents and their children are often hungry. A lot of young children have jobs. They earn money for food for themselves and their families.

Making jewellery has always been important in India.
Young women get jewellery from their parents when they marry.

Indian dancing is very old and very beautiful.

India also has a big film industry in Bombay – Indians call it Bollywood! You can see posters of the film stars on every street.

India is famous for its food.

MIRZA I live in a village near Bangalore. I teach English and maths in a school. There are 900 children at the school. Sometimes I teach outside.

GEETA I work in a computer company in Bangalore.
The computer industry is becoming important in India.

UNIT FOUR
A city project

SHEFFIELD – OLD AND NEW

- Sheffield is famous for steel. But today the steel industry needs fewer factories and fewer workers. So a lot of people are out of work. Some parts of the city look old and dirty.
- Now Sheffield needs new companies and new jobs. So the city council is cleaning the city. Today there are cafés and shops in the old factories. And the city council is cleaning Sheffield's rivers and canals.
- Sheffield has many new attractions: modern trams, Sheffield Arena (where they have concerts for 12,000 people), a new football stadium and a big sports centre. The National Centre for Popular Music has just opened. Now Sheffield wants to build an airport.
- New attractions bring new jobs and more tourists to the city. But some people say that tourists bring more traffic, noise and pollution to the city.

- What's your town/city famous for?
- Are there new attractions in your town/city?
- Is there a lot of traffic and pollution in your town/city?

W 22, 1

A In the first week of April, Ray brought information about a competition to the youth club.

Help to clean up Sheffield!

Competition

for all schools and youth clubs in Sheffield

We need new ideas for old problems!

**Clean up a park or a garden.
Clean up part of a river or a canal.**

Recycle your own great ideas!

Win a group ticket to Alton Towers fun park!

- Send us
  – the name of your school or youth club
  – your address
  – the name of your team leader
- Send us your suggestions before April 30th

W 22, 2

Talk about pollution in your town or city.
There's too much noise/rubbish/traffic in …

B Abbeydale Youth Club decided to enter the competition. The members started making plans. They decided to clean part of a small canal near the club. Ray, the youth club leader, and a team of members met by the canal on a Saturday morning.

RAY OK. Where should we start?
DANIEL Let's start cleaning up this part of the canal first. It's full of rubbish.
TANYA And broken glass! Perhaps we can plant some trees by the canal soon.
STEVE Yes, but first we must take all those old cans and bottles out of the canal.
SHELLINA Oh, come on! Stop talking. Let's start working! Take this bucket, Daniel.

EXERCISE 1 ■ The canal project

collecting ▪ putting ▪ telling ▪ working (2x)

1 RAY Marian and Steve, can you start … over there?
2 TANYA I've started … the bottles. Put them all in my bucket.
3 STEVE Stop … those terrible jokes, Marian!
4 MIKE Ray, should we start … the rubbish into the bags?
5 RAY It's almost one o'clock! Stop … Let's have our lunch.

W 22, 3a

C The youth club members worked hard. They didn't see any fish in the canal, but they saw two old wheels. They found some plastic bags and even some money! "We can collect those cans and bottles for recycling," said Ray.

EXERCISE 2 ■ What did they find in the canal? What didn't they find?
They found some …   They didn't find any …

W 23, 3b

> **Do you collect things for recycling?**
> batteries ▪ bottles ▪ cans ▪ clothes ▪ paper ▪ plastic ▪ …
>
> – Yes, I do. I collect empty/old … for recycling. But I don't collect empty/old …
> – No, I don't. I don't collect anything for recycling.

They started making plans.

D On Sunday morning the youth club members worked by the canal again.

TANYA I've forgotten my bucket. Can I have yours, Daniel?
DANIEL I need my bucket too. But does Ray need his?
RAY My bucket? No, I don't need mine. Here you are, Tanya.
TANYA Thanks, Ray. Shellina, here's some compost from my garden. Can we start planting the trees soon?
SHELLINA No, we can't. We need some garden tools. Ours are old and broken.
DANIEL My parents have some garden tools. We can use theirs.
TANYA That's OK. My sister lives near the canal. We can use hers.

EXERCISE 3 ■ Cleaning the canal

mine ▪ yours ▪ his ▪ hers ▪ ours ▪ theirs

1 Can I have your bucket?
   I've forgotten (my bucket). – I've forgotten mine.
2 We don't have any garden tools. Let's ask my parents. (Their garden tools) are new.
3 Take this plastic bag. (Your plastic bag) is broken.
4 We need more buckets. There's too much rubbish in (our buckets).
5 I'll take away these bottles. They're broken. And Shellina can collect (her bottles).
6 Let's take a photo. Oh no, I've forgotten my camera. We can ask Ray for (his camera).

W 23, 4

EXERCISE 4 ■ Daniel has found a camera by the canal.

1 I've just found this camera. Is it …?
2 No, it isn't … Ask Steve. I think it's …
3 No. But ask Tanya. It must be …

4 No. Look, there are two people. Perhaps it's …
5 No, it isn't …
   OK. It doesn't belong to anybody here. I'll give it to Ray.

✓ CHECKPOINT

mine, yours, his, hers, ours, theirs
I've forgotten my dictionary. – Use mine.
His trainers are nice, but hers are nicer.

My pen is broken. Can I have yours?
Your house is really big. Ours is much smaller.

E Mary Stokes, an environment officer from Sheffield City Council, visited the youth club. She showed a video about Sheffield.

1 These old steel factories were near the M1 motorway. When the factories were closed, a shopping centre was planned.

2 The old buildings were pulled down. And the new *Meadowhall* shopping centre was built.

3 The rivers were cleaned. And new trees were planted. A lot of people got new jobs. It was good for the environment too.

4 A new airport was planned for Sheffield. And work was started. But not everybody thinks an airport is good for the environment.

EXERCISE 5 ■ **The M1 motorway near Sheffield: Use *was* or *were*.**
1 The motorway near Sheffield (was/were) opened in 1960.
2 When it (was/were) built, lots of houses near Sheffield (was/were) pulled down.
3 Many farms (was/were) pulled down too.
4 But traffic (was/were) taken from the city centre.
5 New shops (was/were) opened near the M1.

W 23, 5

F Marian thought a lot about the new airport and the environment. A week later, she brought information about a demonstration to the youth club.
"Who's coming with me?" asked Marian.

Sheffield City Council wants an airport for Sheffield.
An airport means more noise, more pollution, more traffic.
Say **NO** to the airport project now!
Say **YES** to people and **NO** to planes!
Demonstration: Saturday, 2 pm, Tudor Square

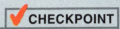 **CHECKPOINT**

Sagen, dass etwas gemacht wurde:
A shopping centre was planned. New buildings were built. A big car park was opened.

The factories were closed. **65**

STORY

Alex changed his mind about the demonstration. Why?

The demonstration

"Hi, Marian. I'm going to work by the canal today." It was Alex on the phone. "I haven't worked there before. And …"
"But, Alex," interrupted Marian. "It's the day of the demonstration. You know, the demonstration against the new airport."
"Yes, I know," answered Alex. "But … Well, demonstrations are a waste of time. Cleaning up the canal is more important, isn't it?"
"But, Alex," said Marian. "If we don't protest now, new projects will destroy more of our environment."
"You're exaggerating," said Alex. "And the new airport isn't very near my house. I won't hear the planes. So it isn't my problem."
"Your problem is that you only think of yourself!" said Marian. "I think the demonstration is important and I want to go. Goodbye."

When Marian arrived at Tudor Square, in the city centre, there were hundreds of people there. There were a lot of police officers too. Finding the youth club group wasn't easy.

At two o'clock a man with a megaphone started talking about the airport.
"The city council wants to build an airport," he said. "Our answer is: People, not planes!"
Then everybody started walking towards Pinstone Street. When somebody in front of the crowd shouted, "What do we want?" the crowd answered, "People, not planes!" Marian and her group walked in the crowd and soon they were shouting too.

When the crowd stopped in front of the town hall, the shouting became louder. People got angry. Suddenly a bottle was thrown at the wall of the town hall.

4

⁴⁰ Three police officers ran into the crowd. They looked very nervous.
"Did you throw that bottle?" one of them asked.
"No, I didn't throw it," a boy answered.
"It was a man over there."
⁴⁵ Marian looked at the boy. It was Alex.
"Alex!" said Marian. "What are you doing here?"
Alex smiled. "Hi, Marian," he said. "You're surprised, aren't you?"
⁵⁰ "Yes, I am. Why did you change your mind about the demonstration?" she asked.
"Well, I was fed up this morning," answered Alex. "And then I listened to the news on Radio Sheffield. And do you know what I
⁵⁵ heard? The city council is planning a new road to the airport – behind our house! And I thought: Marian *is* right. The demonstration is important. I should go to the demonstration too. And here I am!"
⁶⁰ "So you heard about the new road behind your house. Then you changed your mind. You aren't really interested in the environment," she smiled.
"OK. OK. You're right. I was only thinking
⁶⁵ of myself," Alex said.

"And what about the canal?" asked Marian.
"That's important too," said Alex. "But I can do that tomorrow."
"*We* can do that tomorrow," said Marian. "If you don't change your mind again …" ⁷⁰

TASK A ■ Find the lines that explain:
1 … why Marian believes the demonstration is important. *(Lines …)*
2 … why Alex doesn't believe the demonstration is important.
3 … why finding the youth club group wasn't easy for Marian.
4 … why the crowd shouted "People, not planes!"
5 … why the police officers were suddenly nervous at the town hall.
6 … why Alex changed his mind about the demonstration.
7 … that Marian didn't believe Alex was really interested in the environment.

TASK B ■■ Tell Alex and Marian's stories.
I saw a man with a bottle.
I changed my mind about Alex.
I met Marian in the crowd at the town hall.
I heard about the new road on the radio.
I walked with the crowd to the town hall.
I didn't want to go to the demonstration.
I wanted to go to the demonstration.
I heard Alex behind me in the crowd.
A police officer asked Alex about a bottle.
I changed my mind about the demonstration.

1 Alex: I didn't want to go to the demonstration. I …
2 Marian: I wanted to go to the demonstration. I …

W 24, 6-9

ACTIVE ENGLISH

ACTIONS Getting information

Where can Jade put her rubbish?

JADE Excuse me. I'm new. Is there a bottle bank in the school?
PAT Yes. It's in the car park.
JADE And is there a container for cans?
PAT Yes, it's the red one in the car park.
JADE Thank you.

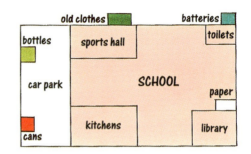

EXERCISE 1 ■ **Make more dialogues about collecting rubbish.**

YOU Is there a … in the school?
A PARTNER Yes. It's …
YOU And is there a container for …?
A PARTNER Yes. It's …
YOU Thank you.

bottle bank ▪ paper bank
container for:
cans ▪ batteries ▪ old clothes

behind the toilets ▪ in the car park
near the library ▪ behind the sports hall

Where can Phil take batteries?

PHIL Excuse me. Can you tell me where the nearest recycling containers are?
WOMAN Yes, they're over there.
PHIL Can I get rid of batteries too?
WOMAN Oh, yes. Put them in the red container.

EXERCISE 2 ■ **Make more dialogues.**

cans ▪ bottles ▪ old clothes ▪ magazines

grey ▪ green ▪ black ▪ white

YOU Excuse me. Can you tell me where the nearest recycling containers are?
A PARTNER Yes, they're over there.
YOU Can I get rid of … too?
A PARTNER Oh, yes. Put them in the … container.

Can Cathy get a ticket?

CATHY Hallo. Can you tell me if there are still tickets for the concert tonight?
MAN Yes, there are a few.
CATHY Can you tell me how much they are?
MAN Well, there are two prices: £15 or £9.

EXERCISE 3 ■ Ask the questions. Find the right answer (or make your own answer).

Can you tell me
- if the museum is open on Mondays?
- if you've repaired my walkman?
- when I can visit the dentist?
- how much a ticket to Bradford costs?
- how long the journey takes?
- when the last train from London arrives?

- Three hours and twenty minutes.
- A single is £4.50 and a return £7.25.
- At 10.35 pm, on platform 2.
- You can come at 2.30 pm.
- Yes, it only needed new batteries.
- No, I'm sorry, not on Mondays.

EXERCISE 4 ☐ Make dialogues.
Get information in Britain.

a
Frage, ob er/sie dir sagen kann, wie lange die Reise dauert.
▼
Sage, dass sie 3 Stunden dauert.

b
Frage, ob die Schule einen Altglascontainer hat.
▼
Sage ja. Der Behälter ist auf dem Parkplatz.

c
Frage, ob es noch Karten für das Konzert gibt.
▼
Sage ja. Es gibt noch ein paar.

EXERCISE 5 ■■ Make dialogues.
Get information in Britain.

Frage, ob er/sie dir sagen kann, wo die nächsten Recyclingbehälter sind.
▼
Sage, dass es vier Behälter auf dem Parkplatz hinter dem Supermarkt gibt.
▼
Frage, ob du auch deine leeren Dosen loswerden kannst.
▼
Sage nein. Der Behälter ist hinter dem Museum.
▼
Frage, ob er/sie dir sagen kann, ob das Museum freitags geöffnet ist.
▼
Sage, dass es freitags geschlossen ist.

W 25, 10-12

*ACTIVE ENGLISH OPTIONS

*CONTEXTS Recycling and the environment

If you want to be environmentally aware, you need "green information".

Which sentence belongs to which photo (A-G)?
1 These containers are only for glass.
2 This is made from old paper.
3 Leave your car at home and travel by bus.
4 They didn't use animals when they tested this product.
5 These eggs come from hens that don't live in cages.
6 They caught this fish in a net that doesn't hurt dolphins.
7 Don't put glass, plastic bags or old clothes in here, please.

* SONG 🎧 Where do the children play?

Well, I think it's fine,
Building jumbo planes,
Taking a ride,
On a cosmic train,
Switch on summer,
From a slot machine.
Get what you want if you want,
Because you can get anything.

I know, we've come a long way.
We're changing day to day,
But tell me,
Where do the children play?

Well, you roll on roads,
Over fresh, green grass,
For your lorry loads,
Pumping petrol gas.
And you make them long,
And you make them tough,
But they just go on and on,
And it seems you can't get off.

* ACTIVITY Do a class survey.

Work in groups. Find out if the students in your class are environmentally aware. Ask questions. Find out who collects these things for recycling:
- batteries, bottles, cans, magazines, newspapers and old clothes.

Each student can get between 0 – 10 points.

Find out the number of points for each student.
- Under 3 isn't environmentally aware.
- Over 7 is environmentally aware.

Now find out the average number of points for your class.

 3 points
 2 points
 2 points
 2 points
 1 point

* ACTION CARDS 📁 Getting information

■ Make action cards with useful words and phrases from this unit. Your cards can have phrases about:
Asking where something is ▪ Asking when something starts
Asking how long something takes ▪ Asking how much it costs

PRACTICE PAGES

STRUCTURES

EXERCISE 1 ■ Find the right sentence for each picture.

- It isn't only your street. It's hers too!
- He recycles his rubbish. What do you do with yours?
- Don't destroy your environment. It's his too!
- Children must learn that the environment is everybody's problem – theirs too!
- Traffic causes pollution – pollution destroys the environment.

EXERCISE 2 ■ The old canal in Sheffield city centre

1 Between 1960 and 1980 the canal	the canal was cleaned up.
2 But about ten years ago	by the canal.
3 The old buildings	was opened in a boat on the canal.
4 A restaurant	were opened in the old buildings.
5 New offices	wasn't used.
6 New shops and cafés were built	were cleaned.

EXERCISE 3 ☐ Tanya was at the shops. What did/didn't she buy?

1 She bought some …
2 She didn't buy any …

EXERCISE 4 ■■ Write six sentences about the Supertrams in Sheffield.

1 any / weren't / in Sheffield / there / 1993 / trams / Before
2 Supertrams / Some / to Sheffield / in 1993 / were delivered
3 There / from / isn't / any / Supertrams / pollution
4 noise / Supertrams / any / don't make
5 were / in Germany / Supertrams / Some / built
6 some Supertrams / to buy / cities / Other / in Britain / want

1 Before 1993 …   2 …

SITUATIONS

Wie fragst du auf Englisch …
1 … wofür die Stadt berühmt ist?
2 … wo ihr anfangen sollt?
3 … warum jemand seine Meinung änderte?
4 … ob es einen Altglascontainer gibt?
5 … ob es für das Konzert noch Karten gibt?
6 … wie lange die Reise dauert?

Tip: Look again at pages 62-69.

WORDPOWER

WORDPOWER 1 ■ Put the rubbish in the right container.

 compost fruit
 glass …
 paper …
 plastic …

a broken mirror · a cassette
an old biro · broken glasses · bus tickets
fruit · ketchup bottles · magazines
newspapers · old brochures
old flowers · peas · phone cards
postcards · potatoes · tea · leaves

WORDPOWER 2 ■ Find 5 words with *-tion*.
1 TIONSTA
2 PETIONTICOM
3 STRAMONDETION
4 POLTIONLU
5 TIONACDAMOCOM

1 Where the train stops.
2 Enter it, and you can win something.
3 Protesting in a crowd of people.
4 Rubbish, dirty water, lots of noise.
5 A place where you can stay.

WORDPOWER 3 ☐ One word is wrong.

an animal · housework
on TV · a building · water

1 soap, news, letter, advert
2 road, canal, lake, river
3 sheep, rabbit, traffic, cow
4 town hall, noise, airport, stadium
5 cleaning up, tidying, washing, planting

1 letter: it isn't on TV   2 …: it isn't …

WORDPOWER 4 ■■ Make a word web.

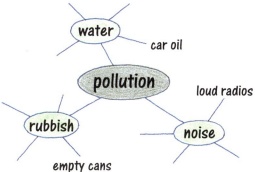

USING A DICTIONARY

DICTIONARY 1 ■ Some words mean two different things. What's the right German word in these sentences?

open 1 *(Verb)* aufmachen
open 2 *(Nomen)* offen
call 1 *(Verb)* nennen
call 2 *(Nomen)* Anruf

1 "*Open* the door!" shouted Sally.
2 "It's *open*," answered her mum.
3 "*Call* me Tom," said Thomas.
4 "There's a *call* for you," said Bob.

DICTIONARY 2 ■■ Find the right German word in the dictionary. Then write the sentences in German.
1 The group hurried through the dark *wood*.
2 Ray *welcomed* the new members.
3 In the *break* the students play cards.
4 *Train* your dog well and it won't hurt anybody.

PRACTICE PAGES

READING From a brochure

Tip: You can find new words in the *Dictionary* (page 140).

the National Centre for Popular Music

- If you listen to music on the radio,
- if you follow the music charts,
- if you want to play in a band,
- if you're interested in music, – then the National Centre for Popular Music is for you!

- We're in the heart of Sheffield:
  – five minutes from the bus station, railway station and the Supertram
  – 15 minutes from the M1 motorway.

The centre has four sections:

1 The museum

Find out about the history of:
- popular music
- Jazz, Reggae, Rock, Soul, Folk, Country and other styles of music
- music from all five continents
- music and dance
- music and films

2 The studios

Find out how:
- famous pop songs were written
- different instruments work
- companies make CDs
- a CD gets from a studio to a CD shop
- your favourite pop video was made
- a DJ spends his/her day

3 The concert hall

Enjoy:
- listening to music
- a musical journey around the world
- live music
- light shows and special videos
- special music programmes for schools
- outdoor live music shows

4 The exhibitions hall

Find out about:
- the life of your favourite pop star
- pop stars' clothes and instruments
- fan clubs and pop magazines
- new stereo equipment
- pop stars' visits to the Centre
- buying and selling your favourite CDs

A steel building in a city famous for steel

EXERCISE 1 ■ Basic reading: Find the right sign for the right section.

A Listen to live music and watch light shows.

B Learn all about pop stars' lives.

C Learn all about the history of pop music.

D Learn all about CDs, videos and musical instruments.

Sign A is for section …   Sign B is for section …   Sign C is for section …   Sign D is for section …

EXERCISE 2 ■ Reading for details: *Yes/No*. Does the brochure say …
1 … that students can visit the centre?
2 … how far the centre is from an airport?
3 … that you can watch videos at the centre?
4 … that you need a day if you visit the four sections?
5 … that they have indoor and outdoor concerts?
6 … how much a ticket for the centre costs?
7 … when the centre opens and closes?
8 … that you can get information about fan clubs?

EXERCISE 3 ■ Language tasks   Tip: All the words are on page 74.
1 Which is the odd one out? *stereo equipment, studio, DJ, CD, instrument*
2 Find the missing words:
   a) Europe is a …
   b) Look in the … for the top ten CDs.
   c) Guitars are the most important … in most pop bands.
   d) Soul and Reggae are different … of music.

LISTENING 🎧 A programme about a competition

The *Radio Sheffield Show:* An interview about the *Clean up Sheffield* competition.

EXERCISE 1 ■ Which photo (A-D) belongs to which project?
1 Tinsley: Photo …
2 Hillsborough: Photo …
3 Heeley: Photo …
4 Fulwood: Photo …

EXERCISE 2 ■■ What's right?
1 The park near Tinsley Youth Club was full of (attractions/rubbish).
2 Hillsborough School worked on (a river / a canal).
3 Members of Heeley Youth Club worked at the City Farm (in their holidays / at weekends).
4 (Heeley Youth Club / Hillsborough School) won the first prize for their canal project.

Weitere Fragen: W 37

SUMMARY

start ... ing, stop ... ing

Die *ing*-Form kann eine Tätigkeit bezeichnen (vgl. Seite 22). Sie wird auch nach *start/stop* verwendet.

Lara loves skiing. She started skiing when she was very young.
   Lara läuft sehr gerne Ski. Sie fing mit dem Skilaufen an, als sie sehr jung war.
It rained an hour ago. But it has stopped raining.
   Es regnete vor einer Stunde, aber es hat aufgehört zu regnen.

mine, yours, ...

I've just found this biro. Is it yours? – No. Mine is blue.

I like your poster. Ours is OK. But yours is nicer.

Sue and Phil have drawn pictures. Hers is better than his.

| mine |
| yours |
| his/hers |
| ours |
| yours |
| theirs |

Mit *mine, yours* usw. sagst du, wem etwas gehört.

Diese Wörter werden ohne ein darauf folgendes Substantiv gebraucht. Vergleiche:

I don't think that's *your* bus. No, it isn't *yours*.
I think that's *my* bus. Yes, it's *mine*.

That isn't Barbara's bike. Hers is black.   Das ist nicht Barbaras Fahrrad. Ihres ist schwarz.
Peter's computer is older than yours.   Peters Computer ist älter als deiner.

Das Passiv

This paper was thrown away.   This car was made in Mannheim in 1885.   These flats were built in 1997.

Mit dem Passiv kann man sagen, dass etwas getan wurde.

Martin's camera was made in Jena.   Martins Kamera wurde in Jena hergestellt.
Two films were shown.   Zwei Filme wurden gezeigt.

BILDUNG
Das Passiv wird aus zwei Teilen zusammmengesetzt:

was/were + Partizip Perfekt (wie z.B. *used, made, taken*)

Bei regelmäßigen Verben endet das Partizip Perfekt auf *-ed,* wie *cooked, played.*

Bei unregelmäßigen Verben gibt es besondere Formen, z. B. *written, worn, forgotten.*

Weitere unregelmäßige Verben findest du auf Seite 158.

IN DIESER UNIT HAST DU GELERNT, …

… wie du sagst, dass etwas angefangen hat.   ➡ *The group has started protesting.*

… wie du sagst, dass etwas aufgehört hat.   ➡ *The clock has stopped working.*

… wie du sagst, wem etwas gehört.   ➡ *Which is your house? – This is ours.*

… wie man sagt, was getan wurde.   ➡ *This tree was planted in 1950.*
Those houses were built 2 years ago.

in einer neuen Umgebung

… Informationen einzuholen.   ➡ *Is there a bottle bank in this road?*
Can you tell me where it is?

*LOOK AROUND 4
Canada

Canada is one of the largest countries in the world. About 30 million people live there.

The south of Canada is warm in summer. The weather can be dangerous. Tornadoes sometimes destroy buildings.

Canada is very cold in winter. In the north life is hard and few people live there. But tourists can see many interesting animals there.

* Fakultativ

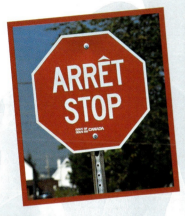  

English and French are the most important languages in Canada. Over 7 million Canadians speak French. Signs in Canada are sometimes in French and English.

The first people in Canada were the Inuit and other Native Canadians.
The Inuit lived in igloos in the coldest parts of Canada. Now they live in houses.

A lot of Canadians enjoy canoeing on Canada's many lakes and rivers.

Companies use the rivers when they have to move wood.

Ice hockey is very popular.

12 million people visit the Niagara Falls every year.

UNIT FIVE
Choosing a job

WORK EXPERIENCE IN BRITAIN

- Most students in Britain do work experience in Year 10, when they're 14 or 15.
- Schools find jobs for students in factories, offices, hospitals and shops.
- Some information about work experience:
  – Students have two weeks work experience.
  – They don't earn any money.
  – A teacher visits students who are doing work experience.
  – Work experience is usually in spring or summer.
  – Students write a diary about their work experience.

- When do students in your school do work experience?
- What was your work experience like?

W 29, 1

A At the youth club, Daniel, Shellina and Marian are talking about work experience and jobs. Marian has an article from a Sheffield newspaper.

MARIAN Look, this is interesting – the five most popular jobs for boys and girls in Germany and here in the North of England.

DANIEL Yes, it *is* interesting. What do you want to be when you leave school? Do you want to be a hairdresser?

MARIAN Not really. It's hard work. I want to be an office clerk.

SHELLINA An office clerk – that's boring. I want to be a shop assistant – in a computer shop or perhaps a music shop. I'm interested in learning more about computers. What about you, Daniel?

DANIEL I don't really know. But I don't want to be a builder. I'm not interested in working outside.

Popular jobs for boys and girls in the North of England and Germany

North of England	Germany
GIRLS	**GIRLS**
1 Hairdresser	1 Doctor's assistant
2 Office clerk	2 Office clerk
3 Shop assistant	3 Shop assistant
4 Secretary	4 Dentist's assistant
5 Factory worker	5 Hairdresser
BOYS	**BOYS**
1 Builder	1 Car mechanic
2 Farm worker	2 Electrician
3 Fisherman	3 Builder
4 Car mechanic	4 Joiner
5 Hairdresser	5 Plumber

What do you want to be when you leave school? What are you interested in doing?
– I want to be a/an …
– I'm interested in …
– I don't want to be a/an …
– I'm not interested in …

W 29, 2

I'm interested in learning …

B Now Alex is with his three friends. He isn't going to do work experience this year.
He did it last year. He worked in a garage – it was fun.

ALEX When's your work experience?
SHELLINA It's in three weeks.
ALEX Where is it?
MARIAN At a travel agency. I'm looking forward to working there.
DANIEL Mine is at a day centre. I'm looking forward to working with old people.
SHELLINA I'm waiting for a place at *Sheffield Computer Games*. I'm looking forward to doing something different.

EXERCISE 1 ■ Who said what? Finish the sentences.

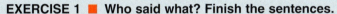

1 "I'm looking forward to talking | new computer games," said Shellina.
2 "But I'm not looking forward to working | school for two weeks," said Shellina.
3 "I'm looking forward to trying | some office work," said Marian.
4 "I'm looking forward to leaving | in the kitchen at the day centre," said Daniel.
5 "I'm looking forward to planning | to old people," said Daniel.
6 "I'm looking forward to doing | holidays for people," said Marian.
7 "And I'm looking forward to hearing | about your work experience in three weeks," said Alex.

What are you looking forward to?		
I'm looking forward to I'm not looking forward to	going out meeting my friends doing a test watching TV doing jobs playing games	tomorrow. this evening. next week/month/year. next Sunday/Monday/… after school.

C Daniel has a place at the Leopold Street Day Centre for his work experience.
He's looking forward to working there.

The Leopold Street Day Centre

Open 10 am to 5 pm.
Drinks, meals and snacks from 10 am to 4 pm.
We need new members over 60.

◆ Meet old friends
◆ Make new friends
◆ Drink tea or coffee
◆ Have lunch or a snack
◆ Read newspapers and magazines
◆ Use our library
◆ Chat with our helpers
◆ Go on a trip every month
◆ Talk to us about your problems

W 29, 3

D Daniel left his house at 9 am. It was his first morning at the day centre. Although he was looking forward to working there, he was a bit nervous. He didn't know anybody at the day centre. When Daniel arrived, Pete was outside. Pete was the warden of the centre. He looked very friendly.
"Hi," he said. "You must be Daniel. How are you this morning?"
Although he was nervous, Daniel smiled. "I'm OK," he said.

EXERCISE 2 ■ **Put the sentences together. Start with *although*.**
1 Daniel was nervous. He smiled. – Although Daniel was nervous, he smiled.
2 Daniel was very busy. He chatted with the other helpers. – Although …
3 Daniel had to work hard. He enjoyed his first day. – Although …
4 The day centre closed at 5 pm. Daniel had to work till 6 pm. – …
5 Daniel was tired after his first day. He went to the cinema in the evening. – …

W 30, 4

E Daniel had to write a diary about his work experience.

MONDAY 9th
I started working at 9.30 am. First I served tea. Then I cleared everything away.
Of course, I dropped one of the cups – and it broke! But the other helpers weren't angry. They laughed.
In the afternoon I chatted with some of the old people. They're fond of chatting. I worked till 6 pm.

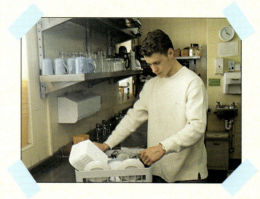

TUESDAY 10th
I spent the morning in the kitchen. At home, I hate working in the kitchen – but here it was great. I had fun and laughed with the other helpers. After lunch, I cleared away the plates. Then I tidied the bookshelves.
I didn't drop anything today!
Another good day.

EXERCISE 3 ■ **What happened on Wednesday 11th? Write Daniel's diary.**
1 Only five people (come) to the day centre.
2 I (not have) a lot of work.
3 I (not help) in the kitchen.
4 I (chat) with some of the helpers.
5 Then I (tidy) the room.
6 I (clear) away the tea things.
7 Pete (not need) me after three o'clock.
8 So I (go) home early.

1 Only five people came to the day centre. 2 I didn't have … 3 … 4 …

F Marian did her work experience in a travel agency. But she didn't like it. When she arrived on her first day nobody talked to her. Everybody was busy. The manager, Mrs Barnes, wasn't very friendly.
She gave Marian a lot of boring jobs:
First Marian opened all the letters – more than 100! Then she made coffee for everybody – but nobody said thank you! And after she had made the coffee, she washed up the cups – alone! Then she unpacked new brochures – that was boring! And after she had unpacked the brochures, she put them in envelopes – that was terrible too!
And after she had finished all those jobs – she was tired. What a morning!

EXERCISE 4 ■ **The afternoon was busy too. Put the sentences in the right order.**
– After she had finished lunch, she tidied the office.
– After she had put the letters in envelopes, she went to the post office.
– After she had tidied the office, she put the letters in envelopes.
– Marian had lunch at 1.30.
– After she had bought stamps at the post office, she remembered the envelopes – they were still on her table!

1 Marian had lunch at 1.30. 2 After she had … 3 …

W 30, 5

G While Marian, Daniel and Shellina were busy with work experience, Alex applied for a place at Midlands College. He wanted to do a car mechanic's course. So he filled in an application form.

MIDLANDS COLLEGE

Application form

Family name: Barker
First names: Alexander Stephen
Age: 16
Address: 17 Bessemer Close, Sharrow, Sheffield S7 5DL
School: Abbeydale School
Hobbies and interests: Cars
Music
Member of youth club
Jobs: Work experience: 2 weeks in a garage
Summer job: 6 weeks in a supermarket
Babysitting

Courses
Hairdresser ☐
Builder ☐
Joiner ☐
Secretary ☐
Plumber ☐
Doctor's/Dentist's assistant ☐
Car mechanic ☒
Bus driver ☐
Ambulance driver ☐
Fitness trainer ☐
Shop assistant ☐

Now you!
You want to apply for a place at Midlands College.
– Choose a course.
– Make an application form.
– Fill it in.

After she had made the coffee, …

STORY 🎧

Shellina has an idea. Will it work?

The Coffee Pot

It was the first week of work experience. At 8.30 am on Wednesday, Shellina went to work.

In the weeks before work experience Shellina had been very unlucky. She had wanted to work at *Sheffield Computer Games*, but the company had closed. Then she had tried to find a place in an office, but she had had no luck. In the end she had found a place as a waitress in a café. It was called *The Coffee Pot* and it belonged to Mr and Mrs Jones.

At 9 am on Wednesday, Shellina arrived at *The Coffee Pot*. Mr Jones was in the kitchen. Mrs Jones was at her computer in the office. Shellina started cleaning the tables and chairs. When some customers came in, she served them. There were never many customers, so the work was easy. But it was a bit boring.

After lunch Marian and Daniel came into *The Coffee Pot*. They wanted two coffees. Shellina sat at their table.
"Are you enjoying the day centre, Daniel?" asked Shellina.
"It's great!" said Daniel, and he told Shellina all about the old people.
"I bet it's more fun than the travel agency," said Marian. "I can't stand the things I have to do. But what's it like here, Shellina?"
"Well," answered Shellina, "Mr and Mrs Jones are very nice. The problem is … well, we don't have enough customers."
"I'm not surprised," said Marian. "It looks a bit dead, doesn't it? And I think we're the only people under fifty!"
"But I have an idea," Shellina smiled.
"Oh?" said Marian. "What is it?"
"Come back next week," said Shellina. "You'll see."

Later Shellina talked about her ideas with Mr and Mrs
Jones. Shellina made a suggestion.
"Why don't we make *The Coffee Pot* into an Internet café?" Shellina asked. "Perhaps only on one day a week – on Saturdays. We could use the computer from your office, and I could bring my computer from home. We could surf the Internet, and ..."
"But that's expensive, isn't it?" interrupted Mr Jones.
"No," said Shellina. "It doesn't cost so much. And customers could pay for every 30 minutes on the Internet. We could advertise in schools and ..."
"Let's try it," said Mrs Jones.

When Marian and Daniel came into *The Coffee Pot* a week later, they were surprised: the café was full! A group of young people were in front of the two computers. More young people had to wait for a place in front of a computer.
People, young and old, were at every table. Shellina was very busy. Daniel and Marian had to wait before they could talk to her. Suddenly Alex came into the café.
"Hi! Good news. I have a place at Midlands College. My course starts in September."

"Brilliant idea!" Daniel told Shellina, when she stopped at their table.
"It has been hard work," said Shellina. "We had to advertise, we had to find out about the Internet ... I've learned so much in the last ten days. Work experience is a great idea."

TASK A ■ Find the lines.
1 Daniel and Marian's first visit to *The Coffee Pot*: lines 19 to ...
2 Wednesday morning at *The Coffee Pot*: lines ... to ...
3 Shellina's clever suggestion: lines ... to ...
4 What had happened before Shellina started her work experience: lines ... to ...
5 Daniel and Marian's second visit to *The Coffee Pot*: lines ... to ...

TASK B ■■ Answer the questions.
1 Shellina didn't work at *Sheffield Computer Games*. Why not?
2 Why was Shellina's job boring?
3 How do we know that most of Shellina's customers were old?
4 Shellina needed two computers. Where did they come from?
5 How did the new customers find out about the Internet café?
6 What was different at *The Coffee Pot* when Daniel and Marian went back there again? Find three things.

W 31, 6-8

ACTIVE ENGLISH

ACTIONS Talking about work

Jenny is talking to a youth worker about a summer job. How many hours a week will she work?

YOUTH WORKER I have a job for you – working in a shop.
JENNY Oh great! When can I start?
YOUTH WORKER On Monday July 10th.
JENNY What will my job be?
YOUTH WORKER Serving the customers and filling the shelves.
JENNY What are my hours?
YOUTH WORKER From 10 am till 5 pm, Monday to Friday.

EXERCISE 1 ■ Make dialogues with a partner about summer jobs.

A PARTNER I have a job for you – …
YOU Oh great! When can I start?
A PARTNER On …
YOU What will my job be?
A PARTNER …
YOU What are my hours?
A PARTNER From … till …

SHEFFIELD JOB CENTRE

Summer jobs for young people:

Where	When	Jobs	Hours
The Tea Shop	5.8. – 5.9.	helping in the kitchen cleaning the tables	Saturdays & Sundays 10.30 am – 6 pm
Babysitting	4.8. – 20.8.	looking after 2 children cleaning the kitchen cooking for children	Mondays and Wednesdays 9 am – 2 pm
The Trend clothes shop	3.8. – 7.9.	helping in the office cleaning	Saturdays 9 am – 6 pm
Carr's supermarket	28.7. – 29.8.	filling the shelves tidying the shop	Monday – Friday 5 pm – 8 pm
The Bookworm bookshop	28.7. – 23.8.	tidying the shelves serving customers	9 am – 3 pm Monday – Saturday

EXERCISE 2 ■ More ideas for summer jobs: Make sentences.

I'd like to work	in a clothes shop, in a fitness centre, in a hotel kitchen, on a farm, in a garage,	because	I'm good at cooking. I like clothes. I'm interested in sport. I'm interested in working with cars. I like working with animals.

Sam is telling his teacher, Mr Blake, about his work experience.

TEACHER What work did you do, Sam?
SAM I worked in a flower shop.
TEACHER Did you enjoy it?
SAM Well, yes and no.
TEACHER What do you mean?
SAM I enjoyed working with flowers.
But I didn't enjoy serving customers.

EXERCISE 3 ■ Make dialogues about work experience.

What work did you do? ■ Did you enjoy it?
What do you mean? ■ What did you enjoy?
What didn't you enjoy?

– I worked in a/an shoe shop/second-hand shop/market/factory/library/bank/office/travel agency/...
– I worked with a builder/joiner/plumber/TV engineer.
– Yes, I did. / No, I didn't. / Well, yes and no.
– I enjoyed / didn't enjoy serving customers / cleaning / answering the phone / chatting with people / working hard / filling the shelves / ...

EXERCISE 4 ☐ Make a dialogue about work experience.

| Frage, was für Arbeit er/sie gemacht hat. |
| Sage, dass du in einem Blumenladen gearbeitet hast. |
| Frage, ob er/sie dies gern gemacht hat. |
| Sage ja. |
| Frage, was ihr/ihm Spaß gemacht hat. |
| Sage, dass du gern Kunden und Kundinnen bedient hast. |

EXERCISE 5 ■■ Make a dialogue about your work experience.

| Sage, welches Berufspraktikum du gemacht hast. |
| Frage, wie es war. |
| Sage, ob es dir Spaß gemacht hat oder nicht. |
| Frage nach den Gründen. |
| Erkläre, was du gern bzw. nicht gern gemacht hast. |
| Frage nach den Arbeitszeiten. |
| Sage, von wann bis wann du gearbeitet hast. |

W 32, 9-10

87

* ACTIVE ENGLISH OPTIONS

* CONTEXTS Different jobs

Which sentence belongs to which photo (A-J)?
1. Apply here if you can repair bikes.
2. Apply for this job if you like helping people who are ill.
3. If you'd like to sell fruit and flowers, apply here.
4. Apply here if you're interested in hairstyles.
5. This is a hard job and it's for people who like working outside.
6. If you're good at painting, you can apply here.
7. In this job you usually work outside and you have to be good at cleaning.
8. This job is for people who like cooking.
9. In this job you wear a uniform and deliver letters.
10. If you're interested in music, perhaps you can sell these.

* LIMERICKS Work

There was a young joiner from Crewe,
Who wanted to build a canoe.
She got to the river,
And found with a shiver,
That she hadn't used waterproof glue.

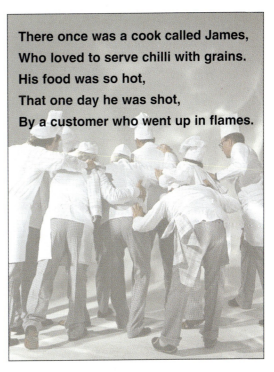

There once was a cook called James,
Who loved to serve chilli with grains.
His food was so hot,
That one day he was shot,
By a customer who went up in flames.

* ACTIVITY Job poster

Find some pictures of an interesting job in magazines. Make a poster with them.
What things do you use in this job? Find some pictures. Use a dictionary and find the words.
Write them on the poster too.
Now write some sentences about the job.
- What's the name of the job?
- Where does the person work?
- What things does the person do?
- Is it inside or outside?
- Is it a difficult job?
- Do you need tools?
- What things do you need?
- Do you know somebody who does this job? Does he/she like it?
- Would you like to do this job?

* ACTION CARDS Talking about work

- Make action cards with useful words and phrases from this unit.
  Your cards can have phrases about:
  Jobs • Work experience • Summer jobs

* Fakultativ **89**

PRACTICE PAGES

STRUCTURES

EXERCISE 1 ■ **A summer job: Put in the *ing*-forms.**

… a summer job in our town is difficult. But I started … for jobs early – and I was lucky. My job for this summer is … at a swimming-pool. That's great because I'm fond of … and I enjoy … outside. I'm looking forward to … work on July 10th. Of course, some things aren't so good. … away other people's rubbish isn't much fun, I know.

applying • clearing
starting • finding
being • swimming
working

EXERCISE 2 ■ **Why weren't they at the film? Make the sentences.**

There was a film at the youth club last week, but some people didn't go.

1 Cathy / because / she had seen the film before / didn't go to the youth club
2 Brian and Jenny / they had heard it was boring / because / didn't watch the film
3 Toby / he had broken his leg / was in hospital / because
4 Gemma / and she wanted / had bought a new CD / to listen to it
5 Ian / so his parents / hadn't done his homework / said no
6 Robert / his ticket / he had lost / because / stayed at home

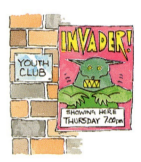

EXERCISE 3 □ ***Although*: Make sentences.**

	although	
1 Sue would like to be a police officer,		I had gone to bed late on Saturday.
2 Fatima had a great holiday in Paris,		his grandmother is German.
3 Kevin can't speak German,		she can't speak French.
4 Mike works in a library,		our CD player is broken at the moment.
5 I've just bought a new CD,		the work is sometimes dangerous.
6 I got up early on Sunday morning,		he isn't fond of reading.

EXERCISE 4 ■■ **What would they like to do? Write sentences and use *although*.**

1 **TESS** I'd like to work in Germany.
   ALI Oh? But you can't speak German.

2 **SUE** I'd like to be a police officer.
   LIZ Oh? But you hate wearing a uniform.

3 **PAUL** I'd like to work in a restaurant.
   JOE But you aren't good at cooking.

4 **JANE** I'd like to get an office job.
   TINA But you hate being inside all day.

5 **BOB** I'd like to be a mechanic.
   IAN Oh? But you can't even repair your bike!

6 **LUKE** I'd like to be a fisherman.
   ANN But it's very dangerous.

1 Tess would like to work in Germany, although she can't speak German.
2 Sue would like to be a police officer, although she …

SITUATIONS

Wie sagst du auf Englisch, dass …
1 … du Verkäufer/in werden willst?
2 … du in einem Reisebüro arbeiten wirst?
3 … du dich darauf freust dort zu arbeiten?
4 … du es hasst in der Küche zu arbeiten?
5 … etwas dich nicht überrascht?
6 … etwas eine großartige Idee ist?

Wie fragst du auf Englisch …
7 … was jemand werden will, wenn er/sie die Schule verläßt?
8 … nach deiner Arbeitszeit?
9 … was für eine Tätigkeit du haben wirst?
10 … ob jemandem etwas gefiel?
11 … was jemandem nicht gefiel?

Tip: Look again at pages 80-87

WORDPOWER

WORDPOWER 1 ■ Look at the clothes. Think of the job.

WORDPOWER 2 ☐ A job quiz
1 It's a man who works on a boat – with fish.
2 It's somebody who puts lights in houses and other places.
3 If you have problems in the bathroom or kitchen, you can phone him/her.
4 He/She builds houses.
5 He/She looks after places like day centres or youth hostels.
6 It's somebody who helps at a day centre or other places.

> a helper
> a warden
> a plumber
> a fisherman
> an electrician
> a builder

WORDPOWER 3 ■ Find the jobs.

> ecoffi klerc • hardisserer • injoer
> inchemac • yacsterer • axit erdriv
> vt ginreene • aetehcr • taiwre
> posh tassisnat

WORDPOWER 4 ■■ Make a word web.

- serve meals
- waiter
- what you must do
- jobs
- work
- restaurant
- where people work

WORDPOWER 5 ■ What's the wrong word in the group?
1 letter, envelope, stamp, shelf
2 competition, waitress, fitness trainer, joiner
3 chat, speak, fill in, talk
4 choose, serve, decide, pick
5 fond of, hate, enjoy, interested in
6 application form, paper bank, diary, notice

PRACTICE PAGES

READING Applying for a job

Tip: You can find new words in the *Dictionary* (page 140).

CV

Family name	Mushtaq
First name	Mohammed
Age	16
Place of birth	Sheffield, England
Nationality	British
Address	23 Cherry Tree Road, Darnall, Sheffield S9 4TU
Telephone	0114 843 068
Languages	Urdu, some German
School subjects	Maths, English, physics, biology, history, German, design & technology, art
Hobbies	Computers, playing the guitar, cooking, gardening
Sports	Hockey, cricket, mountain-biking, inline-skating
Evening and weekend jobs	Delivering newspapers (2 years) Working at a garden centre in Darnall (1 year)
Work experience	2 weeks in Brightways supermarket
Travel abroad	School trip to Germany Family holidays in Pakistan

23 Cherry Tree Road,
Darnall
Sheffield S9 4TU
June 26th

The Manager
Highgate Garden Centre
Highgate Road
Sheffield

Dear Sir/Madam,

I saw your advert in the Sheffield News for a job in your garden centre this summer. I'm very interested in gardening and I'd like to apply for the job.

I worked at a garden centre in Darnall on Saturdays last year. That job has finished now because the centre had to close. I served customers and looked after the plants there. The manager, Mr Davis, was very happy with my work and I was always punctual and reliable. I've had other jobs too. I delivered newspapers for a year and I did my work experience in a supermarket in Sheffield.

When I leave school I want to do a course in gardening. I'm interested in learning as much as possible about plants and gardens. I'm sure that a summer job at your garden centre will be good experience.

I'm fit, I do a lot of sport and I can carry heavy things. I can start working from July 13th.

I'm looking forward to hearing from you.

Yours faithfully,

Mohammed Mushtaq

EXERCISE 1 ■ Basic reading: Is it a) in the cv only, b) in the letter only, c) in the cv *and* in the letter or d) not in the texts?

1 Mohammed wants a job at a garden centre.
2 He lives in Sheffield.
3 He has no sisters.
4 He has lots of hobbies and interests.
5 He's interested in gardening.
6 He's British.
7 He wants to work in the summer.
8 He hates working in an office.

EXERCISE 2 ■ Reading for details: One thing is wrong. What is it? Can you correct it?

1 Mohammed can speak Urdu and French.
2 He doesn't learn history at school.
3 He has never been outside Europe.
4 Mohammed works at the Darnall garden centre.
5 Mr Davis is the manager of the Highgate garden centre.
6 Mohammed hasn't had other jobs.
7 When he leaves school he wants to do a course in German.
8 Mohammed can start work in June.

EXERCISE 3 ■ Language tasks   Tip: All the words are on page 92.
1 Which word is wrong here: *physics, biology, nationality, technology*?
2 And which word is wrong here: *advert, plant, garden centre, flower*?
3 Find the missing words: a) Mohammed … customers.   d) He … after plants.
   b) He … newspapers.   e) He's … for a job.
   c) He can … heavy things.   f) He can … working soon.

LISTENING 🎧 An interview for work experience

Tracy is in a shoe shop in Sheffield. An interview between Tracy and Mrs Singh, the manager.

EXERCISE 1 ■ Listen to Part 1 of the interview. What's right – a or b?

Application form for work experience

	(a)	(b)
1 Name of school	Moorfoot School	Burford School
2 Name of student	Tracy Midmer	Tracy Midler
3 Age	16	15
4 Address	43 Abbeydale Grove	34 Abbeydale Grove
5 Telephone number	323648	323698
6 School subjects	English, maths, science geography, German	English, maths, science history, French

1 a   2 …   3 …   4 …   5 …   6 …

EXERCISE 2 ■■ Listen to Part 2 of the interview. Right or wrong?
1 Tracy likes working with people.
2 Last year she worked in a bank.
3 Now she works in a day centre.
4 She doesn't like the old people there.
5 After school Tracy wants to go to college.
6 She has an aunt in Australia.

Weitere Fragen: W 38

SUMMARY

ing-Form

Du kannst die *ing*-Form nach **interested in ▪ look forward to ▪ fond of** gebrauchen.

Are you interested in working with computers?
   Bist du daran interessiert, mit Computern zu arbeiten?
I'm looking forward to meeting you.
   Ich freue mich darauf, Sie kennen zu lernen.

Bob is **fond of reading** newspapers.

I'm so happy we're interested in doing the same things. That's important for friends.
I'm looking forward to reading your next letter.
Jake

I'm very interested in working with animals. So I'm looking forward to working in this zoo.

although

Mit *although* (= *obwohl* oder *obgleich*) kannst du Sätze verbinden und gegenüberstellen.

Although it was cold, the children went swimming.

Although we played well, we didn't win the match.

Mary went to work, although she was ill.
   Mary ging zur Arbeit, obwohl sie krank war.
   Mary ist zur Arbeit gegangen, obwohl sie krank war.
I buy CDs, although they're expensive.
   Ich kaufe CDs, obwohl sie teuer sind.

The past perfect

Bei mehreren Ereignissen in der Vergangenheit drückt man mit dem *past perfect* (Vorvergangenheit) aus, welches weiter zurücklag.

Jenny finished her homework.   She went to bed.

After Jenny had finished her homework, she went to bed.

After I had washed up, I put the things in the cupboard.
    Nachdem ich abgespült hatte, stellte ich die Sachen in den Schrank.
We had closed all the windows before we left the house.
    Wir hatten alle Fenster geschlossen, bevor wir das Haus verließen.
Before the students went to London, they had read a lot about the city.
    Bevor die Schüler London besuchten, hatten sie viel über die Stadt gelesen.

Das *past perfect* wird gebildet mit *had* und dem Partizip Perfekt des Verbs.
Bei regelmäßigen Verben endet das Partizip Perfekt auf *-ed*:

    When mum came home, we had cooked lunch.

Bei unregelmäßigen Verben gibt es besondere Formen des Partizip Perfekts.

    When dad came home, we had eaten lunch.

Weitere unregelmäßige Verben findest du auf Seite 158.

IN DIESER UNIT HAST DU GELERNT, …

… zu sagen, was dich interessiert.	➡ I'm interested in working outside.
… zu sagen, dass du dich auf etwas freust.	➡ I'm looking forward to visiting you.
… zu sagen, dass du etwas doch tust.	➡ Although I'm busy, I'll help you.
bei einem Vorstellungsgespräch	
… nach Arbeitsbedingungen zu fragen.	➡ What will my job be? What hours will I work?
… über dein Berufspraktikum zu sprechen.	➡ I worked in a café. I didn't enjoy working late.

*LOOK AROUND 5
Living abroad

A lot of Germans find jobs in other countries. What's it like to live away from your family and home? What's it like to speak a foreign language every day? Is it easy to make friends? Do people miss their old friends and neighbours? Here are some young people who are talking about their lives in other countries.

SABINE My family lives near Freudenstadt. When I left school, I became a skiing instructor.
My aunt lives in Canada. With her help I found a job here. I teach skiing in Canada now. Skiing in Germany is great, but the mountains in Canada are the best! I teach swimming in the summer.
Canadians are very friendly – they always talk to strangers. I feel at home here but I miss my old friends and my family. I have my own life here. I have a Canadian boyfriend and I want to stay in Canada.

JÜRGEN I live in Jamaica. When I was 9, my father started a new job with an American fruit company in Jamaica. I didn't like leaving Germany but now I really like Jamaica. The weather is great and I can swim in the sea every day. I like the food too.
Some people are very poor here and there's a lot of crime. It can sometimes be dangerous on the streets at night. But most people here are friendly. I have made a lot of friends in school and I speak English well now. I play in the school cricket team.
I don't want to go back to Germany.

FRANZISKA I was born in Germany and I started school in Stuttgart. When I was 13, my mother married my stepfather, who's Indian. We moved to India and my mother became a teacher at a German language school in Chennai (Madras). I spoke German with my mother and English at school. My Indian friends taught me a lot of Tamil words. But we spoke English most of the time.
I'm 28 now and I'm an engineer. I went to college in Germany. After college I came back to India because I found a job with a German company which has big projects in India. I enjoy living in India.

ANDREAS When I was a teenager in Ihringen, I often worked in vineyards. I left school 2 years ago and I work in a vineyard in Australia now. I can work here for a year.
In the first few weeks here, I didn't understand the Australian accent. Now I understand everybody and I speak English with an Australian accent!
I want to work here for a while and learn English. The people are very friendly.
Australia is very beautiful, but I also miss Germany. Australia is so big and Germany is so far away. I would like to go back to Germany next year.

*EXTRA UNIT ONE

A JOINING A CLUB

Why do teenagers join clubs? Some young people join clubs because they want to make new friends. Other teenagers want to practise a sport or hobby. They usually have to pay an annual membership fee (for example, £15 a year). Then members pay less money per session at the club every week.

Jean Smart joined the Swimming Club because her boyfriend, Tony, was a member. Jean isn't his girlfriend now, but she's still a member of the Swimming Club. Jean's parents aren't always happy when she goes to her club. "When will you do your homework?" they ask.

But some parents are happy when their children go out. Jack Bolt's family moved to Sheffield six months ago, so he doesn't have many friends yet. Jack's parents hope he'll make some new friends at the youth club.

> Talk about a club.
> Are you a member?
> Would you like to join? Why?
> What does it cost?
> Do members pay less money per session?

EW 1, 1*

B

Last year Jean joined the Swimming Club.

JEAN Hallo. I'd like to join the Swimming Club.
WOMAN Great! Can you fill in this form, please?
JEAN OK. What does it cost?
WOMAN If you're under 16, it's £15 a year. And 40p per session.
JEAN And when do we meet?
WOMAN Monday and Wednesday evenings from 6.20 till 7.30.

EXERCISE 1 ■ Jack is joining the Photo Club.
What are the missing words?

1 Hallo. I'd like to … the Photo Club.
2 Great! Can you … in this form, please?
3 OK. What does it …?
4 It's … per session.
5 And when do we …?
6 Saturday mornings … 10.00 … 12.00.

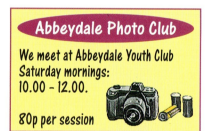

Abbeydale Photo Club
We meet at Abbeydale Youth Club
Saturday mornings:
10.00 – 12.00.
80p per session

EW 1, 2-4

EXERCISE 2 ■ You want to join two clubs. Make dialogues with a partner.

■ ABBEYDALE
■ AEROBICS
■ CLUB
We meet every Wednesday evening (7.30 - 8.30) at Abbeydale Youth Club.
Membership: £10 a year (if you're under 18: £3.50)

Sparkbrook Indoor Tennis Club
Saturdays: 2.00 - 5.00 pm
Annual membership: £18

SHARKS! SKI CLUB
Saturday mornings
10.00 - 12.00
at
Sheffield Ski Village
Annual membership: £15
(Two hour card: £7.50)

EW 2, 5

C AT THE SWIMMING-POOL

A lot of people don't live near an indoor swimming-pool. Jean is lucky.
She lives near a swimming-pool. If you go there, you can …

… swim – or dive from a diving-board,   … go down a water chute,   … listen to music and do exercises in the water,   … have a snack or talk to your friends.

EXERCISE 3 ■ **Tell your partner about your nearest swimming-pool (or sports centre).**
What can/can't you do there? Look at the photos on this page. For example:
1 You can swim there.   2 You can't go down a water chute.   3 You …

EW 3, 6–7

D

Last August, Jean and her old boyfriend Tony were often able to go to the outdoor swimming-pool. He wasn't a good swimmer. But he was able to dive very well. He was very confident. He even dived from the 8-metre board. Jean sometimes dived from the 1-metre board. But she wasn't able to dive very well and she didn't like it. She sometimes went up to the high diving-board, but then she walked down again. She was afraid of diving from the 8-metre board. Tony and Jean weren't able to talk about her problem. Tony always laughed. "Don't be a coward!" he said. That didn't help.

EW 3, 8

> And you? How fast can you swim 100 metres? Are you afraid of diving?

EXERCISE 4 ■ **At the outdoor swimming-pool last summer. Make eight sentences.**

Tony Jean Tony and Jean	was able to wasn't able to were able to weren't able to	go to the outdoor swimming-pool together in August. swim well. dive well. dive from the 8-metre board. dive from the 1-metre board. talk about Jean's problem together.

EW 4, 9–10

✓ **CHECKPOINT**

Was jemand (nicht) tun konnte: *was/wasn't able to*
My grandma was able to swim.   She wasn't able to dive very well.

E A GROUP HOLIDAY

Abbeydale Youth Club organises short holidays for small groups of members. This year they want to go to the Peak District. The Peak District is a National Park outside Sheffield. Jack has written a letter to an outdoor centre for young people.

> Abbeydale Youth Club
> 273 Abbeydale Road
> Sheffield S2 9DL — Your address
>
> Grindleford Outdoor Centre
> Grindleford
> Derbyshire DE4 2HH — This is the postcode.
>
> 21st September — Date
>
> You start a formal letter like this. — Dear Sir or Madam,
>
> Seven members of our youth club in Sheffield are planning to spend three days in the Peak District at the end of October. Could you send us a brochure about the Outdoor Centre, please?
>
> Is there accommodation for boys and girls? Can we have meals at the centre? What does it cost per night? Will we be able to go potholing near the centre?
>
> We're looking forward to hearing from you.
>
> You finish a formal letter like this. — Yours faithfully,
>
> Jack Bolt
>
> You can have a PS at the end of your letter. — PS Could you send us a map of the National Park, please? Thank you.

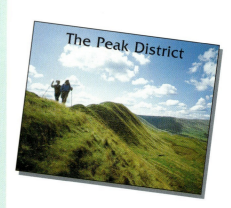

EW 4, 11

EXERCISE 5 ■ For each picture, write a question from the letter.

1  2  3 4  5

1 Could you send us a brochure about the Outdoor Centre, please?
2 … 3 … 4 … 5 …

EXERCISE 6 ■ Drop two pencils on the letter. Then copy the letter.

EXERCISE 7 ■ Write a letter to the Tourist Information Centre in Sheffield.
You and two friends are going to spend a week in Sheffield next year.
Ask for brochures and information about *your* interests.

EW 5, 12

EXTRA UNIT ONE

THE OUTDOOR CENTRE

Jean, David and Jack went on the trip to the Outdoor Centre. Jack's younger sister, Susan, wanted to go too. But her father said, "No. You're too young." So she wasn't allowed to go.
At the centre, Cabin A was for the girls and Cabin B for the boys. The boys weren't allowed to go into Cabin A. No girl was allowed to go into Cabin B. There were other rules too. An instructor said, "We're going to do a lot in a very short time. So breakfast is at 7 am. In the evening you'll be tired. So you aren't allowed to stay up after 10 pm. And nobody is allowed to play music after 10.15. But, believe me, you'll have fun." Jean and her friends practised abseiling. They went pony-trekking. Then they started an orienteering course in a wood that they didn't know. They had to use a map and find their way out again. On the last day they went down into some beautiful caves. The instructor was right. It was a great holiday.

EXERCISE 8 ■ Put in *was/were allowed to* or *wasn't/weren't allowed to*.
1 Susan … go on the trip.
2 No boy … go into Cabin A.
3 The girls … go into Cabin B.
4 Nobody … stay in bed after 7 am.
5 They … stay up after 10 pm.
6 They … play music till 10.15.
7 In the wood, they … use a map.
8 They … go into some caves.

EXERCISE 9 ■ Talk to your partner about your last school trip.
What were you allowed to do? What weren't you allowed to do?

EW 5, 13-14

LISTENING Down in the caves

You're going to hear about the last day at the Outdoor Centre.

EXERCISE 10 ■ Listen to the story. What's right? What's wrong?
1 Sixteen people went down into some caves.
2 In the first cave they saw a man.
3 The group had to walk along a tunnel.
4 Jean, David and Mr Jackson went into the tunnel first.
5 Jean wasn't afraid of the tunnel.
6 There were beautiful green rocks in the last cave.

Weitere Fragen: EW 6, 15-16

Soon after the trip, Jean met Tony at the swimming-pool. He got a big surprise. Jean went up to the 8-metre board. And she was able to do it – she dived from the 8-metre board. Tony swam to her. "Cool," he said. "You aren't a coward now."
"No," Jean said. "If you can do it, I can do it too. I learned that when I was in a cave. But I must go. I have to meet David in an hour."

Weitere Übungen: EW 7/8

Was jemand (nicht) tun durfte: *was allowed to*
Brendan was allowed to watch TV till 10 pm.   He wasn't allowed to go to bed late.

*EXTRA UNIT TWO

DANGEROUS DOGS

In this magazine last month there was an article about John Saunders (10):

He was watching TV with his grandmother, Mrs Helen Homan. They were in her living-room. Sammy, Mrs Homan's young Rottweiler dog, was sleeping in front of the fire. But when Mrs Homan left the room, Sammy jumped at John. He bit the boy's left arm. John had to go to hospital. He still has problems with his arm.

EW 9, 1

Here are two of our readers' letters about this article:

Dear Animal World

Your story about John Saunders made me angry! I think the government should ban Rottweilers and other dangerous dogs now!
If we don't ban these dogs, the streets won't be safe. If the government changes the law, these dogs won't attack people in the future.
It's easy, really – why can't people have a friendly dog? I can't understand why people want to own dangerous dogs. People can't always have their favourite animal as a pet. They aren't allowed to have pet tigers – so ban dangerous dogs too.

Yours faithfully,
Paul Hudson, London

Dear Animal World

I read your article about a dog that attacked a child. It's very sad when these attacks happen. But why do people always blame the dog?
I blame the owner of the dog! If an owner trains a dog well, it won't attack people. But if an owner doesn't train a dog well, the dog will become aggressive. Then it's the owner's fault. It isn't the dog's fault!
Banning Rottweilers isn't the answer. We must punish owners who don't train their dogs well.

Yours faithfully,
Natalie Chandler, Birmingham

EXERCISE 1 ■ Find the person who …

1 … has a problem with his left arm.
2 … owns a Rottweiler dog.
3 … believes people can't always have special pets.
4 … thinks owners must train dogs well.
5 … says an aggressive dog is the owner's fault.
6 … thinks the government must ban some dogs.

EW 9, 2

EXERCISE 2 ■ How many sentences can you make?

1 If we don't ban dangerous dogs,	more people will buy dangerous pets.
2 If you don't train a dog well,	it isn't the dog's fault.
3 If a dog attacks somebody,	more dogs will bite people.
4 If the government doesn't change the law,	you aren't a good dog owner.

EW 9, 3

EXERCISE 3 ■ Write a letter to the magazine about the article.

Who's right, Natalie or Paul? Say why.
Who's wrong? Say why.
Dear Animal World, …

Was unter bestimmten Bedingungen geschehen wird:
If the dog **stays** in the water, **it'll** get cold.   If you **train** your dog, it **won't** attack people.

*Fakultativ   If we don't ban these dogs, the streets won't be safe. (Wiederholung)

B DOGS FOR PEOPLE WITH DISABILITIES *Animal World Magazine*

Guide Dogs for the Blind is an association that trains dogs. These dogs help blind people in Britain. Another association that trains dogs is *Hearing Dogs for the Deaf*. These dogs become the ears of deaf people. Now read about two people who have special dogs – dogs that help them inside and outside their homes.

Gerald is blind. But he has a guide dog, Betsy. Gerald and Betsy are a team. When he wants to cross a road, Gerald stops at the side of the road. Then he says "Forward" to Betsy. The dog only starts crossing the road when there's no traffic. So Gerald knows he's safe. Gerald doesn't like it when people touch or feed his dog. Betsy is a working dog. When he needs help, Gerald asks a person who can see.

Rebecca is deaf. When her baby cries, she can't hear him. Her alarm clock can't wake her. Rebecca can't hear the telephone or the doorbell. But Flash, her hearing dog, helps her. When he hears a noise, Flash touches Rebecca with his nose. He then takes her to the place where the noise is coming from. "Flash hears for me," says Rebecca.

EW 10, 4-5a

EXERCISE 4 ■ Find sentences that mean:
1 These associations teach dogs to help people.
2 Gerald can't see.
3 Gerald and Betsy work together.
4 Gerald asks people for help.
5 Rebecca can't hear.
6 "Flash has become my ears now."

EXERCISE 5 ■ Finish the sentences.
1 Guide dogs help …
2 Hearing dogs help …
3 Special dogs can help people …
4 Betsy helps Gerald when …
5 Betsy is a working dog. Other people mustn't …
6 Rebecca can't hear her baby when …
7 Flash touches Rebecca when …

EW 10, 5b

LISTENING 🎧 An interview with Matthew

The *Radio Sheffield Show:* An interview with Matthew, a deaf person.

EXERCISE 6 ■ Which photo (A-D) comes first? Which photo comes next?

EXERCISE 7 ■ Find the wrong word(s) in each sentence.
1 Matthew has problems because he can't see.
2 Sleeping is a problem for Matthew.
3 Matthew wakes Jess up in the morning.
4 Matthew missed his family on his birthday.
5 Jess knows Matthew's address.
6 A bus driver attacked Matthew.

Weitere Fragen: EW 11, 6

TWO NEWSPAPER STORIES

C *A lucky dog*

Emma Short and her grandfather were taking his dog Daisy for a walk in January. Suddenly Daisy saw a bird on a frozen lake. She ran after the bird onto the thin ice. The dog broke through the ice into the cold water.
"I wanted to rescue my dog," Mr Short told our reporter. "I went onto the ice. But the ice started breaking and I had to turn back." Mr Short wanted to phone the fire brigade. But then Emma saw a boat. There was a rope in it.

"If you hold the rope, I can rescue Daisy," she said to her grandfather. He wasn't so sure. Emma climbed into the boat and Mr Short pushed it into the lake. It broke the ice. With a paddle, Emma moved the boat nearer to Daisy. Emma pulled the dog into the boat. Mr Short pulled the boat back to the side of the lake.

"Daisy was very cold but she was still alive," said the happy owner.

D *Man drowns in lake*

Edward Morris (54) drowned last Sunday. His dog ran onto a frozen lake near Sheffield. The ice was too thin. The dog broke through the ice into the water. Mr Morris jumped into the water and tried to rescue the dog. But the water was too cold. Mr Morris started shouting for help. Jill Cox (15) was taking her dog for a walk near the lake. She heard the shouting and saw Mr Morris in the water. She ran to a telephone and phoned the fire brigade.
Two other people went into the water but they weren't able to help Mr Morris. Later, a police diver found Mr Morris under the ice. He was dead.

A police officer told our reporter, "Dog owners mustn't try to rescue their pets from frozen lakes. It's too dangerous. Most dogs get out of the water without help – like Mr Morris' dog."

EW 11, 7-8

> Emma and Mr Morris: were they brave or very silly? What do you think?

EXERCISE 8 ■ Find what happened in text C, text D or texts C and D.
1. A dog ran onto a frozen lake. *C and D.*
2. A dog broke through the thin ice.
3. An owner wanted to rescue his dog.
4. Nobody phoned the fire brigade.
5. A girl phoned the fire brigade.
6. Two people tried to help a man in a lake.
7. A man pushed a boat into a lake.
8. A girl rescued her grandfather's dog.
9. A man drowned.
10. The dog didn't die.

EXERCISE 9 ■ Answer the questions in full sentences.
1. Who did Daisy belong to?
2. Why did Daisy run onto the ice?
3. How did Mr Short try to rescue his dog?
4. Where was Emma when she rescued Daisy?
5. How did Mr Short help Emma?
6. When did Mr Morris jump into the lake?
7. Why did Mr Morris shout for help?
8. How did Jill Cox try to help Mr Morris?
9. Where did the diver find Mr Morris?
10. Do dogs usually die in water?

EW 12, 9

EXTRA UNIT TWO

EXERCISE 10 ■ What did Emma think? Write six sentences.
1 If my grandfather (go) onto the ice, it (break). *If my grandfather goes onto the ice, it'll break.*
2 If we (wait) for the fire brigade, it (be) too late.
3 If Daisy (stay) too long in the cold water, she (die).
4 If I (go) into the water, I (die).
5 If we (push) the boat into the water, it (break) the ice.
6 If Daisy (die), my grandfather (be) very sad.

EXERCISE 11 ■ A reporter is interviewing Emma. Work with a partner.
Write the missing questions and answers. Then practise the interview together.

REPORTER
1 Where did you go for a walk?
2 Why did Daisy go onto the ice?
3 But the ice was too thin, wasn't it?
4 Why didn't your grandfather rescue his dog?
5 …?
6 …?
7 …?
8 …?

EMMA
We went for a walk near a lake.
…
…
…
No, that was my idea. I saw the boat first.
The rope was in the boat.
I used a paddle.
He pulled the boat back to the side of the lake.

EW 13, 10-11

EXERCISE 12 ■ Tell the story. Write two sentences for each picture.

1 Jenny/Rob/walk/town
2 want/go swimming

3 suddenly/see/fire/house
4 see/child/upstairs/window

5 Rob/phone/fire brigade
6 but/Jenny/go/house

7 Jenny/go/upstairs
8 find/small boy/bedroom

9 Jenny/come/window/child/arms
10 3 minutes/fire brigade/arrive

1 Jenny and Rob were walking through town.
2 They wanted to go swimming.
3 Suddenly …

EW 14, 12-13
Weitere Übungen: EW 15/16

*EXTRA UNIT THREE

AN ALTERNATIVE LIFESTYLE

It's two o'clock at the fair in Sligo, in the West of Ireland. Sally Proudfoot and Ross Langley are enjoying themselves. They aren't winning prizes or eating ice-creams. They're putting on a puppet show.

Sally and Ross left school in Liverpool a year ago. "We didn't want to go to college," said Sally. "And we didn't want a nine-to-five job. We wanted a different lifestyle."

Sally had an old van. Ross was good at making puppets. So they decided to travel in the van and put on puppet shows.

They came to Ireland last May. "Our first fair was in the capital, Dublin," said Ross. "We were a bit nervous, of course, but our puppet show went very well. The children laughed and enjoyed the show. And now we travel from fair to fair. It's great. We love it."

They live and sleep in the van. "That's a bit uncomfortable, isn't it?" I asked. "Yes, but it's cheap. We needn't pay for accommodation," answered Sally.

"Living in a van is great. But cooking isn't easy," explained Ross. "It gets too hot. We eat a lot of fresh food so we needn't cook every day."

"And we needn't cook tonight," said Sally. "We've made friends with some people in town. We can sleep in their house tonight. Now, that's luxury!"

And what do their parents think about their alternative lifestyle? "Oh, our parents needn't worry about us," said Ross. "We're safe, we're happy, and we earn a bit of money. Our parents should be happy."

I don't know if Ross and Sally's parents are happy. But I saw the children who watched the puppet show. And they looked very happy.

EW 17, 1-2

EXERCISE 1 ■ Write the sentences about Sally and Ross.

1 Sally/come from/Liverpool/Ross and
2 go to/didn't/They/college/want to
3 decided to/puppet shows/put on/They
4 Ireland/travel/They/to fair/from fair/in
5 sleep/Sally/live/and/Ross/in a van/and
6 very happy/They're/their/with/lifestyle

1 Sally and Ross come from Liverpool.

EXERCISE 2 ■ Sally is telling a reporter about her lifestyle. Make the sentences.

1 We needn't cook tonight
2 Our show never starts before 2 pm
3 We eat a lot of fresh food
4 We needn't stay in hotels
5 Our parents needn't worry about us
6 We've done this show many times

so we needn't cook meals every day.
because we live in the van.
so we needn't get nervous before the show.
because we're staying with friends.
so we needn't work from nine to five.
because we're safe.

EW 17, 3-5

Was jemand nicht zu tun braucht: *needn't*
You **needn't** check the sports equipment. I've already checked it.
Cheer up. You **needn't** worry about the test. You've learned all the new words.

* Fakultativ   We needn't pay for accommodation.

THE STREETS OF LONDON

In the last few years, the number of young homeless people has increased. How do they live? Where do they sleep? We met Lisa in a shop doorway near Victoria Station. We asked her a few questions.

QUESTION *When did you leave home?*
LISA A year ago. My parents argued a lot. My dad was often drunk. One day he hit me. That's when I left home.
QUESTION *Why did you come to London?*
LISA I have a few friends here. I knew there weren't any jobs. I wanted to earn some money.
QUESTION *How do you earn money?*
LISA I play my guitar in the streets. And I sell *The Big Issue* at a station.
QUESTION *Where do you sleep?*
LISA Sometimes I spend a few nights with friends. But sometimes I sleep rough – in shop doorways. When it's too cold, I go to a hostel.
QUESTION *What's it like in the streets?*
LISA The streets are frightening at night. Sometimes I'm lonely. But I have my dog. He's my best friend.
QUESTION *Are people nice to you?*
LISA Some train passengers smile or chat with me. I've learned that there are a lot of good people in the world. But not everybody likes homeless people.

Some homeless people sell *The Big Issue*

THE BIG ISSUE

Many homeless people in Britain sell *The Big Issue* magazine. They buy the magazine for 40p and sell it for 80p. Selling *The Big Issue* means that they can earn some money.

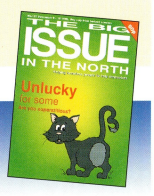

EW 19, 6

EXERCISE 3 ■ What's right?
1 Lisa *comes / doesn't come* from London.
2 She has *no / a few* friends in the capital.
3 Lisa *earns / doesn't earn* enough money.
4 She sleeps rough if *it's / it isn't* too cold.
5 The homeless girl *is/isn't* alone at night.
6 She *meets / doesn't meet* a lot of nice people.

EXERCISE 4 ■ Find the questions.
1 It's frightening at night.
2 I sell a magazine and I play the guitar.
3 Some are nice, some aren't.
4 I left home when my dad hit me.
5 With friends, in hostels or shop doorways.
6 I wanted to earn some money.

EXERCISE 5 ■ Work with a partner. Use the notes and write an interview with David.

QUESTION *When did you leave home?*
DAVID About nine months ago.
QUESTION *Why did you come to London?*
DAVID …

- left home about 9 months ago
- friends in London
- sell *The Big Issue*
- sleep rough – sometimes in a hostel
- streets are lonely and dangerous
- other homeless people are my friends

EW 19, 7-10

C A SOCIAL PROJECT

WHEELS

What's joyriding?
Some young people enjoy driving cars – other people's cars! They drive too fast and there are a lot of accidents. Some joyriders are already dead.

That's joyriding.   • Dangerous • Fast • Illegal

What's Wheels?
Wheels is a project that gives young people an alternative. Young people learn to repair old cars in our garage. When they've repaired the cars, they can drive them – on our own track. They *don't* use public roads.

That's Wheels   • Safe • Exciting • Legal

Who is Wheels for?
We welcome all young people who are interested in cars and driving.

Why does Wheels need your help?
We have to buy equipment. We have to pay for our garage. We need money. Please support us. Give a donation. Become a Wheels supporter.

EXERCISE 6 ■ *Wheels:* Correct these sentences. Write them again.

1 Joyriders drive their own cars.
2 Joyriding is legal and dangerous.
3 Most joyriders die in accidents.
4 *Wheels* teaches joyriders to drive.
5 Members of *Wheels* drive on public roads.
6 *Wheels* is for people who enjoy joyriding.
7 *Wheels* buys old cars with the money.
8 The supporters give old cars to *Wheels*.

EW 21, 11

LISTENING *Wheels*

Martin is new at *Wheels*. Jason and Linda are telling him about the project.

EXERCISE 7 ■ Which poster is right?

A WHEELS
… is for everybody, from 9 – 99
… meets every day, Mon – Fri
… costs nothing

B WHEELS
… is for people over 18
… meets every month
… costs £15 per session

C WHEELS
… is for young people under 24
… meets two days a week
… costs £1 per session

EXERCISE 8 ■ Listen again. What's right?

1 *50/15/5* members are usually there.
2 The youngest member is *12/30/13*.
3 The oldest member is *14/24/21*.
4 Members pay *10p/£10/£1* per session.
5 Jason goes to *Wheels* on *Mondays / twice a week / on Sundays*.
6 The Rover is *Linda's/Jason's/Martin's* favourite car.

Weitere Fragen: EW 21, 12

EXTRA UNIT THREE

LETTERS ABOUT *WHEELS*

People in Sheffield have different opinions about the *Wheels* project.
Here are some letters in the local newspaper.

Why should we support car thieves? People who steal cars should pay a fine. Or they should go to prison. I give donations to young people who work hard.
For example, some teenagers want to go to college but they don't have enough money. They need our support. *Wheels* is a silly idea!

Clare Palmer

Wheels offers an alternative. The young people who go to *Wheels* learn about cars. Perhaps some of them will get jobs as drivers or mechanics. That's good for them. And they'll all become better drivers. That's good for everybody. I've already given my donation to *Wheels*.

Stephen Hardy

In my part of the town, young people have nothing to do. Many are unemployed. Many are bored. Going to the cinema is too expensive. That's why they take cars.
Of course joyriding isn't OK. But complaining doesn't help. We should help the young people instead. That's why I think *Wheels* is a great idea. We should all support it.

Jody Canfield

What do the young people learn at *Wheels*? I'm sure they learn about breaking into cars. And then they learn to drive fast – so that they can escape from the police. No, I'm not going to give a donation to *Wheels*. It should stop its work.

Rod Longhurst

EW 22, 13

EXERCISE 9 ■ Who supports *Wheels*? Who doesn't support it?
1 Clare Palmer …   3 Jody Canfield …
2 Stephen Hardy … 4 Rod Longhurst …

EXERCISE 10 ■ Who says this: a) Clare b) Jody c) Stephen d) Rod?
1 *Wheels* teaches the wrong things.
2 If they go to *Wheels*, more young people will find work when they leave school.
3 We should help students who don't have a lot of money.
4 Young people don't have enough to do.
5 At *Wheels* young people will learn to drive well.

EXERCISE 11 ■ What's *Wheels*?
- Who goes to *Wheels*?
- What do the members do there?
- What does *Wheels* need?
- Why is *Wheels* a good idea?

EXERCISE 12 ■ What's your opinion?
Write a letter to the newspaper.
What's your opinion of *Wheels*:
- Is it a good project?
- Say why/why not.

Tip: Look at the information on page 108.

Tip: Look at the letters on this page.   EW 22, 14

Weitere Übungen: EW 23/24

*EXTRA UNIT FOUR

A A NEW START

It isn't easy to leave everything behind and start a new life in a new place. It's tough to say goodbye to old friends, to school mates and to relations. It's sometimes difficult to settle in a new country, where people speak another language and have another culture – where people are just different. Jutta Lang knows all this. She emigrated from Germany to England last year.

Jutta's father, an engineer, had lost his job two years before when his factory closed down. He tried and tried to get other work, but without success. He was depressed about this. Jutta's mother was a chemist in another factory, but she didn't like her job very much. So one day Frau Lang had an idea – they should start looking for jobs abroad. "Jobs in foreign countries are often in the German newspapers," she said to her husband. "These days, more people go abroad to work and live. It could be a new start for us too."

Surprisingly it didn't take long to find something. They both found jobs at a new chemical factory near Bristol. So they decided that the whole family should move from Riedlingen in the south of Germany to England. Jutta (16) and her two younger brothers Sven (10) and Paul (8) were very excited about the move.
In the first weeks in England, the Langs were very busy. They found a nice house with a large garden. They were very happy in their new home.

But not everything was easy for the Langs. They had to get used to a new school, lessons in English, school lunches, different food and new neighbours. And they missed a lot of things from home: their favourite TV programmes on German TV, the visits to their school friends, chatting on the phone with their old friends.
"Will we ever really settle here?" Jutta asked herself.

EW 25, 1

EXERCISE 1 ■ Right, wrong or not in the text?

1 Jutta Lang is English.
2 Jutta's father had no work in Germany.
3 Jutta's mother had no work.
4 Herr Lang tried to get a job in Stuttgart.
5 You can find jobs abroad in German newspapers.
6 Only Frau Lang found a job in England.
7 The Langs stayed with friends in their first weeks in England.
8 The Lang children started school in England.

EXERCISE 2 ■ Find the words in the text for …

1 it's *difficult* to say goodbye – *tough*
2 school *friends* – …
3 *people in your family* – …
4 they *went* from Germany to a new home in England – …
5 he was *very unhappy* – …
6 jobs *in another country* – …
7 *talking* on the phone – …
8 will we ever really *feel at home* here? – …

EW 25, 2

110 *Fakultativ

B A YEAR LATER

How do the Langs feel about their new home after a year?

People are nice. They speak very politely in shops and they stand in queues at bus stops.
But on the roads it's sometimes different. People don't always drive very carefully. And you can't drive very fast – not like in Germany.

I like it here. In Germany, we lived in a small flat. Here, we live in a house – and the rent isn't too high. We live comfortably here.

The food is very different here, but you get used to it. People eat a lot of white bread. You can eat cheaply in fish and chip shops. The cakes aren't very good. But the different puddings are good: jelly, trifle, custard … delicious!

School is difficult. My teacher in Germany always spoke slowly. Here people speak quickly and I sometimes can't understand them.
Or they speak quietly! Some people in school think my accent is funny and they laugh about it. And sometimes I miss my old friends in Germany.

Sport is fun here. I've started playing rugby. I can't play very well – not yet.

EW 26, 3

EXERCISE 3 ■ What the Langs like in England and what they don't like. Finish the sentences.

1 The Langs live … in their new house.
2 People speak … in shops.
3 You can eat … in fish and chip shops.

4 People don't always drive …
5 You can't drive … on English roads.
6 People don't speak … They speak … and …

EXERCISE 4 ■ The Lang family. Finish the sentences.

1 Jutta is a quick reader. She reads *quickly*.
2 Paul is a slow reader. He reads …
3 Sven is good at hockey. He plays …
4 Mr Lang is a quiet man. He speaks …
5 Mrs Lang's car is fast. She drives …
6 People in shops are often polite. They speak …

EW 26, 4-5

> **What can people from other countries say about Germany?**
> – People are …   – People speak …   – People drive …
> – People live …   – People eat …   – The cakes are …

> **Adjektive beschreiben, wie etwas ist:**
> John is a <mark>quiet</mark> man.
> **Viele Adverbien enden auf -ly:** quick – quick**ly**, angry – angri**ly**, nice – nice**ly**
> ⚠ **Beachte aber:** good – well, fast – fast
>
> **Adverbien sagen, wie jemand etwas macht:**
> John speaks <mark>quietly</mark>.

C FEELING LONELY

Jutta has made some good friends in Bristol. But sometimes she thinks of her old friends in Germany.

LOUISE Do you ever miss Germany?
JUTTA Yes, a little. I sometimes miss my old friends.
LOUISE Do you phone them?
JUTTA No, that's too expensive. And I don't write letters very regularly.
LOUISE You have a computer at home – you should get a modem for it.
JUTTA A modem? What's that?
LOUISE A modem is used for sending e-mail – like electronic letters. You can send e-mail to your friends, if they have modems. You can send e-mail to your old school, I'm sure.
JUTTA A great idea. Perhaps I can get one for my birthday …

EW 27, 6-8

EXERCISE 5 ■ What are these inventions used for? Finish the sentences.

> answering the phone ▪ cooking food quickly ▪ drying hair ▪ toasting bread
> sending e-mail and surfing the Internet ▪ sending faxes ▪ washing clothes ▪ washing dishes

1 a modem   2 a toaster   3 a microwave   4 a fax machine

5 a dishwasher   6 a hair-drier   7 a washing-machine   8 an answerphone

1 A modem is used for sending e-mail and surfing the Internet.
2 A toaster is used for …
3 A microwave …

EW 29, 9

EXERCISE 6 ■ More helpful inventions: Answer the questions.

1 What's used for recording TV programmes? – …
2 What's used for playing CDs? – …
3 What's used for taking photos? – …
4 What's used for telling the time? – …
5 What's used for phoning people? – …

EW 29, 10

> **Do you know other inventions?**
> Ask your teacher or look for the words in the dictionary.
> What machines would you like to have?
> ▪ a machine that does my homework / …

 CHECKPOINT

Das Passiv: was gemacht wird
A computer is used for lots of things.   Today computers are used in most offices.

EXTRA UNIT FOUR

AN INVENTIONS QUIZ

What do you know about inventions? When did people invent these things?
What do you think? What does your partner think?
Write your answers. The correct answers are on page 137.

1 When were toasters invented?
a) 1809
b) 1909
c) 1989

2 When were cornflakes invented?
a) 1794
b) 1896
c) 1994

3 When were CDs invented?
a) 1959
b) 1969
c) 1979

4 When were walkmans invented?
a) 1977
b) 1987
c) 1997

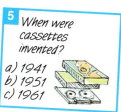

5 When were cassettes invented?
a) 1941
b) 1951
c) 1961

6 When were mountain bikes invented?
a) 1973
b) 1983
c) 1993

7 When were snowboards invented?
a) 1956
b) 1976
c) 1996

8 When were inline-skates invented?
a) 1960
b) 1980
c) 1990

EXERCISE 7 ■ Write correct sentences.
1 Toasters were invented in …
2 Cornflakes were …
3 CDs …
4 Walkmans …
5 Cassettes …
6 Mountain bikes …
7 Snowboards …
8 Inline-skates …

EW 30, 11

LISTENING 🎧 The journey to England

Jutta Lang is going to tell us about her journey to England.
EXERCISE 8 ■ Listen to the story. Which pictures (a or b) are right?

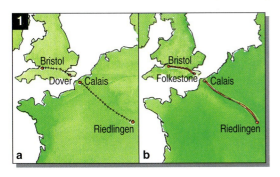

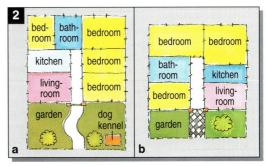

EXERCISE 9 ■ Look at these sentences. Then listen again
and make the correct sentences.
1 The Langs went to England *(in the summer / in the winter)*.
2 It was a long drive to Calais – *(2 days / 3 days)*.
3 The journey to England *(was/wasn't)* very comfortable.
4 In Bristol the family stayed in a hotel for *(2 days / 2 weeks)*.
5 Their house has a big *(living-room/kitchen)*.
6 The three Lang children sleep in *(one bedroom / different bedrooms)*.

Weitere Fragen: EW 30, 12
Weitere Übungen: EW 31/32

*EXTRA UNIT FIVE

 A **TIMES HAVE CHANGED … AND JOBS TOO!**

Find the right words for photos A-D.

> growing and selling food ▪ spraying cars ▪ working hours ▪ selling food

1 I'm a farmer and my father was a farmer. He used lots of chemicals on the land and grew bigger vegetables. Today I don't use any chemicals. I grow organic vegetables. It's more work so I have to sell them for more money.

2 I started work when I was 16. I worked in a baker's shop in the town centre. Today most small baker's shops have closed. People buy their bread in a supermarket. I still sell bread and cakes – in a supermarket.

3 My uncle started work in the car industry in 1960. In those days spraying parts of cars was dangerous. Today lots of the dangerous jobs are done by robots.

4 When I started work here, we closed at 5.30 every evening. And we weren't open on Sundays. But now the chemist's is open every Sunday from 11.00 till 4.00 and on three evenings a week till 8.00.

EXERCISE 1 ■ Which texts go with which photos?
Text 1: Photos …   Text 2: Photos …   Text 3: Photos …   Text 4: Photos …   EW 33, 1

EXERCISE 2 ■ Who are they?

> shop assistant ▪ farmer
> factory worker ▪ chemist

1 Her shop is open 7 days a week.
2 She grows vegetables without chemicals.
3 He doesn't spray cars today.
4 She has the same job in a different shop.

EXERCISE 3 ■ Find the partners in the text.
1 buy – sell   5 aunt
2 less   6 safe
3 finished   7 stopped
4 large   8 opened

EW 33, 2

*Fakultativ

B OLD JOBS, NEW JOBS

When Kate Rogers was a child, her father was a butcher. He liked his work and he had to work very hard. Every year he had fewer customers. People started buying cheaper meat from supermarkets.

When Kate inherited her father's business, she closed the butcher's shop. She opened a sandwich bar in the shop instead. Kate's customers are office workers who don't have a long lunch break. She sells sandwiches, crisps, chocolate and cans of lemonade and cola. Now she earns more money than a butcher but she doesn't have to work so hard.

When Ben Toft left school in Sheffield, he got a job in the steel industry. His parents and grandparents had worked in the steel industry too. Ben had his first job for five years.

Two years ago more steel was made in Sheffield than ever before. But the industry needed fewer workers. A lot of people lost their jobs – including Ben. Ben had to find a new job. He trained as a lorry driver. Then he got a job as a courier. Now Ben earns more money than before. But his life is different now. He often has to work in the evenings and at weekends.

EXERCISE 4 ■ **Put these key phrases about Kate Rogers in the right order.**

he had to work very hard ■ earns more money ■ Kate inherited a business ■ customers are office workers ■ opened a sandwich bar ■ cheaper meat from supermarkets ■ doesn't have to work so hard ■ father was a butcher ■ fewer customers ■ closed the butcher's shop

KATE ROGERS 1 … 2 … 3 …

EXERCISE 5 ■ **What's right about Kate's story (a or b)?**

1 a) Kate's father had a butcher's shop.
   b) Kate's father worked in a butcher's.

2 a) Mr Rogers' meat was cheaper than meat in supermarkets.
   b) Mr Rogers lost customers when supermarkets opened.

3 a) Kate closed the butcher's shop she inherited.
   b) Kate inherited a good business.

4 a) Kate opened a shop that sold food to office workers.
   b) Kate went to another shop near some offices.

5 a) Kate earns more money than a butcher in her sandwich bar.
   b) Kate's customers buy meat in their lunch break.

EW 34, 3

EXERCISE 6 ■ **Find 6 key phrases in the text about Ben.**

EXERCISE 7 ■ **Write 10 sentences about Ben. Five should be right, five wrong. Give the sentences to a partner. Does he/she know the right sentences?**

EW 34, 4

115

C   MOBILE PHONES

When mobile phones were invented, they were used by people in mobile jobs – people like joiners, plumbers and travelling salespeople who worked in different places every day. Their customers or companies could phone them while they travelled from job to job.

But today mobile phones (people often say 'mobiles') are used by all sorts of people. One in three British adults lives in a home with a mobile. In Britain mobiles have become cheaper and more common.

In 1997 11% of mobile phone owners were under 25. New technology is very attractive to young people. Instant communication with your family and friends has now become part of everyday life. Teenagers are often given mobiles by their parents. They can then phone their parents at night if they miss the last bus home. Their parents can also find out where they are at any time.

People who enjoy doing extreme sports like mountain-climbing often carry a mobile phone. They can get help quickly if they have an accident. Mobiles also help to make life easier for people with disabilities and old people who can't move very quickly.

People like farmers and foresters often work in isolated places. They can now save a lot of time if they have a mobile phone.

But mobile phones aren't popular in some places. People often complain about the noise from mobile phones in cinemas, trains and even churches. Some restaurants have special rooms for customers who want to make or receive calls on their mobile phones.

All new inventions have good and bad effects on the people who use them. Some scientists believe that if you use a mobile phone too often it could damage your brain. But will people stop using their mobile phones?

EXERCISE 8 ■ Find these words.
1 People who visit shops and offices and sell their companies' products.
2 Somebody between 13 and 19.
3 Dangerous sports.
4 People who can't walk well, for example.
5 A new thing that somebody has made.

EXERCISE 9 ■ Put in the verbs in the passive form.
1 Today mobile phones (use) by more and more people.
   – Today mobile phones *are used* by more and more people.
2 Business people bought the first mobile phones.
   Today they (buy) by everybody.
3 Many young people (give) mobile phones by their parents.
4 Mobile phones (use) by many farmers.
5 People get angry when calls (receive) in cinemas or churches.

"I've told you before: Don't phone me at work."

EW 35, 5

People often call a mobile phone a 'mobile'. The word 'handy' isn't used in Britain.

EW 35, 6-9

EXTRA UNIT FIVE

Phoning and driving

After work last Tuesday, Susan Gordon was driving home. A friend called her on her mobile phone. Susan spoke to her friend. She didn't see a bend in the road. She was driving too fast and her car crashed into a tree.

Susan's legs were hurt and she wasn't able to get out of the car. She was a long way from the nearest phone. But that wasn't a problem. She dialled 999 on her mobile phone. The emergency services arrived 6 minutes later.

EW 37, 10

EXERCISE 10 ■ Write Susan's dialogue with the emergency services.

EXERCISE 11 ■ Tell the story. Use the right form of the verb.

1 Last Saturday/Sally and John/go/important football match
2 long queue/in front of/stadium
3 Suddenly/John/remember/the tickets
4 They/be/his old jeans/at home
5 John/phone/father/about the tickets
6 His father/bring/tickets/stadium

1 Last Saturday Sally and John went to an important football match.
2 There was a long queue …
3 …

7 John and Sally/be/happy
8 They/not lose/place/long queue

LISTENING 🎧 Mobile phones users

You're going to hear five people. They're speaking on their mobiles.

EXERCISE 12 ■ Which picture (A-E) goes with which person?

1st person: …   3rd person: …   5th person: …
2nd person: …   4th person: …

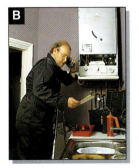 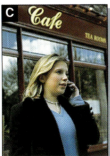  

Weitere Fragen: EW 37, 11-12   Weitere Übungen: EW 38/39

The English alphabet

a	[eɪ]	j	[dʒeɪ]	s	[es]
b	[biː]	k	[keɪ]	t	[tiː]
c	[siː]	l	[el]	u	[juː]
d	[diː]	m	[em]	v	[viː]
e	[iː]	n	[en]	w	[ˈdʌbljuː]
f	[ef]	o	[əʊ]	x	[eks]
g	[dʒiː]	p	[piː]	y	[waɪ]
h	[eɪtʃ]	q	[kjuː]	z	[zed]
i	[aɪ]	r	[ɑː]		

English sounds

[iː] team, see, he
[ɑː] ask, class, start
[ɔː] or, ball, four, door
[uː] ruler, blue, too, two, you
[ɜː] girl, her, early, work
[ɪ] in, big, enough
[e] yes, bed
[æ] cat, black
[ʌ] bus, colour
[ɒ] on, dog, what
[ʊ] put, good, woman
[ə] again, sister, today
[i] radio, video, coffee, happy
[u] July, usually

[eɪ] eight, name, play, great
[aɪ] I, time, right, my
[ɔɪ] boy, toilet
[əʊ] old, no, road, yellow
[aʊ] house, now
[ɪə] near, here, we're
[eə] there, repair
[ʊə] you're, plural

[b] bike, hobby, table, job
[p] pen, pupil, shop
[d] day, window, good
[t] ten, matter, at
[k] car, lucky, book
[g] go, again, bag
[ŋ] wrong, morning
[l] like, old, small
[r] ruler, friend, biro
[v] very, seven, have
[w] we, where, quarter
[s] six, poster, yes
[z] zoo, present, his
[ʃ] she, station, English
[tʃ] child, teacher, match
[dʒ] jeans, German, badge
[ʒ] garage, usually
[j] yes, you, young
[θ] thing, maths, tooth
[ð] the, father, with

Vocabulary

Dieses Wörterverzeichnis enthält alle neuen Wörter des Buches in der Reihenfolge, in der sie im Buch zum ersten Mal vorkommen.

Der Pfeil bedeutet: Schau in die rechte Spalte.

Dieses Zeichen bedeutet „Aufgepasst!".

Die ganz schwarz gedruckten Wörter sind besonders wichtig.

In der eckigen Klammer steht, wie die Wörter ausgesprochen werden.

Diese Zahl gibt die Seite an, auf der die Wörter zum ersten Mal vorkommen.

Normal gedruckte Wörter sind wichtig für das Kapitel, in dem sie vorkommen.

Dieses Sternchen bedeutet: Achtung, unregelmäßiges Verb! Du findest dieses Verb mit seinen drei Formen in dem Kasten „Irregular Verbs".

Schräg gestellte Wörter kommen z.B. in Liedern und *activities* vor.

In diesem Abschnitt kannst du selbst überprüfen, ob du Wörter richtig verstanden hast.

UNIT TWO VOCABULARY

travel around the city [əˈraʊnd] — durch die Stadt fahren
passenger [ˈpæsɪndʒə] — Fahrgast, Passagier/in
multiscreen cinema [ˈmʌltɪskriːn] — Multiplex-Kino, Kinocenter
*****spend** [spend] — (Zeit) verbringen →
go window-shopping — einen Schaufensterbummel machen
meeting place — Treffpunkt
fountain [ˈfaʊntɪn] — Springbrunnen
club — Musikkneipe, Disko
hurry — schnell gehen
still [stɪl] — immer noch →
27 **hat** [hæt] — Hut
try on — anprobieren
herself [hɜːˈself] — sich (selbst)
himself [hɪmˈself] — sich (selbst)
myself [maɪˈself] — mir/mich (selbst)
yourself [jɔːˈself] — dir/dich (selbst)
she'll enjoy herself — sie wird sich amüsieren, sie wird viel Spaß haben
*****hurt** [hɜːt] — verletzen →
dry ski slope [draɪˈskiːsləʊp] — Trockenskipiste
slope [sləʊp] — Abhang, Piste
28 **themselves** [ðəmˈselvz] — sich (selbst)
on the phone — am Telefon
mobile phone [ˈməʊbaɪlˈfəʊn] — Mobiltelefon, Handy
argue [ˈɑːɡjuː] — (sich) streiten →
ourselves [aʊəˈselvz] — uns (selbst)
Help yourselves to milk. [ˈhelpjɔːˈselvztəˈmɪlk] — Nehmt euch (selbst) Milch!
yourselves [jɔːˈselvz] — euch (selbst); sich (selbst)
sugar [ˈʃʊɡə] — Zucker

STORY
30 **minibus** [ˈmɪnɪbʌs] — Kleinbus
nervous [ˈnɜːvəs] — nervös
ambulance [ˈæmbjʊləns] — Krankenwagen
ski-lift [ˈskiːlɪft] — Skilift
towards [təˈwɔːdz] — auf ... zu, in Richtung
unhappy [ʌnˈhæpi] — unglücklich
31 **room** — Platz
knee [niː] — Knie →
*****bet** [bet] — wetten
leg [leɡ] — Bein →
scream [skriːm] — schreien
instructor [ɪnˈstrʌktə] — Lehrer/in, Betreuer/in
show off [ʃəʊˈɒf] — angeben

ACTIVE ENGLISH
32 **Can he cheer her up?** [ˈtʃɪərˈʌp] — Kann er sie aufmuntern? →
Cheer up! — Kopf hoch!
down — „down", bedrückt →
I'm fed up with going to the cinema. [fedˈʌp] — Ich habe es satt, ins Kino zu gehen.
33 **grumpy** [ˈɡrʌmpi] — schlecht gelaunt, mürrisch →
That's what friends are for. — Dazu sind Freunde da.
Australian [ɒˈstreɪliən] — australisch

Sorry, I can't take so many *passengers*.

I know why you're always tired. You *spend* too much time in front of your computer.

Are you *still* waiting for your friend?

⚠ **still** (engl.) = immer noch
quiet (engl.) = **still**, leise

Robert *hurt* himself last week. He fell over when he was on his inline-skates.

Amy and Tom are friends, but they *argue* about everything.

Please *help yourselves to* cake. There's more cake in the kitchen.

FREE TIME
I talk on my mobile phone.
I read a book.
I go window-shopping.
I go dancing.
I go to the cinema.
I play basketball.
I spend time with friends.
I enjoy myself.

← knee
leg →

Let's listen to my new CD. Perhaps it'll *cheer* us *up*.

What's the matter? You look *down*.

Aren't you *fed up with* sitting at h...
Don't talk to B...

Hier sind Wörter in Gruppen zusammengefasst. Das macht das Lernen leichter.

TEST YOURSELF

a OLD BUILDINGS
clean up
p _ _ l d _ _ _
d _ _ _ _ _ y

b WHO DOES IT BELONG TO?
It's mine.
It's o _ _ s.
It's th _ _ _ s.
It's he _ _.

c Ergänze.
1 There are very ... houses in the north of Scotland.
2 I want to sleep. Please don't make so much ...
3 Where's the newspaper? – It's ... the chair.
4 You have so many old shoes you don't wear. Please ... ... them.

119

UNIT ONE VOCABULARY

8 **member** ['membə] — Mitglied
against [ə'genst] — gegen
interested in — interessiert an →
make friends — Freundschaft(en) schließen
coffee bar ['kɒfibɑ:] — Cafeteria
sports hall ['spɔ:tshɔ:l] — Sporthalle
church hall ['tʃɜ:tʃhɔ:l] — Gemeindesaal der Kirche
disco ['dɪskəʊ] — Disko
local council [ləʊkəl'kaʊnsl] — Gemeindeverwaltung
church [tʃɜ:tʃ] — Kirche
indoor football ['ɪndɔ:] — Fußball in der Halle, Hallenfußball
snooker ['snu:kə] — (eine Art) Billard

She's only *interested in* computers.

9 **I like playing** table-tennis. — Ich spiele gern Tischtennis. →
do sports — Sport treiben
outdoor sports ['aʊtdɔ:] — Sport im Freien
I enjoy swimming. [ɪn'dʒɔɪ] — Ich habe Spaß am Schwimmen. Ich schwimme gern. →
ice-skating ['aɪsskeɪtɪŋ] — Schlittschuhlaufen
tenpin bowling [tenpɪn'bəʊlɪŋ] — Bowling
ski [ski:] — Ski fahren

Robbie *likes playing* football. But his team never wins.

Does Linda *enjoy* working in a shop? – Yes, she really enjoys her new job.

10 **I'm good/bad at skiing.** — Ich bin gut/schlecht im Skifahren. Ich kann gut/schlecht Ski fahren. →

★**teach** [ti:tʃ] — beibringen, unterrichten
earn [ɜ:n] — verdienen
the job pays well — die Arbeit wird gut bezahlt
★**babysit** ['beɪbɪsɪt] — „Babysitten" (auf kleine Kinder aufpassen)

11 **news** [nju:z] — Nachricht(en), Neuigkeit(en) →
equipment [ɪ'kwɪpmənt] — Ausstattung, Ausrüstung
dartboard ['dɑ:tbɔ:d] — Dartscheibe
the black one — der/die/das schwarze →
dart [dɑ:t] — (Wurf-)Pfeil
fair [feə] — Volksfest, Jahrmarkt, Kirmes
★**bring: I've brought** [brɔ:t] — (mit)bringen: ich habe (mit)gebracht

I think Ms Davis is a good teacher. She's *good at* explaining words.

Have you heard the *news*? There's going to be a new girl in our class.

Which pullover do you like? – The pink *one*.

⚠ a **fair** = Volksfest
she's **fair** = sie ist fair, sie ist gerecht

STORY

12 **upside down** [ʌpsaɪd'daʊn] — mit dem Kopf nach unten; verkehrt herum →
★**eat: I ate** [et] — essen: ich aß / ich habe gegessen
mirror ['mɪrə] — Spiegel
tall [tɔ:l] — lang, groß →
fat [fæt] — dick, fett
★**throw** [θrəʊ]: **I threw** [θru:] — werfen: ich warf / ich habe geworfen
disappointed [dɪsə'pɔɪntɪd] — enttäuscht
ghost train ['gəʊstreɪn] — Geisterbahn

13 **ghost** [gəʊst] — Gespenst, Geist
eye [aɪ] — Auge →
kiss [kɪs] — küssen

Careful! Your cup is *upside down*.

Linda isn't very *tall*. But she likes tall boys.

Chris has beautiful *eyes*.

ACTIVE ENGLISH

14 ★**go out** [gəʊ'aʊt] — ausgehen, weggehen
make a date [deɪt] — sich verabreden
mosque [mɒsk] — Moschee
date — Verabredung

15 they **should** [ʃʊd, ʃəd]   sie sollten, sie sollen →   *Should* we go to the cinema?
    stadium ['steɪdɪəm]   Stadion   – No, it's late. We *should* go home now.
16 *ring* [rɪŋ]   Ring
    around a toy [əˈraʊnd]   um ein Spielzeug herum
    score [skɔː]   (Punkte) erzielen
    bucket [ˈbʌkɪt]   Eimer
    prize [praɪz]   Preis, Gewinn
17 *short* [ʃɔːt]   kurz, klein
    prize [praɪz]   Preis, Gewinn
    ride on carousels   auf Karussells fahren
      [raɪdɒnˈkærəˈselz]
    spin [spɪn]   (schnell) drehen
    round and round   rundherum
      [ˈraʊndəndˈraʊnd]
    climb [klaɪm]   klettern
    slowly [ˈsləʊli]   langsam
    sky [skaɪ]   Himmel
    towards [təˈwɔːdz]   auf ... zu, in Richtung
    ground [graʊnd]   Boden, Erde
    still [stɪl]   trotzdem
    a day out at the fair   ein Ausflug zum Jahrmarkt
    chart [tʃɑːt]   Schaubild, Diagramm
    bar chart [ˈbɑːtʃɑːt]   Balkendiagramm
    pie chart [ˈpaɪtʃɑːt]   Kreisdiagramm

FRIENDS
make friends
make a date
go out
go to a disco
go to a football stadium
have fun
kiss
girlfriend
boyfriend

PRACTICE PAGES

19 **dictionary** [ˈdɪkʃənri]   Wörterbuch →   What's "Nachrichten" in English?
    alphabetical [ˈælfəˈbetɪkl]   alphabetisch   – I don't know. Let's look in the *dictionary*.
    order [ˈɔːdə]   Reihenfolge

★ IRREGULAR VERBS

INFINITIVE FORM	SIMPLE PAST FORM	PRESENT PERFECT FORM
babysit [ˈbeɪbɪsɪt]	I babysat [ˈbeɪbɪsæt]	I've babysat [ˈbeɪbɪsæt]
bring [brɪŋ]	I brought [brɔːt]	I've brought [brɔːt]
eat [iːt]	I ate [et]	I've eaten [ˈiːtn]
go [gəʊ]	I went [went]	I've gone [gɒn]
teach [tiːtʃ]	I taught [tɔːt]	I've taught [tɔːt]
throw [θrəʊ]	I threw [θruː]	I've thrown [θrəʊn]

LOOK AROUND 1

24 *(the) Caribbean* [kærəˈbiːən]   Karibik, karibisch   25 *Afro-Caribbean*   afrokaribisch
    island [ˈaɪlənd]   Insel   [æfrəʊkærəˈbiːən]
    state [steɪt]   Staat   *Creole* [ˈkriːəʊl]   kreolisch
    a lot   viel   *carnival* [ˈkɑːnɪvl]   Karneval
    hot [hɒt]   heiß

TEST YOURSELF

a **PLACES**
coffee bar
?
?
?

b **SPORTS**
indoor football
outdoor ?
ice- ?
tenpin ?

c **Ergänze.**
1 Leroy doesn't go to parties. He's only ... ... computers.
2 Does Peter ... working in a restaurant? – No, he doesn't really ... his new job.
3 Mrs Davis is about 1,80 metres. She's ...
4 You can find English words in the ...

UNIT TWO VOCABULARY

26 **travel around the city** [əˈraʊnd] — durch die Stadt fahren
passenger [ˈpæsɪndʒə] — Fahrgast, Passagier/in →
multiscreen cinema [ˈmʌltɪskriːn] — Multiplex-Kino, Kinocenter
*****spend** [spend] — *(Zeit)* verbringen →
go window-shopping — einen Schaufensterbummel machen
meeting place — Treffpunkt
fountain [ˈfaʊntɪn] — Springbrunnen
club — Musikkneipe, Disko
hurry — schnell gehen
still [stɪl] — immer noch →

27 **hat** [hæt] — Hut
try on — anprobieren
herself [hɜːˈself] — sich (selbst)
himself [hɪmˈself] — sich (selbst)
myself [maɪˈself] — mir/mich (selbst)
yourself [jɔːˈself] — dir/dich (selbst)
she'll enjoy herself — sie wird sich amüsieren, sie wird viel Spaß haben
*****hurt** [hɜːt] — verletzen →
dry ski slope [draɪˈskiːsləʊp] — Trockenskipiste
slope [sləʊp] — Abhang, Piste

28 **themselves** [ðəmˈselvz] — sich (selbst)
on the phone — am Telefon
mobile phone [ˈməʊbaɪlˈfəʊn] — Mobiltelefon, Handy
argue [ˈɑːgjuː] — (sich) streiten →
ourselves [aʊəˈselvz] — uns (selbst)
Help yourselves to milk. [ˈhelpjɔːˈselvztəˈmɪlk] — Nehmt euch (selbst) Milch! →
yourselves [jɔːˈselvz] — euch (selbst); sich (selbst)
sugar [ˈʃʊgə] — Zucker

STORY

30 **minibus** [ˈmɪnɪbʌs] — Kleinbus
nervous [ˈnɜːvəs] — nervös
ambulance [ˈæmbjʊləns] — Krankenwagen
ski-lift [ˈskiːlɪft] — Skilift
towards [təˈwɔːdz] — auf … zu, in Richtung
unhappy [ʌnˈhæpi] — unglücklich

31 **room** — Platz
knee [niː] — Knie →
*****bet** [bet] — wetten
leg [leg] — Bein →
scream [skriːm] — schreien
instructor [ɪnˈstrʌktə] — Lehrer/in, Betreuer/in
show off [ʃəʊˈɒf] — angeben

ACTIVE ENGLISH

32 **Can he cheer her up?** [ˈtʃɪərˈʌp] — Kann er sie aufmuntern? →
Cheer up! — Kopf hoch!
down — „down", bedrückt →
I'm fed up with going to the cinema. [fedˈʌp] — Ich habe es satt, ins Kino zu gehen. →

33 **grumpy** [ˈgrʌmpi] — schlecht gelaunt, mürrisch →
That's what friends are for. — Dazu sind Freunde da.

34 *Australian* [ɒˈstreɪliən] — australisch

Sorry, I can't take so many *passengers*.

I know why you're always tired. You *spend* too much time in front of your computer.

Are you *still* waiting for your friend?

⚠ **still** (engl.) = immer noch
quiet (engl.) = **still**, leise

Robert *hurt* himself last week. He fell over when he was on his inline-skates.

Amy and Tom are friends, but they *argue* about everything.

Please *help yourselves to* cake. There's more cake in the kitchen.

> **FREE TIME**
> I talk on my mobile phone.
> I read a book.
> I go window-shopping.
> I go dancing.
> I go to the cinema.
> I play basketball.
> I spend time with friends.
> I enjoy myself.

← knee

leg

Let's listen to my new CD. Perhaps it'll *cheer* us *up*.

What's the matter? You look *down*.

Aren't you *fed up with* sitting at home and watching TV?
Don't talk to Ben this morning. He's very *grumpy*.

	soap [səʊp]	Seifenoper, Unterhaltungsserie
35	*I may not follow ...* [meɪ]	Vielleicht folge ich nicht ...
	I may not lead ... [liːd]	Vielleicht führe ich nicht ...
	just	nur
	hardly ['hɑːdli]	kaum
	lose [luːz]	verlieren
	Chinese [tʃaɪˈniːz]	chinesisch
	proverb ['prɒvɜːb]	Sprichwort
	silver ['sɪlvə]	Silber
	gold [gəʊld]	Gold
	true [truː]	wahr
	secret ['siːkrət]	geheim

★ IRREGULAR VERBS

INFINITIVE FORM	SIMPLE PAST FORM	PRESENT PERFECT FORM
bet [bet]	I bet [bet]	I've bet [bet]
hurt [hɜːt]	I hurt [hɜːt]	I've hurt [hɜːt]
spend [spend]	I spent [spent]	I've spent [spent]

LOOK AROUND 2

42	*Australia* [ɒˈstreɪliə]	Australien	43	*Aborigine* [æbəˈrɪdʒəni]	Ureinwohner/Ureinwohnerin (Australien)
	it takes 4 days to drive ...	es dauert 4 Tage, um ... zu fahren		*protect* [prəˈtekt]	schützen
	square [skweə]	Quadrat		*plant* [plɑːnt]	Pflanze
	by radio	über Funk		*love* [lʌv]	lieben, gern mögen
	sun [sʌn]	Sonne		*cricket* [ˈkrɪkɪt]	Kricket
	suncream [ˈsʌnkriːm]	Sonnencreme		*Australian* [ɒˈstreɪliən]	australisch
	kangaroo [kæŋɡəˈruː]	Känguru		*beside* [bɪˈsaɪd]	neben
	kookaburra [ˈkʊkəbʌrə]	Rieseneisvogel			
	platypus [ˈplætɪpəs]	Schnabeltier			

TIPS

Wörter zum Selbermachen

Manchmal ist es ganz einfach, aus einem englischen Wort ein neues Wort zu bilden: z.B. wird aus *happy* ganz schnell *unhappy*, aus *friendly* wird *unfriendly*. Versuche aus den Wörtern rechts neue Wörter zu bilden.

Manchmal kannst du auch durch Anhängen von *-er* aus einem Tätigkeitswort ein Wort für die Person bilden, die diese Tätigkeit ausübt: z.B. *read* kann zu *reader* werden. Du musst nur die Endung *-er* an das Verb hängen. Aber aufgepasst! Manchmal gibt es in der Schreibweise Unterschiede: z.B. *swim – swimmer*, *drive – driver*. Versuche aus den Wörtern rechts neue Wörter zu bilden.

Vielleicht hilft dir das *Dictionary* (ab S. 140) noch mehr neue Wörter zu bilden.

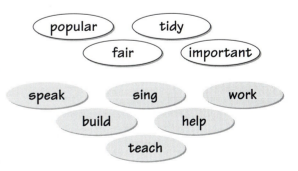

UNIT THREE VOCABULARY

44	alone [ə'ləʊn]	allein
	housework ['haʊswɜːk]	Hausarbeit →
	they do their shopping	sie machen ihre Einkäufe
	Meals on Wheels ['miːlzɒn'wiːlz]	Essen auf Rädern
	hot [hɒt]	heiß; warm
	old people's home	Altersheim
	day centre	Altentagesstätte, Seniorentreff
	grandparents ['grænpeərənts]	Großeltern
	short [ʃɔːt]	kurz; klein →
45	foot, feet [fʊt, fiːt]	Fuß, Füße
	shoe [ʃuː]	Schuh
	hair [heə]	Haar, Haare
	comb [kəʊm]	kämmen
	top 10 [tɒp]	die Top 10, die wichtigsten 10
	kind [kaɪnd]	liebevoll, freundlich
	promise ['prɒmɪs]	Versprechen
	(a) sense of humour ['sensəv'hjuːmə]	(Sinn für) Humor
	*hit [hɪt]	schlagen
	*ring [rɪŋ]: it rang [ræŋ]	klingeln, läuten: es klingelte / es hat geklingelt
46	go out (together)	miteinander gehen →
	voice [vɔɪs]	Stimme
47	What's wrong with him?	Was hat er? Was ist los mit ihm? →
	they got on his nerves [nɜːvz]	sie gingen ihm auf die Nerven
	complain [kəm'pleɪn]	sich beschweren
	*think of	denken an →

STORY

48	mistake [mɪ'steɪk]	Fehler →
	snow [snəʊ]	Schnee
	earring ['ɪərɪŋ]	Ohrring
	*lose [luːz]: I've lost [lɒst]	verlieren: ich habe verloren →
	bell [bel]	(Tür-)Klingel, Glocke
	recognize ['rekəgnaɪz]	erkennen
49	decide [dɪ'saɪd]	beschließen, (sich) entscheiden
	spray [spreɪ]	(be)sprühen, sprayen
	hairstyle ['heəstaɪl]	Frisur
	look the same	gleich aussehen
	correct [kə'rekt]	korrigieren, berichtigen

ACTIVE ENGLISH

50	Australia [ɒ'streɪliə]	Australien
	documentary [dɒkjuˈmentri]	Dokumentarfilm
	soap [səʊp]	Seifenoper, Unterhaltungsserie
	I can't stand soaps. [stænd]	Ich kann Seifenopern nicht ausstehen.
	police drama [pəˈliːsdrɑːmə]	Krimi
	channel ['tʃænəl]	Programm, Sender, Kanal
	advert ['ædvɜːt]	Werbespot; Werbung →
	cable ['keɪbl]	Kabel; Kabel-
	satellite dish ['sætəlaɪtdɪʃ]	Satellitenschüssel
	age [eɪdʒ]	Alter; Altersstufe

Al is doing the *housework*. He's cleaning and cooking.

Is Julie very *short*? – No, she isn't. She's very tall.

⚠ one f**oo**t – two f**ee**t

> **A NICE GIRL OR BOY …**
> is kind.
> has a sense of humour.
> is friendly.
> is polite.
> keeps promises.
> listens to you.

Helen is Gavin's girlfriend. They're *going out together*.

What's wrong with Nina?
– I think she has had a bad day.

Is it true that young people never *think of* old people?

How many *mistakes* did you make? – About five.

Oh no, I think *I've lost* my ticket! – Sorry, young man, you have to get off the bus then.

> **WINTER**
> There's a lot of snow.
> It rains.
> It's cold.
> It's windy.
> It's cloudy.
> You're cold.
> You go snowboarding.
> You go skiing.

Do you enjoy watching *adverts*? – No, I don't. But my sister Aysha loves watching them.

3

51	**What sort of …?** [sɔːt]	Was für …? →
	cartoon [kɑːˈtuːn]	Zeichentrickfilm; Cartoon
52	they're allowed to see this film [əˈlaʊd]	sie dürfen diesen Film sehen
53	I'm bored	ich langweile mich
	I don't want to be nobody's fool [fuːl]	ich will mich von keinem zum Narren machen lassen
	I want to be me	ich möchte ich selbst sein
	sweet [swiːt]	süß; lieb
	neat [niːt]	ordentlich
	I don't want someone living my life for me	ich will nicht, dass jem. anders mein Leben für mich lebt
	turn this world inside out [ˈɪnsaɪdˈaʊt]	diese Welt umstülpen, diese Welt umdrehen
	turn suburbia upside down [sʌˈbɜːbɪə]	die Vorstädte auf den Kopf stellen
	walk the streets	durch die Straßen irren
	scream [skriːm]	schreien, kreischen
	alleyway [ˈælɪweɪ]	schmale Gasse
	I don't want to be told what to wear	ich will nicht, dass mir gesagt wird, was ich anziehen soll
	who cares? [keəz]	wen kümmert es?
	so what?	… und wenn schon!
	dye [daɪ]	färben
	a brain up there [breɪn]	ein Gehirn dort oben
	choose [tʃuːz]	aussuchen, (aus)wählen
	on time	pünktlich

What sort of music do you like? – Rap, of course.

PRACTICE PAGES

55 rhyme [raɪm]   (sich) reimen →

Tell me a word that *rhymes* with "shoe". – "Flu".

★ IRREGULAR VERBS

INFINITIVE FORM	SIMPLE PAST FORM	PRESENT PERFECT FORM
hit [hɪt]	I hit [hɪt]	I've hit [hɪt]
lose [luːz]	I lost [lɒst]	I've lost [lɒst]
ring [rɪŋ]	I rang [ræŋ]	I've rung [rʌŋ]
think [θɪŋk]	I thought [θɔːt]	I've thought [θɔːt]

LOOK AROUND 3

60	*India* [ˈɪndɪə]	Indien	*sugar-cane* [ˈʃʊɡəkeɪn]	Zuckerrohr
	official language [əˈfɪʃlˈlæŋɡwɪdʒ]	Amtssprache	*rice* [raɪs]	Reis
			wheat [wiːt]	Weizen
	also [ˈɔːlsəʊ]	auch	*poor* [pʊə]	arm
	Indian [ˈɪndɪən]	Inder/Inderin; indisch	61 *jewellery* [ˈdʒuːəlri]	Schmuck
	grow [ɡrəʊ]	anbauen	*marry* [ˈmæri]	heiraten

TIPS

Wörter zum Vorführen

Zu manchen Wörtern kann man sich (Hand-)Bewegungen oder Geräusche vorstellen. Lies deine Liste mit den neuen Wörtern laut und mache zu allen Wörtern, bei denen dir etwas einfällt, ein Geräusch oder eine (Hand-)Bewegung, so als wolltest du jemandem das Wort vorführen. Welches Wort stellt das Mädchen rechts dar?

UNIT FOUR VOCABULARY

62 **steel** [stiːl] — Stahl
   few [fjuː] — wenige →
   worker ['wɜːkə] — Arbeiter/Arbeiterin
   dirty ['dɜːti] — schmutzig →
   city council ['kaʊnsl] — Stadtrat
   canal [kə'næl] — Kanal
   attraction [ə'trækʃn] — Attraktion, Anziehungspunkt
   concert ['kɒnsət] — Konzert
   national ['næʃnəl] — national, National-
   noise [nɔɪz] — Lärm; Geräusch →
   What ... for? — Wofür ...? →
   competition [kɒmpə'tɪʃn] — Wettbewerb
   clean up — säubern, reinigen
   recycle [riː'saɪkl] — recyceln, wieder verwerten
   leader ['liːdə] — Leiter/Leiterin

63 **enter** ['entə] — sich beteiligen (an); sich (an)melden für
   by the canal [baɪ] — (nahe) beim Kanal →
   plant [plɑːnt] — (an)pflanzen
   bucket ['bʌkɪt] — Eimer
   wheel [wiːl] — Rad
   paper ['peɪpə] — Papier

64 *forget: **I've forgotten** [fə'gɒtn] — vergessen: ich habe vergessen
   yours [jɔːz] — deine(r, s); Ihre(r, s); eure(r, s)
   his [hɪz] — seine/seiner/seines
   mine [maɪn] — meine/meiner/meines
   compost ['kɒmpɒst] — Kompost
   ours ['aʊəz] — unsere/unserer/unseres →
   theirs [ðeəz] — ihre/ihrer/ihres →
   hers [hɜːz] — ihre/ihrer/ihres

65 environment officer — Umweltbeauftragte/r
   motorway ['məʊtəweɪ] — Autobahn
   the factories **were closed** — die Fabriken wurden geschlossen →
   building ['bɪldɪŋ] — Gebäude →
   pull down [pʊl'daʊn] — abreißen, niederreißen
   demonstration [demən'streɪʃn] — Demonstration

STORY

66 **he changed his mind** [tʃeɪndʒd, maɪnd] — er änderte seine Meinung
   interrupt [ɪntə'rʌpt] — unterbrechen →
   a waste of time [weɪst] — Zeitverschwendung
   protest [prə'test] — protestieren
   destroy [dɪ'strɔɪ] — zerstören
   exaggerate [ɪg'zædʒəreɪt] — übertreiben
   megaphone ['megəfəʊn] — Megaphon
   crowd [kraʊd] — (Menschen-)Menge

67 **line** [laɪn] — Zeile

ACTIVE ENGLISH

68 **bottle bank** — Altglascontainer
   paper bank — Altpapiercontainer
   get rid of [get'rɪdəv] — wegwerfen, loswerden →
   grey [greɪ] — grau

70 *environmentally aware* [ɪnvaɪrən'mentəliə'weə] — umweltbewusst
   product ['prɒdʌkt] — Produkt, Erzeugnis

Very *few* people live in the north of Scotland.

The windows are really *dirty*. Let's clean them tomorrow.

Don't make so much *noise*, please. The baby is sleeping.
What's this tool *for*?

> **What ...**
> What time is it?
> What's your name?
> What's this in English?
> What colour is ...?
> What's the matter?
> What ... for?
> What sort of ...?

Can I use your phone? – Yes, of course. It's over there, *by* the window.

⚠ This book is **his**.
His book is new.

Those places are *ours*, not *theirs*.

This house is very old. It *was built* 120 years ago.
I don't like modern *buildings*. Do you like them?

⚠ **building** = Gebäude
we're **building** = wir bauen gerade

Can I *interrupt* you for a minute? I need your help.

There's no room in my cupboard.
– Why can't you *get rid of* some clothes?

	hen [hen]	Huhn, Henne	
	cage [keɪdʒ]	Käfig	
	they caught [kɔːt]	sie fingen / sie haben gefangen	
	net [net]	Netz	
	dolphin [ˈdɒlfɪn]	Delphin	
	in here	hier hinein	
71	*it's fine* [faɪn]	es ist gut, es ist in Ordnung	
	jumbo plane [ˈdʒʌmbəʊ]	Jumbojet	
	take a ride	eine Fahrt machen	
	cosmic train [ˈkɒzmɪk]	ein Zug aus dem Weltall	
	switch on [swɪtʃˈɒn]	einschalten	
	from a slot machine [ˈslɒtməˈʃiːn]	an einem Münzautomaten	
	because you can get anything [bɪˈkɒz]	weil du alles bekommen kannst	
	we've come a long way	wir haben es weit gebracht	
	change	sich ändern	
	day to day	von Tag zu Tag	
	roll [rəʊl]	rollen, fahren	
	fresh [freʃ]	frisch	
	for your lorry loads, pumping petrol gas [ˈlɒrɪləʊdz, ˈpʌmpɪŋˈpetrəlgæs]	mit euren Lastwagenladungen, die Abgase ausstoßen	
	tough [tʌf]	widerstandsfähig, hart	
	they just go on and on	sie hören einfach nicht mehr auf	
	it seems [siːmz]	es scheint	
	survey [ˈsɜːveɪ]	Umfrage; Untersuchung	
	find out	herausfinden	
	0 (=zero) [ˈzɪərəʊ]	Null	
	point [pɔɪnt]	Punkt	
	number	Anzahl	
	average [ˈævərɪdʒ]	durchschnittlich	

★ IRREGULAR VERBS

INFINITIVE FORM	SIMPLE PAST FORM	PRESENT PERFECT FORM
forget [fəˈget]	I forgot [fəˈgɒt]	I've forgotten [fəˈgɒtn]

LOOK AROUND 4

78	*Canada* [ˈkænədə]	Kanada	
	tornado, tornadoes [tɔːˈneɪdəʊ, tɔːˈneɪdəʊz]	Tornado, Tornados	
	destroy [dɪˈstrɔɪ]	zerstören	
79	*language* [ˈlæŋgwɪdʒ]	Sprache	
	Canadian [kəˈneɪdɪən]	Kanadier/Kanadierin	
	Native Canadian [ˈneɪtɪv]	Ureinwohner/Ureinwohnerin aus Kanada	
	igloo [ˈɪgluː]	Iglu	
	ice hockey [ˈaɪshɒki]	Eishockey	
	Niagara Falls [naɪˈægərəˈfɔːlz]	Niagarafälle	

TEST YOURSELF

a | OLD BUILDINGS
clean up
p _ _ l d _ _ _
d _ _ _ _ _ y

b | WHO DOES IT BELONG TO?
It's mine.
It's o _ _ s.
It's th _ _ _ s.
It's he _ _.

c Ergänze.
1 There are very … houses in the north of Scotland.
2 I want to sleep. Please don't make so much …
3 Where's the newspaper? – It's … the chair.
4 You have so many old shoes you don't wear. Please … … … them.

UNIT FIVE VOCABULARY

80 *choose [tʃuːz] — (aus)wählen, aussuchen →
work experience ['wɜːkɪk'spɪərɪəns] — Berufspraktikum
diary ['daɪəri] — Tagebuch
hairdresser ['heədresə] — Friseur/Friseurin
office clerk — Büroangestellte/r
secretary ['sekrətri] — Sekretär/Sekretärin
builder ['bɪldə] — Bauarbeiter/Bauarbeiterin
fisherman ['fɪʃəmən] — Fischer
mechanic [mə'kænɪk] — Mechaniker/Mechanikerin
doctor's assistant ['dɒktəzə'sɪstənt] — Arzthelfer/Arzthelferin
dentist's assistant — Zahnarzthelfer/in
electrician [ɪlek'trɪʃn] — Elektriker/Elektrikerin
joiner ['dʒɔɪnə] — Tischler/in, Schreiner/in
plumber ['plʌmə] — Installateur/in, Klempner/in

81 garage — (Reparatur-)Werkstatt
I'm looking forward to working there. ['lʊkɪŋ'fɔːwədtu] — Ich freue mich darauf, dort zu arbeiten. →
chat [tʃæt] — sich unterhalten, plaudern
helper ['helpə] — Helfer/Helferin

82 although [ɔːl'ðəʊ] — obwohl →
a bit (of) [ə'bɪt] — ein bisschen, ein wenig
warden — Heimleiter/Heimleiterin
How are you? — Wie geht es dir/Ihnen? →
I'm OK. — Mir gehts gut. →
serve [sɜːv] — servieren, bedienen
clear away ['klɪərə'weɪ] — abräumen, wegräumen
*break: I broke [brəʊk] — zerbrechen: ich zerbrach / ich habe zerbochen
They're fond of chatting. ['fɒndəv] — Sie mögen es, sich zu unterhalten. Sie unterhalten sich gern. →
I hate working in the kitchen. — Ich arbeite sehr ungern in der Küche.
(book-)shelf, shelves [ʃelf, ʃelvz] — (Bücher-)Regal, Regale

83 after — nachdem →
she had made — sie hatte gemacht →
envelope ['envələʊp] — Briefumschlag
while [waɪl] — während →
apply (for) [ə'plaɪ] — sich bewerben (um) →
course [kɔːs] — Kurs, Lehrgang
fill in [fɪl'ɪn] — ausfüllen
application form [æplɪ'keɪʃnfɔːm] — Bewerbungsformular
first name — Vorname
interest ['ɪntrəst] — Interesse →
ambulance driver ['æmbjələns'draɪvə] — Sanitäter/Sanitäterin

STORY

84 luck [lʌk] — Glück
in the end [end] — schließlich
waitress ['weɪtrəs] — Kellnerin

85 advertise ['ædvətaɪz] — Reklame machen, werben
brilliant ['brɪliənt] — großartig
find out — herausfinden

You can't have a new CD and a new T-shirt. You can *choose* only one new thing.

⚠ garage = Garage
garage = (Reparatur-)Werkstatt

He's *looking forward to* going on holiday.

Although she liked school, she was happy when school was over.

Hi. *How are you?*
– *I'm OK*, thanks. How are you?

Bob is very *fond of* listening to rock music.

After Pat *had cleaned* the kitchen, she chatted with the old people.

While Dave was at school, somebody stole his bike.
There's a job at the supermarket. Why don't you *apply*?
– I've already applied for it.

What are your *interests*? – Well, I'm interested in films and film stars.

> **SATZANFÄNGE/ SATZVERBINDUNGEN**
> after
> before
> while
> although
> but
> because

ACTIVE ENGLISH

86 youth worker — Jugendpfleger/in
fill — (auf)füllen, voll machen →
my **hours** — meine Arbeitszeit →
88 paint [peɪnt] — malen, (an)streichen
uniform ['juːnɪfɔːm] — Uniform
89 limerick ['lɪmərɪk] — Limerick *(kurzes, humorvolles Gedicht)*

find — herausfinden; entdecken
shiver ['ʃɪvə] — Schauder
waterproof ['wɔːtəpruːf] — wasserfest
glue [gluː] — Klebstoff, Leim
once [wʌns] — einmal
cook [kʊk] — Koch
chilli ['tʃɪli] — (scharfe) Peperoni; Chili
grain [greɪn] — Korn
hot [hɒt] — scharf
one day — eines Tages
he was shot [ʃɒt] — er wurde niedergeschossen; er wurde erschossen
by a customer — von einem Kunden/einer Kundin
who went up in flames [fleɪmz] — der/die in Flammen aufgig
person ['pɜːsn] — Person
inside [ɪn'saɪd] — im Haus, drinnen

Greg works at a supermarket. He has to *fill* the shelves and serve the customers.
What are your *hours*? – From 9 am to 5 pm.

*IRREGULAR VERBS

INFINITIVE FORM	SIMPLE PAST FORM	PRESENT PERFECT FORM
choose [tʃuːz]	I chose [tʃəʊz]	I've chosen ['tʃəʊzn]
break [breɪk]	I broke [brəʊk]	I've broken ['brəʊkən]

LOOK AROUND 5

96 abroad [ə'brɔːd] — im Ausland
foreign ['fɒrən] — fremd
language ['læŋgwɪdʒ] — Sprache
life, lives [laɪf, laɪvz] — Leben
skiing instructor [ɪn'strʌktə] — Skilehrer/Skilehrerin
Canadian [kə'neɪdiən] — Kanadier/Kanadierin
stranger ['streɪndʒə] — Fremde/Fremder
sea [siː] — Meer
poor [pʊə] — arm
crime [kraɪm] — Kriminalität
cricket ['krɪkɪt] — Kricket
97 I was born [bɔːn] — ich bin geboren
marry ['mæri] — heiraten

Indian ['ɪndiən] — Inder/Inderin
move to ['muːvtu] — umziehen nach
most of the time — meistens
college ['kɒlɪdʒ] — (Fach-)Hochschule
vineyard ['vɪnjəd] — Weinberg
sun [sʌn] — Sonne
in the first few weeks — in den ersten paar Wochen
Australian [ɒ'streɪliən] — australisch
helpful ['helpfl] — hilfsbereit
countryside ['kʌntrɪsaɪd] — Landschaft
also ['ɔːlsəʊ] — auch
next year — im nächsten Jahr

TIPS

Verben mit Präpositionen

Look kann verschiedene Bedeutungen haben, wenn eine Präposition folgt. Eine Präposition ist z.B. *after, at, in, on, out, to, up.* So gibt es *look* (schauen), *look after* (sich kümmern um), *look at* (sich anschauen). Finde heraus, welche Bedeutungen die Wörter, die du rechts siehst, haben können.

ask	get
ask for	get to
ask about	get on

EXTRA UNIT ONE VOCABULARY

98 **joining a club** ['dʒɔɪnɪŋ]   einem Club beitreten
    join [dʒɔɪn]   beitreten, Mitglied werden →
    make friends   Freundschaft(en) schließen
    practise ['præktɪs]   üben, trainieren
    annual ['ænjuəl]   jährlich →
    membership ['membəʃɪp]   Mitgliedschaft
    fee [fiː]   Beitrag, Gebühr
    member ['membə]   Mitglied
    less [les]   weniger →
    per [pɜː]   pro
    session ['seʃn]   Treffen; Sitzung
    Swimming Club   Schwimmverein
    still [stɪl]   immer noch
    *****go out**   ausgehen, weggehen
    move (to) [muːv]   umziehen (nach), ziehen (nach)

    not ... yet [jet]   noch nicht →
    fill in [fɪl'ɪn]   ausfüllen
    form [fɔːm]   Formular
    aerobics [eər'əʊbɪks]   Aerobic
    indoor tennis ['ɪndɔː]   Tennis in der Halle

99 **swimming-pool** ['swɪmɪŋpuːl]   Schwimmbad
    dive [daɪv]   Kopfsprung machen
    diving-board ['daɪvɪŋbɔːd]   Sprungbrett
    water chute ['wɔːtəʃuːt]   Wasserrutsche
    they were able to swim ['eɪbltu, 'eɪbltə]   sie konnten schwimmen →
    outdoor swimming-pool ['aʊtdɔː]   Freibad
    swimmer ['swɪmə]   Schwimmer/Schwimmerin
    confident ['kɒnfɪdənt]   selbstbewusst
    board [bɔːd]   Brett
    she was afraid (of) [ə'freɪd]   sie hatte Angst (vor) →
    coward ['kaʊəd]   Feigling

100 **short** [ʃɔːt]   kurz; klein
    National Park ['næʃnəl'pɑːk]   Nationalpark
    outdoor centre   Erlebnisurlaub *(für Jugendliche)*, Ferienlager
    postcode ['pəʊstkəʊd]   Postleitzahl
    formal ['fɔːməl]   offiziell, formell →
    like this   so, auf diese Weise →
    Dear Sir or Madam, ... [dɪə'sɜːrɔː'mædəm]   Sehr geehrte Damen und Herren, ... →
    *****spend** [spend]   *(Zeit)* verbringen
    at the end of October [end]   Ende Oktober
    go potholing ['pɒthəʊlɪŋ]   auf Höhlenforschungstour gehen
    potholing   Höhlenforschung
    look forward to [lʊk'fɔːwədtu]   sich freuen auf
    Yours faithfully, ... [jɔːz'feɪθfəli]   Mit freundlichen Grüßen ... →
    copy ['kɒpi]   abschreiben; kopieren
    ask for   bitten um →
    interest ['ɪntrəst]   Interesse

Ann didn't have many friends, so she *joined* a youth club.

Our school's *annual* party is in December.

Peter has *less* free time now because he has a part-time job.

I haven*'t* had breakfast *yet*.
  – But it's already 12 o'clock.

When Michael was a child, he *wasn't able to* speak English, but now his English is very good.

Jamie *is afraid of* dogs.

You can start a *formal* letter *like this*: *Dear Sir or Madam, ...*

POST
letter
postcard
address
postcode
stamp
post office
postman

You can finish a formal letter with:
  Yours faithfully, ...

Claire didn't understand what the teacher said so she *asked* Bill *for* help.

EXTRA UNIT ONE

101 **she was allowed to** go
[əˈlaʊdtu, əˈlaʊdtə]
cabin [ˈkæbɪn]
instructor [ɪnˈstrʌktə]

stay up
abseiling [ˈæbseɪlɪŋ]
pony-trekking [ˈpəʊnitrekɪŋ]
orienteering course
[ɔːriənˈtɪərɪŋkɔːs]
wood [wʊd]
down in the caves
*swim: **I swam** [swæm]

sie durfte gehen →

Hütte
Betreuer/Betreuerin,
  Lehrer/Lehrerin
aufbleiben
Abseilen
Ponyreiten *(übers Land)*
Orientierungslauf

Wald →
unten in den Höhlen
schwimmen: ich schwamm /
  ich bin geschwommen

You *aren't allowed to* ride
your bike here.

⚠ **stay** = 1. bleiben; 2. übernachten
stay up = aufbleiben

Let's go for a walk in the *wood*. – Oh no, let's have
coffee in a nice café.

*IRREGULAR VERBS

INFINITIVE FORM	SIMPLE PAST FORM	PRESENT PERFECT FORM
go [gəʊ]	I went [went]	I've gone [gɒn]
spend [spend]	I spent [spent]	I've spent [spent]
swim [swɪm]	I swam [swæm]	I've swum [swʌm]

TEST YOURSELF

a SWIMMING CLUB: A – E – I – O – U?
sw?mming-p??l: swimming-pool
?nd??r swimming-pool
sw?mm?r
d?v?
d?v?ng-b??rd

b Ergänze.
1 Because Ian wanted to make more friends, he … a youth club.
2 I'm so hungry. It's already 2 pm and we haven't had lunch …
3 After two years in Germany Jenny … … … speak German.
4 My sister jumps on a chair when she sees a mouse.
  She's … … mice.
5 When you write a formal letter, you start with "… … … …".
  And you finish with "… …".

TIPS

Wörter, die sich reimen

Wenn du manchmal Schwierigkeiten hast, dir ein neues Wort zu merken, kannst du mit Tricks arbeiten. Du kannst dir z.B. ein anderes englisches Wort suchen, das sich auf das neue Wort reimt *(still – ill)*. Bilde aus diesen beiden Wörtern anschließend einen Satz, z.B. *Is Jill still ill?* Versuche einmal einen Satz mit *Clive – dive – five* oder *we – fee* zu bilden. Vielleicht fallen dir manchmal auch lustige Sätze ein und es gibt etwas zu lachen? Dann solltest du diese Sätze unbedingt deinen Mitschülern und Mitschülerinnen vorlesen!

EXTRA UNIT TWO VOCABULARY

102 fire — Kaminfeuer
   jump at ['dʒʌmpət] — anspringen →
   ★**bite** [baɪt]: **he bit** [bɪt] — beißen: er biss / er hat gebissen →
   reader ['riːdə] — Leser/Leserin
   government ['gʌvənmənt] — Regierung →
   ban [bæn] — verbieten →
   change [tʃeɪndʒ] — (sich) ändern
   law [lɔː] — Gesetz →
   attack [əˈtæk] — 1. angreifen; 2. Angriff
   own [əʊn] — besitzen
   as [æz, əz] — als →
   tiger ['taɪgə] — Tiger
   blame [bleɪm] — beschuldigen
   owner ['əʊnə] — Besitzer/Besitzerin
   train [treɪn] — dressieren, abrichten
   aggressive [əˈgresɪv] — aggressiv, angriffslustig
   punish ['pʌnɪʃ] — bestrafen →
   person ['pɜːsn] — Person, Mensch
   Who's wrong? — Wer hat Unrecht? →

103 disability [dɪsəˈbɪləti] — (Körper-)Behinderung
   guide dog ['gaɪddɒg] — Blindenhund
   the blind [ðəˈblaɪnd] — die Blinden
   association [əsəʊsɪˈeɪʃn] — Vereinigung, Verband
   blind [blaɪnd] — blind
   hearing dog — „hörender Hund" (Hund für Gehörlose)
   the deaf [ðəˈdef] — die Gehörlosen
   ear [ɪə] — Ohr
   deaf [def] — gehörlos
   inside [ɪnˈsaɪd] — innerhalb (von); (nach) drinnen →
   side of the road — Straßenrand
   forward ['fɔːwəd] — vorwärts
   touch [tʌtʃ] — berühren, anfassen →
   working dog — „arbeitender Hund" (für eine bestimmte Arbeit abgerichteter Hund)
   alarm clock [əˈlɑːmklɒk] — Wecker →
   ★**wake** [weɪk] — wecken, aufwecken
   doorbell ['dɔːbel] — Türglocke, Türklingel
   noise [nɔɪz] — Geräusch; Lärm
   nose [nəʊz] — Nase

104 frozen ['frəʊzn] — zugefroren; gefroren
   ★**run: I ran** [ræn] — rennen: ich rannte / ich bin gerannt
   she ran after it — sie rannte hinter ihm her
   onto ['ɒntu, 'ɒntə] — auf (... hinauf/herauf) →
   thin [θɪn] — dünn
   ice [aɪs] — Eis (gefrorenes Wasser)
   ★**break: it broke** [brəʊk] — brechen: es brach / es ist gebrochen
   rescue ['reskjuː] — retten
   turn back [tɜːn] — umkehren, zurückgehen →
   fire brigade ['faɪəbrɪˈgeɪd] — Feuerwehr
   rope [rəʊp] — Seil
   ★**hold** [həʊld] — halten
   climb [klaɪm] — klettern, steigen
   push [pʊʃ] — schieben; stoßen
   paddle ['pædl] — Paddel
   move [muːv] — (sich) bewegen →
   pull [pʊl] — ziehen

Jennifer doesn't like dogs. Two years ago a dog *jumped at* her and *bit* her.

The *government has banned* dangerous drugs.

You mustn't ride your bike without lights at night. It's dangerous and against the *law*.

Simon has a job *as* a judo teacher.

Do your parents *punish* you if you come home late in the evenings? – Yes, I get less pocket-money then.

Bill says that the English word for "Eis" is "eyes". But *he's wrong*.

> Wendy **owns** a house.
> It's her **own** house.
> Wendy is the **owner** of the house.

They went *inside* because it started raining.

Don't *touch* that tiger!

alarm clock

> **KÖRPERTEILE**
> eye
> ear
> nose
> tooth/teeth
> arm
> hand
> finger

The child climbed *onto* the tree.

I can't walk to the top of the mountain. Let's *turn back*.

She can't *move* her left arm.

EXTRA UNIT TWO

side of the lake — Seeufer
she was alive [ə'laɪv] — sie war am Leben
drown [draʊn] — ertrinken
shout for help — um Hilfe rufen →
the shouting — das (laute) Rufen
diver ['daɪvə] — Taucher/Taucherin
get — kommen, gelangen
brave [breɪv] — mutig, tapfer →

Two children fell into a river. They *shouted for* help.

I was afraid of going into the old, dark house. But Sue was very *brave*. She went in and found the lights.

*IRREGULAR VERBS

INFINITIVE FORM	SIMPLE PAST FORM	PRESENT PERFECT FORM
bite [baɪt]	I bit [bɪt]	I've bitten ['bɪtn]
break [breɪk]	I broke [brəʊk]	I've broken ['brəʊkən]
hold [həʊld]	I held [held]	I've held [held]
run [rʌn]	I ran [ræn]	I've run [rʌn]
wake [weɪk]	I woke [wəʊk]	I've woken ['wəʊkən]

TEST YOURSELF

a REGULAR OR IRREGULAR?

Infinitive Form – Simple Past Form – Present Perfect Form

jump	I jumped	I've jumped
bite	?	?
change	?	?
punish	?	?
wake	?	?
hold	?	?
move	?	?

b Ergänze.
1 You mustn't drive a car when you're 14. That's against the …
2 Asif has a job … a waiter in a restaurant.
3 Let's go … It's too cold outside.
4 She can't … her finger. She hurt her hand yesterday.
5 Brenda is never afraid. She's always very …

EXTRA UNIT THREE VOCABULARY

106 **alternative** [ɔːlˈtɜːnətɪv] — alternativ *(anders)*
lifestyle [ˈlaɪfstaɪl] — Lebensstil
prize [praɪz] — Preis, Gewinn →
*****put on** — aufführen *(Theaterstück, Show)* →
puppet show [ˈpʌpɪt] — Puppentheater →
college [ˈkɒlɪdʒ] — Berufsschule, Fach-(hoch-)schule
nine-to-five job — geregelter Achtstundentag
van [væn] — Lieferwagen, Kleinbus
decide [dɪˈsaɪd] — beschließen, (sich) entscheiden
a bit (of) [bɪt] — ein bisschen, ein wenig →
uncomfortable [ʌnˈkʌmftəbl] — unbequem
hot [hɒt] — heiß; warm
fresh [freʃ] — frisch
luxury [ˈlʌkʃəri] — Luxus
if — ob →

107 **in the last few years** — in den letzten paar Jahren
increase [ɪnˈkriːs] — ansteigen, zunehmen →
doorway [ˈdɔːweɪ] — Eingang
ask a question — eine Frage stellen
he was drunk [drʌŋk] — er war betrunken
one day — eines Tages
*****hit: I hit** [hɪt] — schlagen: ich schlug / ich habe geschlagen
*****sleep rough** [rʌf] — im Freien übernachten
hostel — Wohnheim; Obdachlosenheim
it's frightening [ˈfraɪtnɪŋ] — es macht mir Angst
lonely [ˈləʊnli] — einsam
chat [tʃæt] — sich unterhalten, plaudern →
alone [əˈləʊn] — allein

108 **social** [ˈsəʊʃl] — sozial, Sozial-
joyriding [ˈdʒɔɪraɪdɪŋ] — (Vergnügungs-)Fahrt in einem gestohlenen Auto
accident [ˈæksɪdənt] — Unfall →
joyrider [ˈdʒɔɪraɪdə] — Person, die ein Auto für eine (Vergnügungs-)Fahrt stiehlt
illegal [ɪˈliːgl] — ungesetzlich, illegal
alternative [ɔːlˈtɜːnətɪv] — Alternative
garage — (Reparatur-)Werkstatt
track [træk] — Rennstrecke
public [ˈpʌblɪk] — öffentlich
legal [ˈliːgl] — gesetzlich, legal
welcome [ˈwelkəm] — begrüßen; willkommen heißen
support [səˈpɔːt] — unterstützen
donation [dəʊˈneɪʃn] — Spende
supporter [səˈpɔːtə] — Unterstützer/Unterstützerin
correct — korrigieren, berichtigen
twice [twaɪs] — zweimal

109 **opinion** [əˈpɪnjən] — Meinung →
local newspaper [ˈləʊkl] — Lokalzeitung
thief, thieves [θiːf, θiːvz] — Dieb/Diebin, Diebe/Diebinnen
fine [faɪn] — Geldstrafe
prison [ˈprɪzn] — Gefängnis →
offer [ˈɒfə] — anbieten
mechanic [məˈkænɪk] — Mechaniker/Mechanikerin
*****give: I've given** [ɡɪvn] — geben: ich habe gegeben
unemployed [ˌʌnɪmˈplɔɪd] — arbeitslos →
many are bored [bɔːd] — viele langweilen sich →

You can win great *prizes* at a fair.
We're *putting on* a show about our teachers. The tickets are £1.
I went to a *puppet show* yesterday. I liked the beautiful puppets.

puppets

⚠ prize = Gewinn, Preis
pric**e** = (Kauf-)Preis

I'm always *a bit* nervous before our English tests.

⚠ **a bit** tired/nervous/worried …
a bit of free time/money/help …

I don't know *if* Mandy has already gone home.

The number of cars on the roads *has increased*.

⚠ I **hit** = ich schlage
I **hit** = ich schlug / ich habe geschlagen
I've **hit** = ich habe geschlagen

Jo and I like *chatting*. When we meet, we talk about lots of different things.

Please hurry! There has been an *accident* in Elm Road.

Our neighbour thinks the law should punish joyriders. What's your *opinion*?

Megabilly is in *prison*.

My stepfather was *unemployed* for two years but last week he found a job.
Wendy always watches TV when she's *bored*.

EXTRA UNIT THREE

complain [kəm'pleɪn] — sich beschweren
instead [ɪn'sted] — stattdessen
break into — aufbrechen, einbrechen (in)
escape from the police [ɪ'skeɪpfrəm] — vor der Polizei fliehen, der Polizei entkommen

THIEF/THIEVES
steal
break into
illegal
against the law
escape from the police
prison

*IRREGULAR VERBS

INFINITIVE FORM	SIMPLE PAST FORM	PRESENT PERFECT FORM
hit [hɪt]	I hit [hɪt]	I've hit [hɪt]
give [gɪv]	I gave [geɪv]	I've given ['gɪvn]
put [pʊt]	I put [pʊt]	I've put [pʊt]
sleep [sliːp]	I slept [slept]	I've slept [slept]

TEST YOURSELF

a
HOMELESS PEOPLE
sleep rough
sleep in a ?
are often lo?
are often unem?

b Ergänze.
1. Before English tests I'm usually … … nervous.
2. Do you know … my brother has already left or not?
3. My dad really enjoys … When he talks to his friend, he's on the phone for an hour.
4. Jenny thinks that we should support social projects. What's your …?
5. Mike doesn't have anything to do. He's very …

TIPS

Swimming-pool und alles, was damit zu tun hat

Schreibe kurze Sätze auf, die dir einfallen, wenn du über *swimming-pool* nachdenkst: *It's summer. It's sunny. I'm on holiday. I'm smiling. I'm enjoying myself.*

Jetzt bist du an der Reihe. Was fällt dir z.B. ein, wenn du über *unemployed people* oder *an alternative lifestyle* nachdenkst? Mache dir zwei Zettel. Einen mit der Überschrift *Unemployed people* und einen mit der Überschrift *An alternative lifestyle.* Schreibe unter diesen Überschriften kurze Sätze auf, die dir dazu einfallen.

Überlege dir dann andere Überschriften und schreibe möglichst viele passende Sätze dazu auf.

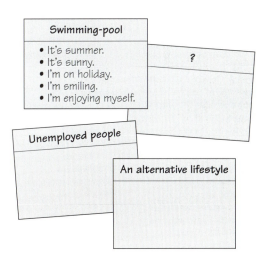

EXTRA UNIT FOUR VOCABULARY

110 *leave behind — zurücklassen, hinter sich lassen →
life, lives [laɪf, laɪvz] — Leben
tough [tʌf] — hart, schwer →
school mate [ˈskuːlmeɪt] — Schulfreund/Schulfreundin
relation [rɪˈleɪʃn] — Verwandte/Verwandter →
settle [ˈsetl] — sich niederlassen; sich einleben

language [ˈlæŋgwɪdʒ] — Sprache →
culture [ˈkʌltʃə] — Kultur
just [dʒʌst] — einfach →
emigrate [ˈemɪgreɪt] — auswandern
he had lost [lɒst] — er hatte verloren
close down [kləʊzˈdaʊn] — schließen →
success [səkˈses] — Erfolg
depressed [dɪˈprest] — deprimiert, niedergeschlagen
chemist [ˈkemɪst] — Chemiker/Chemikerin
like **very much** — sehr (gern mögen) →
look for — suchen →
abroad [əˈbrɔːd] — im Ausland; ins Ausland
in a foreign country [ˈfɒrən] — im Ausland, in einem anderen Land

husband [ˈhʌzbənd] — Ehemann
these days — heutzutage
go abroad to work — ins Ausland gehen, um zu arbeiten

start — Anfang
surprisingly [səˈpraɪzɪŋli] — überraschenderweise →
both [bəʊθ] — beide →
chemical factory [ˈkemɪkl] — Chemiefabrik
whole [həʊl] — ganz
excited [ɪkˈsaɪtɪd] — aufgeregt, begeistert
move [muːv] — Umzug
get used to [ˈjuːstə, ˈjuːstu] — sich gewöhnen an →

111 How do they feel about …? — Was halten sie von …?
*stand [stænd] — stehen
*speak: **I spoke** [spəʊk] — sprechen: ich sprach / ich habe gesprochen →

slow [sləʊ] — langsam →
quick [kwɪk] — schnell
rent [rent] — Miete
comfortable [ˈkʌmftəbl] — bequem, angenehm
bread [bred] — Brot
pudding [ˈpʊdɪŋ] — Nachtisch
jelly [ˈdʒeli] — „Wackelpudding"; Grütze
trifle [ˈtraɪfl] — Trifle *(britische Süßspeise)*
custard [ˈkʌstəd] — Vanillesoße
delicious [dɪˈlɪʃəs] — köstlich, lecker →

112 regular [ˈregjələ] — regelmäßig
it's used for sending e-mails [ˈjuːzdə, ˈjuːzdɔː] — es wird benutzt, um E-Mails zu schicken →
invention [ɪnˈvenʃn] — Erfindung
dry [draɪ] — trocknen, abtrocknen
toast [təʊst] — toasten *(Brot rösten)*
fax [fæks] — Fax(nachricht)
wash the dishes [ˈdɪʃɪz] — (Geschirr) spülen
microwave [ˈmaɪkrəweɪv] — Mikrowelle
fax machine [ˈfæksməˌʃiːn] — Faxgerät
dishwasher [ˈdɪʃwɒʃə] — Geschirrspülmaschine
hair-drier [ˈheədraɪə] — Föhn
washing-machine [ˈwɒʃɪŋməˌʃiːn] — Waschmaschine

Philip often thinks about the friends he *left* behind in his old school.

This is a *tough* exercise. Can we do it together?

We have *relations* in Australia: My uncle, my aunt and my two cousins.

> **tough**
> difficult
> hard

My wife speaks two *languages*: English and Japanese.

If you have a problem, why don't you *just* talk to your teacher about it?

The factory has *closed down* and Anna's mum is unemployed again.

Matthew doesn't like inline-skating *very much*.
What are you doing under the bed? — I'm *looking for* my pen.

Clive and Colleen spent their holidays at home. *Surprisingly* they *both* enjoyed it.

> **GEFÜHLE**
> They were happy.
> They were excited.
> They were depressed.
> They were frightened.
> They were afraid.
> They were sad.
> They were angry.

We had to *get used to* the different food in England.

Could you *speak* more *slowly*, please?

Thanks for the pudding. It was *delicious*.

What's that thing *used for*? — It's used for combing your hair.

EXTRA UNIT FOUR

answerphone	['ɑːnsəfəʊn]	Anrufbeantworter
helpful	['helpfl]	hilfreich
machine	[mə'ʃiːn]	Maschine, Gerät
113 invent	[ɪn'vent]	erfinden
correct	[kə'rekt]	richtig, korrekt
they were invented		sie wurden erfunden →

The telephone *was invented* in 1876.

★ IRREGULAR VERBS

INFINITIVE FORM	SIMPLE PAST FORM	PRESENT PERFECT FORM
leave [liːv]	I left [left]	I've left [left]
speak [spiːk]	I spoke [spəʊk]	I've spoken ['spəʊkən]
stand [stænd]	I stood [stʊd]	I've stood [stʊd]

TEST YOURSELF

a MACHINES
microwave
?
?
?
?

b OPPOSITES
easy – tough
find – ?
sit – ?
slow – ?

c Ergänze.
1. Sally has made many new friends. She doesn't very often think about the friends she … …
2. Do you have … in England? – Yes, my sister and my cousin live there.
3. How many … do you speak? – Two, English and German.
4. My younger brother always wants to eat ice-cream. He likes it … …
5. What are you doing? – I'm … … my pencil-case.
6. I love English puddings. I think they're …

Answers to the quiz on p.113: 1b 2b 3c 4a 5c 6a 7b 8b

EXTRA UNIT FIVE VOCABULARY

114 *****grow** [grəʊ] — anpflanzen, heranziehen → We want to *grow* an apple tree in our garden.
working hours — Arbeitszeit
chemical ['kemɪkl] — Chemikalie → A lot of people complain about too many *chemicals* in the food.
land [lænd] — Land, Boden
vegetable ['vedʒtəbl] — Gemüse
organic [ɔːˈgænɪk] — biodynamisch (nur mit natürlichen Düngemitteln angebaut) → *Organic* food is often very expensive, isn't it?

baker's shop ['beɪkəzʃɒp] — Bäckerladen
by — von, durch → Mr Jackson was attacked *by* a dog yesterday.
robot ['rəʊbɒt] — Roboter

115 butcher ['bʊtʃə] — Fleischer/Fleischerin
meat [miːt] — Fleisch
inherit [ɪnˈherɪt] — erben
business ['bɪznəs] — Geschäft, Betrieb → Jenny lost her job nine months ago. Now she has her own *business*.
sandwich bar ['sænwɪtʃbɑː] — „Sandwichladen", Stehcafé
office worker ['ɒfɪsˌwɜːkə] — Büroangestellte/Büroangestellter

lunch break ['lʌntʃbreɪk] — Mittagspause
including [ɪnˈkluːdɪŋ] — einschließlich
train as ['treɪnəz] — ausgebildet werden zum/zur
lorry ['lɒri] — Lastwagen →

lorry

courier ['kʊriə] — Kurier/Kurierin, Bote/Botin
key phrase ['kiːfreɪz] — Hauptaussage
in a butcher's — in einer Fleischerei

116 mobile job ['məʊbaɪl] — Arbeit, bei der man viel unterwegs ist → I'd like to have a *mobile job* because I like travelling.
travelling salespeople ['seɪlzˌpiːpl] — Handelsreisende, Vertreter/Vertreterinnen
all sorts of people [ɔːlˈsɔːtsəv, ɔːlˈsɔːtsɒv] — alle möglichen Leute → I like *Disco Cool* because they play *all sorts of* CDs: rock, jazz and rap.
one in three — jede/jeder dritte
common ['kɒmən] — häufig, weit verbreitet → It's very *common* now that people live and work in foreign countries.
attractive (to) [əˈtræktɪv] — attraktiv (für), anziehend (für)
instant communication ['ɪnstəntkəmjuːnɪˈkeɪʃn] — unverzügliche Verständigung

everyday life ['evrɪdeɪˈlaɪf] — Alltagsleben
*****find out** — herausfinden
at any time — jederzeit
extreme sport [ɪkˈstriːm] — Extremsport
mountain climbing ['maʊntənˈklaɪmɪŋ] — Bergsteigen →

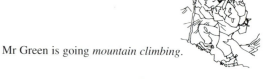

Mr Green is going *mountain climbing*.

carry — bei sich haben
also ['ɔːlsəʊ] — auch
forester ['fɒrɪstə] — Förster/Försterin
isolated ['aɪsəleɪtɪd] — abgelegen, (von der Umwelt) abgeschnitten →

⚠ **also** (engl.) = auch
so (engl.) = also, daher; so

My uncle in Australia lives in a very *isolated* place. His neighbours live about 50 km away.

save [seɪv] — sparen
receive [rɪˈsiːv] — erhalten, bekommen
call [kɔːl] — Anruf
effect [ɪˈfekt] — (Aus-)Wirkung → Waking my brother in the morning had no *effect*. He didn't get up.
scientist ['saɪəntɪst] — (Natur-)Wissenschaftler/Wissenschaftlerin

damage ['dæmɪdʒ] — schädigen; beschädigen → I'm sorry I've *damaged* your microwave.

brain [breɪn] — Gehirn
product ['prɒdʌkt] — Produkt, Erzeugnis

FOOD
fruit
vegetable
meat
fish
bread
pizza
yoghurt

138

EXTRA UNIT FIVE

117
- **passive form** [ˈpæsɪvfɔːm] — Passivform
- **bend** [bend] — Kurve, Biegung
- **crash into** [kræʃ] — fahren gegen, hineinfahren in
- **a long way from** — weit entfernt von
- **dial** [ˈdaɪəl] — wählen *(beim Telefon)*
- **emergency services** [ɪˈmɜːdʒənsiˈsɜːvɪsɪz] — Notdienst
- **user** [ˈjuːzə] — Benutzer/Benutzerin

ACCIDENT
- crash
- rescue
- ambulance
- emergency services
- fire brigade
- hospital
- nurse

★ IRREGULAR VERBS

INFINITIVE FORM	SIMPLE PAST FORM	PRESENT PERFECT FORM
find [faɪnd]	I found [faʊnd]	I've found [faʊnd]
grow [grəʊ]	I grew [gruː]	I've grown [grəʊn]

TEST YOURSELF

a BUYING FOOD
in a baker's shop
?
?

b WHO REALLY NEEDS A MOBILE PHONE?
travelling salespeople
people who do ?
people who go ?
people who live in ? places

c Ergänze.
1. Ms Blair was bitten … a dog yesterday.
2. I don't like travelling, so I don't want a … …
3. I like … … … TV programmes: soaps, police dramas and talk shows.
4. My wife and I enjoy doing extreme sports like … …
5. My friend … our microwave yesterday. Can you repair it?

TIPS

Falsche Freunde?

Manchmal findest du ein englisches Wort, das (fast) genauso aussieht wie ein deutsches Wort. Oft ist die Bedeutung aber unterschiedlich (z.B. *become* – bekommen). *Become* bedeutet aber nicht „bekommen", sondern „werden". Auf Englisch nennt man Paare wie „become – bekommen" *false friends* – falsche Freunde. Überprüfe anhand deines *Dictionary* (ab S. 140), inwieweit die Bedeutung der deutschen Wörter unten mit ähnlichen englischen Wörtern übereinstimmt. Bedeutet z.B. das deutsche Wort „Offizier" dasselbe wie das englische Wort *officer*?

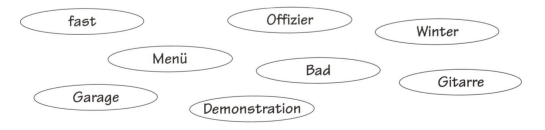

fast · Offizier · Winter · Menü · Bad · Gitarre · Garage · Demonstration

Dictionary

Alphabetische Liste der Wörter aus den Bänden 1 – 4

A

a [ə] ein/eine; **£2 a week** 2 Pfund pro Woche; **seven days a week** sieben Tage in der Woche
able to [ˈeɪbltu, ˈeɪbltə]: **I'm able to swim** ich kann schwimmen
about [əˈbaʊt] 1. über, von; wegen; 2. ungefähr; **The programme is about ...** Die Sendung handelt von ...; **What about ... ?** Wie wäre es mit ... ? Was ist mit ... ?
above [əˈbʌv] über
abroad [əˈbrɔːd] im Ausland; ins Ausland
abseiling [ˈæbseɪlɪŋ] Abseilen
accent [ˈæksənt] Akzent
accident [ˈæksɪdənt] Unfall
accommodation [əkɒməˈdeɪʃn] Unterkunft
action [ˈækʃn] Handlung, Tätigkeit
activity [ækˈtɪvəti] Tätigkeit, Aktivität; Unternehmung
address [əˈdres] Adresse
adult [ˈædʌlt] Erwachsene/Erwachsener
advert [ˈædvɜːt] Werbespot, Werbung; Stellenausschreibung
advertise [ˈædvətaɪz] Reklame machen, werben
aerobics [eəˈrəʊbɪks] Aerobic
afraid (of) [əˈfreɪd]: **I'm afraid (of)** ich habe Angst (vor)
after [ˈɑːftə] 1. hinter ... her; 2. nach; **after school** nach der Schule; 3. nachdem; **after that** danach
afternoon [ˌɑːftəˈnuːn] Nachmittag; **Good afternoon.** Guten Tag. *(nachmittags)*; **in the afternoon(s)** nachmittags; am Nachmittag; **this afternoon** heute Nachmittag
again [əˈgen] (schon) wieder; noch einmal
against [əˈgenst] gegen
age [eɪdʒ] Alter; Altersstufe
agency [ˈeɪdʒənsi]: **travel agency** [ˈtrævleɪdʒənsi] Reisebüro

aggressive [əˈgresɪv] aggressiv, angriffslustig
ago [əˈgəʊ]: **400 years ago** vor 400 Jahren
airport [ˈeəpɔːt] Flughafen
alarm [əˈlɑːm]: **alarm clock** Wecker
alive [əˈlaɪv]: **she's alive** sie ist am Leben
all [ɔːl] alle; alles; **all the time** die ganze Zeit
allowed (to) [əˈlaʊd]: **I'm allowed to go** ich darf gehen
almost [ˈɔːlməʊst] fast, beinahe
alone [əˈləʊn] allein
along [əˈlɒŋ] entlang
alphabetical [ˌælfəˈbetɪkl] alphabetisch
already [ɔːlˈredi] schon
also [ˈɔːlsəʊ] auch
alternative [ɔːlˈtɜːnətɪv] 1. alternativ 2. Alternative
although [ɔːlˈðəʊ] obwohl
always [ˈɔːlweɪz] immer
am [æm]: **I am** ich bin
am [ˈeɪem] morgens, vormittags
ambulance [ˈæmbjələns] Krankenwagen; **ambulance driver** Sanitäter/Sanitäterin
American [əˈmerɪkən] amerikanisch; Amerikaner/Amerikanerin
an [ən] ein/eine
and [ænd, ənd] und
angry [ˈæŋgri] böse, wütend
animal [ˈænɪməl] Tier; **animal home** Tierheim
annual [ˈænjuəl] jährlich
another [əˈnʌðə] ein anderer / eine andere / ein anderes; noch ein/eine/eins
answer [ˈɑːnsə] 1. antworten, beantworten; 2. Antwort
answerphone [ˈɑːnsəfəʊn] Anrufbeantworter
any [ˈeni]: **at any time** jederzeit; **not ... any** kein/keine
anybody [ˈenibɒdi]: **not ... anybody** niemand

anything [ˈeniθɪŋ]: **not ... anything** nichts
apple [ˈæpl] Apfel
application form [æplɪˈkeɪʃnfɔːm] Bewerbungsformular
apply (for) [əˈplaɪ] sich bewerben (um)
April [ˈeɪprəl] April
are [ɑː]: **you are** du bist; ihr seid; Sie sind; **we/they are** wir/sie sind
argue [ˈɑːgjuː] (sich) streiten
arm [ɑːm] Arm
around [əˈraʊnd]: **around the world** überall in der Welt; **travel around the city** durch die Stadt fahren
arrive [əˈraɪv] ankommen
art [ɑːt] Kunst
article [ˈɑːtɪkl] Artikel
as [əz, æz]: als; **as near as** so nah wie; **as you are** wie du bist
Asian [ˈeɪʃn] asiatisch; Asiat/Asiatin
ask [ɑːsk] fragen; bitten; **ask about** fragen nach; **ask a question** eine Frage stellen; **ask for** bitten um
assistant [əˈsɪstənt]: **shop assistant** Verkäufer/Verkäuferin; **dentist's assistant** Zahnarzthelfer/in; **doctor's assistant** Arzthelfer/in
association [əsəʊsiˈeɪʃn] Vereinigung, Verband
at [æt, ət] bei; an; in; **at any time** jederzeit; **at Dave's house/Asif's flat** bei Dave/Asif zu Hause; **at home** zu Hause, daheim; **at night** nachts, in der Nacht; **at school** in der Schule; **at 6 o'clock** um 6 Uhr/18 Uhr; **at that time** damals, zu jener Zeit; **at the moment** zurzeit, im Augenblick; **at the top** auf der Spitze; **at the weekend** am Wochenende; **at work** bei der Arbeit
ate [et]: **I ate** ich aß / ich habe gegessen
athletics [æθˈletɪks] Leichtathletik
attack [əˈtæk] 1. Angriff; 2. angreifen

attraction [əˈtrækʃn] Attraktion, Anziehungspunkt
attractive (to) [əˈtræktɪv] attraktiv (für), anziehend (für)
auction [ˈɔːkʃn] Versteigerung
August [ˈɔːɡəst] August
aunt [ɑːnt] Tante
Australia [ɒˈstreɪliə] Australien
autumn [ˈɔːtəm] Herbst
away [əˈweɪ] weg, entfernt; fort

B

baby [ˈbeɪbi] Baby
babysat [ˈbeɪbisæt]: **I babysat** ich passte auf kleine Kinder auf / ich habe auf kleine Kinder aufgepasst; **I've babysat** ich habe auf kleine Kinder aufgepasst
babysit [ˈbeɪbisɪt] „Babysitten" *(auf kleine Kinder aufpassen)*
back [bæk] zurück
bacon [ˈbeɪkən] Speck
bad [bæd] schlecht, schlimm; **bad at** schlecht in, ungeschickt in
badge [bædʒ] Abzeichen; Anstecker, Button
bag [bæɡ] (Schul-)Tasche, Tüte
baker's shop [ˈbeɪkəzʃɒp] Bäckerladen
ball [bɔːl] Ball
ban [bæn] verbieten
banana [bəˈnɑːnə] Banane
band [bænd] Band, (Musik-)Gruppe
bank [bæŋk] Bank, Sparkasse; **bank clerk** Bankangestellte/Bankangestellter; **bottle bank** Altglascontainer; **paper bank** Altpapiercontainer
bar [bɑː] Bar, Kneipe; **coffee bar** Cafeteria; **sandwich bar** „Sandwichladen", Stehcafé
basketball [ˈbɑːskɪtbɔːl] Basketball
bathroom [ˈbɑːθruːm] Badezimmer, Bad
battery [ˈbætəri] Batterie
be [biː] sein
beach [biːtʃ] Strand
bean [biːn] Bohne
beautiful [ˈbjuːtɪfl] schön, wunderschön
became [bɪˈkeɪm]: **I became** ich wurde / ich bin geworden

because [bɪˈkɒz] weil; **because of** wegen
become [bɪˈkʌm] werden; **I've become** ich bin geworden
bed [bed] Bett; **bed and breakfast** [bedənˈbrekfəst] Zimmer mit Frühstück *(in kleiner Frühstückspension)*; **go to bed** ins Bett gehen; **in bed** im Bett
bedroom [ˈbedruːm] Schlafzimmer
been [biːn, bɪn]: **I've been** ich bin gewesen
before [bɪˈfɔː] 1. vor; 2. bevor; 3. vorher, schon einmal
began [bɪˈɡæn]: **I began** ich begann/ich habe begonnen
behind [bɪˈhaɪnd] hinter
believe [bɪˈliːv] glauben
bell [bel] (Tür-)Klingel, Glocke
belong to [bɪˈlɒŋtu, bɪˈlɒŋtə] gehören (zu)
bend [bend] Kurve, Biegung
best [best] beste/bester/bestes; der/die/das Beste
bet [bet] wetten; **I bet** ich wettete / ich habe gewettet; **I've bet** ich habe gewettet
better [ˈbetə] besser
between [bɪˈtwiːn] zwischen
big [bɪɡ] groß
bike [baɪk] Fahrrad; **bike path** Fahrradweg; **ride a bike** Rad fahren
bingo [ˈbɪŋɡəʊ] Bingo(-spiel)
biology [baɪˈɒlədʒi] Biologie
bird [bɜːd] Vogel
biro [ˈbaɪrəʊ] Kugelschreiber
birth [bɜːθ]: **place of birth** Geburtsort
birthday [ˈbɜːθdeɪ] Geburtstag; **Happy birthday (to you)!** Herzlichen Glückwunsch zum Geburtstag!
bit [bɪt]: **I bit** ich biss / ich habe gebissen
bit [bɪt]: **a bit (of)** ein bisschen, ein wenig
bite [baɪt] beißen
bitten [ˈbɪtn]: **I've bitten** ich habe gebissen
black [blæk] schwarz
blame [bleɪm] beschuldigen
blind [blaɪnd] blind; **the blind** die Blinden
blue [bluː] blau

board [bɔːd] 1. Tafel; 2. Brett
boat [bəʊt] Schiff, Boot
bomb [bɒm] Bombe
book [bʊk] 1. Buch; Heft; 2. buchen, reservieren (lassen), vorbestellen;
bookshelf, bookshelves [ˈbʊkʃelf] Bücherregal, Bücherregale
bored [bɔːd] gelangweilt; **I'm bored** ich langweile mich
boring [ˈbɔːrɪŋ] langweilig
born [bɔːn]: **I was born in England** ich bin in England geboren
both [bəʊθ] beide
bottle [ˈbɒtl] Flasche; **bottle bank** Altglascontainer
bought [bɔːt]: **I bought** ich kaufte / ich habe gekauft; **I've bought** ich habe gekauft;
boutique [buːˈtiːk] Boutique
box [bɒks] Kiste, Karton, Schachtel, Dose
boy [bɔɪ] Junge
boyfriend [ˈbɔɪfrend] (fester) Freund
brain [breɪn] Gehirn
brave [breɪv] mutig, tapfer
bread [bred] Brot
break [breɪk] brechen, zerbrechen, kaputtmachen; **break into** aufbrechen, einbrechen (in); **lunch break** Mittagspause
breakfast [ˈbrekfəst] Frühstück; **for breakfast** zum Frühstück; **have breakfast** frühstücken
bricklayer [ˈbrɪkleɪə] Maurer/Maurerin
bridge [brɪdʒ] Brücke
brilliant [ˈbrɪliənt] großartig
bring [brɪŋ] bringen, mitbringen
Britain [ˈbrɪtn] Großbritannien
British [ˈbrɪtɪʃ] britisch; Brite/Britin
brochure [ˈbrəʊʃə] Broschüre
broke [brəʊk]: **I broke** ich zerbrach, ich habe zerbrochen (usw.)
broken [ˈbrəʊkən] **I've broken** ich habe zerbrochen (usw.); **it has broken** es ist gebrochen; es ist zerbrochen
brother [ˈbrʌðə] Bruder
brought [brɔːt]: **I brought** ich brachte (mit) / ich habe (mit)gebracht; **I've brought** ich habe (mit)gebracht
brown [braʊn] braun
bucket [ˈbʌkɪt] Eimer
budgie [ˈbʌdʒi] Wellensittich

build [bɪld] bauen
builder ['bɪldə] Bauarbeiter/Bauarbeiterin
building ['bɪldɪŋ] Gebäude
built [bɪlt]: **I built** ich baute / ich habe gebaut; **I've built** ich habe gebaut
bus [bʌs] Bus; **bus station** Bushof, Busbahnhof
bus-stop ['bʌstɒp] Bushaltestelle
business ['bɪznəs] Geschäft, Betrieb
busy ['bɪzi] beschäftigt; hektisch, belebt
but [bʌt] aber
butcher ['bʊtʃə] Fleischer/Fleischerin; **in a butcher's** in einer Fleischerei
buy [baɪ] kaufen
by [baɪ] von, durch; **by bike/bus/car/…** mit dem Rad/Bus/Auto/…; **by the canal** (nahe) beim Kanal
Bye. / Bye-bye. [baɪ, baɪ'baɪ] Tschüs. Wiedersehen.

C

cabin ['kæbɪn] Hütte
cable ['keɪbl] Kabel
café ['kæfeɪ] Café
cake [keɪk] (kleiner) Kuchen
calculator ['kælkjuleɪtə] Taschenrechner
call [kɔ:l] 1. Anruf; 2. nennen; **it's called** es heißt
came [keɪm]: **I came** ich kam / ich bin gekommen
camera ['kæmrə] Fotoapparat, Kamera
can [kæn] Dose, Büchse
can [kæn, kən] können, dürfen; **can't** [kɑ:nt] (= **cannot** ['kænɒt]) nicht können, nicht dürfen
canal [kə'næl] Kanal
cane [keɪn] Rohrstock
canoe [kə'nu:] Kanu
canoeing [kə'nu:ɪŋ] Kanufahren, Paddeln
capital ['kæpɪtl] Hauptstadt
car [kɑ:] Auto; Wagen; **car park** (großer) Parkplatz, Parkhaus
caravan ['kærəvæn] Wohnwagen

card [kɑ:d] (Spiel-, Post-)Karte; **youth hostel card** Jugendherbergsausweis
career [kə'rɪə] Karriere, Laufbahn
careful ['keəfl] vorsichtig; sorgfältig
carry ['kæri] 1. tragen; befördern; 2. bei sich haben
cartoon [kɑ:'tu:n] Zeichentrickfilm; Cartoon
cassette [kə'set] Cassette
castle ['kɑ:sl] Burg; Schloss
cat [kæt] Katze
Catholic ['kæθlɪk] Katholik/Katholikin
cave [keɪv] Höhle
CD [si:'di:] CD
CD-player [si:'di:'pleɪə] CD-Player, CD-Spieler
centimetre ['sentɪmi:tə] Zentimeter
centre ['sentə] Zentrum, Mitte, Center
chair [tʃeə] Stuhl
change [tʃeɪndʒ] (sich) ändern; **I've changed my mind** ich habe meine Meinung geändert
channel ['tʃænəl] Programm, Sender, Kanal
charts [tʃɑ:ts]: **music charts** Musikhitparade
chat [tʃæt] sich unterhalten, plaudern
cheap [tʃi:p] billig, preiswert
check [tʃek] (über)prüfen, kontrollieren
cheer ['tʃɪə]: **he cheers her up** er muntert sie auf; **Cheer up!** Kopf hoch!
cheese [tʃi:z] Käse
cheeseburger ['tʃi:zbɜ:gə] Cheeseburger
chemical ['kemɪkl] Chemikalie; **chemical factory** Chemiefabrik
chemist ['kemɪst] 1. Apotheker/Apothekerin, Drogist/Drogistin; **at the chemist's** in der Apotheke/Drogerie; 2. Chemiker/Chemikerin
chewing gum ['tʃu:ɪŋgʌm] Kaugummi
chicken ['tʃɪkɪn] Huhn, (Brat-)Hähnchen
child, children [tʃaɪld, 'tʃɪldrən] Kind, Kinder
chip shop ['tʃɪpʃɒp] Pommes-frites-Bude
chips [tʃɪps] Pommes frites
chocolate ['tʃɒklət] Trinkschokolade; Schokolade

choose [tʃu:z] (aus)wählen, aussuchen
chose [tʃəʊz]: ich wählte (aus) / ich habe (aus)gewählt (usw.)
chosen ['tʃəʊzn]: ich habe (aus)gewählt, ausgesucht
church [tʃɜ:tʃ] Kirche; **church hall** Gemeindesaal der Kirche
chute [ʃu:t]: **water chute** Wasserrutsche
cinema ['sɪnəmə] Kino
city ['sɪti] Stadt, Großstadt; **city council** Stadtrat
class [klɑ:s] Klasse
classroom ['klɑ:sru:m] Klassenzimmer
clean [kli:n] 1. sauber machen, putzen; 2. sauber; **clean up** säubern, reinigen; **I clean my teeth.** Ich putze mir die Zähne.
clear away [klɪərə'weɪ] abräumen, wegräumen
clerk [klɑ:k]: **bank clerk** Bankangestellte/Bankangestellter; **office clerk** Büroangestellte/Büroangestellter, kaufmännische Angestellte/kaufmännischer Angestellter
clever ['klevə] schlau, klug
climb [klaɪm] klettern, steigen
clock [klɒk] Uhr; **alarm clock** Wecker
close [kləʊz] zumachen, schließen; **close down** schließen; stilllegen
clothes [kləʊðz] Kleidung, Kleider
cloudy ['klaʊdi] bewölkt
club [klʌb] 1. Club, Verein; 2. Musikkneipe, Diskothek
coal [kəʊl] Kohle
coffee ['kɒfi] Kaffee; **coffee bar** Cafeteria
cola ['kəʊlə] Cola
cold [kəʊld] 1. kalt; 2. Erkältung; **I'm cold** ich friere
collect [kə'lekt] (ein)sammeln
college ['kɒlɪdʒ] Berufsschule, Fach(hoch-)schule
colour ['kʌlə] Farbe; **What colour is …?** Welche Farbe hat …?
comb [kəʊm] kämmen
come [kʌm] kommen; **I've come** ich bin gekommen; **Come to my house.** Komm zu mir (nach Hause). **Come on!** Komm/t schon! Los!

comfortable ['kʌmftəbl] bequem, angenehm
comic ['kɒmɪk] Comic(heft)
common ['kɒmən] häufig, weitverbreitet
communication [kəmju:nɪ'keɪʃn]: **instant communication** unverzügliche Verständigung
company ['kʌmpəni] Gesellschaft, Firma
competition [kɒmpə'tɪʃn] Wettbewerb
complain [kəm'pleɪn] sich beschweren
compost ['kɒmpɒst] Kompost
computer [kəm'pju:tə] Computer, Rechner
concert ['kɒnsət] Konzert
confident ['kɒnfɪdənt] selbstbewusst
container [kən'teɪnə] Container, Behälter
continent ['kɒntɪnənt] Kontinent, Erdteil
cook [kʊk] kochen
cool [ku:l] cool, toll
copy ['kɒpi] abschreiben; kopieren
cornflakes ['kɔ:nfleɪks] Cornflakes
correct [kə'rekt] 1. richtig, korrekt; 2. korrigieren, berichtigen
cost [kɒst] (Geld) kosten
couch [kaʊtʃ] Couch, Sofa
cough [kɒf] Husten
could [kʊd]: **I could** ich könnte; **Could you ...?** Könntest du / Könnten Sie ...?
council ['kaʊnsl]: **city council** Stadtrat; **local council** Gemeindeverwaltung
count [kaʊnt] zählen
country ['kʌntri] Land; **in the country** auf dem Land; **Country** Country(musik)
courier ['kʊriə] Kurier/Kurierin, Bote/Botin
course [kɔ:s]: Kurs, Lehrgang; **of course** natürlich, selbstverständlich
cousin ['kʌzn] Cousin/Cousine, Vetter
cow [kaʊ] Kuh
coward ['kaʊəd] Feigling
crash into [kræʃ] fahren gegen, hineinfahren in
cricket ['krɪkɪt] Kricket
crime [kraɪm] Verbrechen
crisps [krɪsps] Kartoffelchips
cross [krɒs] überqueren
crowd [kraʊd] (Menschen-)Menge
cry [kraɪ] weinen
culture ['kʌltʃə] Kultur
cup [kʌp] Tasse
cupboard ['kʌbəd] Schrank
custard ['kʌstəd] Vanillesoße
customer ['kʌstəmə] Kunde/Kundin
cv [si:'vi:] (= **curriculum vitae** [kə'rɪkjələm'vi:taɪ]) Lebenslauf

D

dad [dæd] Papa, Vati
damage ['dæmɪdʒ] schädigen; beschädigen
dance [dɑ:ns] 1. Tanz; 2. tanzen
dangerous ['deɪndʒərəs] gefährlich
dark [dɑ:k] dunkel
dart [dɑ:t] (Wurf-)Pfeil; **dart board** Dartscheibe
darts [dɑ:ts] Darts, Pfeilwurfspiel
date [deɪt] 1. Datum; 2. Verabredung; **make a date** sich verabreden
daughter ['dɔ:tə] Tochter
day [deɪ] Tag; **day centre** Altentagesstätte, Seniorentreff; **day out** Ausflug; **day return** Tagesrückfahrkarte; **open day** Tag der offenen Tür
dead [ded] tot
deaf [def] gehörlos; **the deaf** die Gehörlosen
dear [dɪə]: **Dear Sir or Madam, ...** Sehr geehrte Damen und Herren, ...
December [dɪ'sembə] Dezember
decide [dɪ'saɪd] beschließen, (sich) entscheiden
delicious [dɪ'lɪʃəs] köstlich, lecker
deliver [dɪ'lɪvə] austragen, zustellen; liefern
demonstration [demən'streɪʃn] Demonstration
dentist ['dentɪst] Zahnarzt/Zahnärztin; **at the dentist's** beim Zahnarzt / bei der Zahnärztin; **dentist's assistant** Zahnarzthelfer/Zahnarzthelferin
department store [dɪ'pɑ:tmənt stɔ:] Kaufhaus

depressed [dɪ'prest] deprimiert, niedergeschlagen
design [dɪ'zaɪn]: **design and technology** künstlerisches Gestalten und Werken
destroy [dɪ'strɔɪ] zerstören
dial ['daɪəl] wählen *(beim Telefon)*
dialogue ['daɪəlɒg] Dialog, Gespräch
diary ['daɪəri] Tagebuch
dictionary ['dɪkʃənri] Wörterbuch
did [dɪd]: **I did** ich tat / ich habe getan
die [daɪ] sterben
different ['dɪfrənt] andere/anderer/anderes; verschieden, anders; **different from** anders als
difficult ['dɪfɪkəlt] schwierig, schwer
dirty ['dɜ:ti] schmutzig
disability [dɪsə'bɪləti] (Körper-)Behinderung
disappointed [dɪsə'pɔɪntɪd] enttäuscht
disco ['dɪskəʊ] Disko
discrimination [dɪskrɪmɪ'neɪʃn] Diskriminierung, Benachteiligung
dish [dɪʃ]: **satellite dish** Satellitenschüssel
dishes ['dɪʃɪz]: Geschirr; **wash the dishes** (Geschirr) spülen; **dishwasher** Geschirrspülmaschine
dive [daɪv] Kopfsprung machen
diver ['daɪvə] Taucher/Taucherin
diving-board ['daɪvɪŋbɔ:d] Sprungbrett
DJ [di:'dʒeɪ] (= **disc jockey** ['dɪskdʒɒki]) Diskjockey
do [du:] tun, machen; **do sports** Sport treiben
doctor ['dɒktə]: **doctor's assistant** Arzthelfer/Arzthelferin
documentary [dɒkju'mentri] Dokumentarfilm
dog [dɒg] Hund
donation [dəʊ'neɪʃn] Spende
done [dʌn]: **I've done** ich habe getan
door [dɔ:] Tür
doorbell ['dɔ:bel] Türglocke, Türklingel
doorway ['dɔ:weɪ] Eingang
down [daʊn] 1. „down", bedrückt; 2. unten; hinunter/herunter, hinab/herab; **pull down** abreißen, niederreißen
downhill [daʊn'hɪl] bergab

drama ['drɑːmə]: **police drama** Krimi
draw [drɔː] zeichnen
drawn [drɔːn]: **I've drawn** ich habe gezeichnet
drew [druː]: **I drew** ich zeichnete / ich habe gezeichnet
drink [drɪŋk] 1. trinken; 2. Getränk
drive [draɪv] fahren
driver ['draɪvə] Fahrer/Fahrerin; **ambulance driver** Sanitäter/in
drop [drɒp] fallen lassen
drove [drəʊv]: **I drove** ich fuhr / ich bin gefahren
drown [draʊn] ertrinken
drug [drʌg] 1. Droge, Rauschgift; 2. Medikament
drunk [drʌŋk]: **he was drunk** er war betrunken
dry [draɪ] (ab)trocknen
dry ski slope [draɪˈskiːsləʊp] Trockenskipiste

E

each [iːtʃ] jede/jeder/jedes; je
ear [ɪə] Ohr
early ['ɜːli] früh; vorzeitig, zu früh
earn [ɜːn] verdienen
earring ['ɪərɪŋ] Ohrring
east [iːst] Ost-; (nach) Osten; östlich
easy ['iːzi] einfach, leicht
eat [iːt] essen; **eat out** zum Essen ausgehen
eaten ['iːtn]: **I've eaten** ich habe gegessen
effect [ɪˈfekt] (Aus-)Wirkung
egg [eg] Ei
electrician [ɪlekˈtrɪʃn] Elektriker/Elektrikerin
e-mail ['iːmeɪl] (= **electronic mail** [ɪlekˈtrɒnɪkˈmeɪl]) „E-Mail" (= elektronische Post)
emergency services [ɪˈmɜːdʒənsiˈsɜːvɪsɪz] Notdienst
emigrate ['emɪgreɪt] auswandern
empty ['empti] leer
end [end] Ende; **at the end of October** Ende Oktober
engineer [endʒɪˈnɪə] Techniker/Technikerin; Ingenieur/Ingenieurin

England ['ɪŋglənd] England
English ['ɪŋglɪʃ] englisch; Englisch; Engländer/Engländerin
enjoy [ɪnˈdʒɔɪ] Spaß haben an, gern tun; **I enjoy myself** ich amüsiere mich, ich habe viel Spaß
enough [ɪˈnʌf] genug
enter ['entə] sich beteiligen an; sich (an)melden für
envelope ['envələʊp] Briefumschlag
environment [ɪnˈvaɪrənmənt] Umgebung; Umwelt; **environment officer** Umweltbeauftragte/Umweltbeauftragter
equipment [ɪˈkwɪpmənt] Ausstattung, Ausrüstung
escape (from) [ɪˈskeɪp] fliehen (vor), entkommen
Europe ['jʊərəp] Europa
even ['iːvn] sogar; **not even** nicht einmal
evening ['iːvnɪŋ] Abend; **Good evening.** Guten Abend. **in the evening(s)** abends; am Abend; **this evening** heute Abend.
ever ['evə] schon einmal, jemals
every ['evri] jede/jeder/jedes
everybody ['evrɪbɒdi] jeder, alle
everyday life ['evrɪdeɪˈlaɪf] Alltagsleben
everything ['evrɪθɪŋ] alles
exaggerate [ɪgˈzædʒəreɪt] übertreiben
example [ɪgˈzɑːmpl] Beispiel; **for example** zum Beispiel
except [ɪkˈsept] außer
excited [ɪkˈsaɪtɪd] aufgeregt, begeistert
exciting [ɪkˈsaɪtɪŋ] aufregend, spannend
excuse [ɪkˈskjuːz]: **Excuse me, ...** Entschuldigen Sie, ...
exercise ['eksəsaɪz] Übung
exhibition [eksɪˈbɪʃn] Ausstellung; Vorführung
expensive [ɪkˈspensɪv] teuer
experience [ɪkˈspɪərɪəns] Erfahrung
explain [ɪkˈspleɪn] erklären
extra ['ekstrə] extra, zusätzlich
extreme [ɪkˈstriːm]: **extreme sport** Extremsport
eye [aɪ] Auge

F

factory ['fæktri] Fabrik
fair [feə] 1. fair, gerecht; 2. Volksfest, Jahrmarkt, Kirmes
faithfully ['feɪθfəli]: **Yours faithfully, ...** Mit freundlichen Grüßen ...
fall [fɔːl] fallen; **fall over** umfallen, hinfallen
fallen ['fɔːlən]: **I've fallen** ich bin gefallen
family ['fæmli] Familie
famous ['feɪməs] berühmt
fan [fæn] Fan, Anhänger/Anhängerin
far [fɑː] weit
farm [fɑːm] Bauernhof, Farm
farmer ['fɑːmə] Landwirt/Landwirtin
fast [fɑːst] schnell
fat [fæt] dick, fett
father ['fɑːðə] Vater
fault [fɔːlt] Schuld
favourite ['feɪvrət] Lieblings-
fax [fæks] Fax(nachricht); **fax machine** Faxgerät
February ['februəri] Februar
fed up (with) ['fedˈʌp]: satt haben; **I'm fed up with going to the cinema.** Ich habe es satt, ins Kino zu gehen.
fee [fiː] Beitrag, Gebühr
feed [fiːd] füttern, zu essen geben
feel [fiːl] (sich) fühlen; **How do you feel about ...?** Was hältst du von ...?
fell [fel]: **I fell** ich fiel / ich bin gefallen
felt [felt]: **I felt** ich fühlte (mich) / ich habe (mich) gefühlt
felt-tip ['felttɪp] Filzstift
few [fjuː] wenige; **a few** ein paar, einige; **in the last few years** in den letzten paar Jahren
field [fiːld] Feld, Wiese
fighting ['faɪtɪŋ] Kämpfe
fill [fɪl] (auf)füllen, voll machen; **fill in** ausfüllen
film [fɪlm] Film
find [faɪnd] finden; **find out** herausfinden; erfahren
fine [faɪn] Geldstrafe
finger ['fɪŋgə] Finger; **fish finger** Fischstäbchen

finish ['fɪnɪʃ] aufhören (mit); beenden
fire ['faɪə] Feuer; Kaminfeuer
fire brigade ['faɪəbrɪ'geɪd] Feuerwehr
firm [fɜːm] Firma
first [fɜːst] 1. erste/erster/erstes; 2. zuerst; **first name** Vorname
fish [fɪʃ] Fisch; **fish and chips** Fisch und Pommes frites; **fish finger** Fischstäbchen
fisherman ['fɪʃəmən] Fischer
fit [fɪt] fit, in guter (körperlicher) Verfassung
fitness ['fɪtnəs]: **fitness trainer** Fitnesstrainer/Fitnesstrainerin; **fitness training** Fitnesstraining
flat [flæt] Wohnung
flower ['flaʊə] Blume
flower-bed ['flaʊəbed] Blumenbeet
flu [fluː] Grippe
Folk [fəʊk] Folk(musik)
follow ['fɒləʊ] folgen, verfolgen; befolgen
fond of ['fɒndəv]: **I'm fond of dancing.** Ich mag es zu tanzen. Ich tanze gern.
food [fuːd] Essen; Lebensmittel; Futter
foot, feet [fʊt, fiːt] Fuß, Füße; **on foot** zu Fuß
football ['fʊtbɔːl] Fußball
for [fɔː, fə] für; **for breakfast / for lunch** zum Frühstück / zum Mittagessen; **for example** zum Beispiel; **ask for** bitten um; **shout for help** um Hilfe rufen; **I'm late / in time for school.** Ich komme zu spät / rechtzeitig zur Schule. **What ... for?** Wofür ...?
foreign ['fɒrən]: **in a foreign country** im Ausland, in einem anderen Land
forester ['fɒrɪstə] Förster/Försterin
forget [fə'get] vergessen
forgot [fə'gɒt]: **I forgot** ich vergaß / ich habe vergessen
forgotten [fə'gɒtn]: **I've forgotten** ich habe vergessen
form [fɔːm] Formular; **application form** Bewerbungsformular
formal ['fɔːməl] offiziell, formell
forward ['fɔːwəd] vorwärts; **look forward to** sich freuen auf

found [faʊnd]: **I found** ich fand / ich habe gefunden; **I've found** ich habe gefunden
fountain ['faʊntɪn] Springbrunnen
free [friː] frei; kostenlos; **free time** Freizeit
French [frentʃ] französisch; Französisch; Franzose/Französin; **French fries** Pommes frites
fresh [freʃ] frisch
Friday ['fraɪdeɪ, 'fraɪdi] Freitag
friend [frend] Freund/Freundin; **make friends** Freundschaft(en) schließen; **That's what friends are for.** Dazu sind Freunde da.
friendly ['frendli] freundlich
fries [fraɪz]: **French fries** Pommes frites
frightened ['fraɪtnd]: **I'm frightened** ich erschrecke, ich habe Angst
frightening ['fraɪtnɪŋ] beängstigend
from [frɒm, frəm] von; aus; **from 8 till 10** von 8 (Uhr) bis 10 (Uhr)
front [frʌnt]: **in front of** vor; **front of the train** vorn im Zug; Zugspitze
frozen ['frəʊzn] (zu)gefroren
fruit [fruːt] Obst, Früchte
full (of) [fʊl] voll (von, mit); vollständig
fun [fʌn] Spaß; **... is/are fun.** ... macht/machen Spaß. **She's great fun.** Es macht großen Spaß, mit ihr zusammen zu sein. **fun park** Vergnügungspark, Freizeitpark
funny ['fʌni] lustig, komisch
future ['fjuːtʃə] Zukunft

G

game [geɪm] Spiel
garage ['gærɑːʒ] 1. Garage; 2. (Reparatur-)Werkstatt
garden ['gɑːdn] Garten
gardening ['gɑːdnɪŋ] Gartenarbeit
gate [geɪt] Tor; Sperre, Schranke
gave [geɪv]: **I gave** ich gab / ich habe gegeben (usw.)
geography [dʒi'ɒgrəfi] Erdkunde, Geographie
German ['dʒɜːmən] deutsch; Deutsch; Deutsche/Deutscher

Germany ['dʒɜːməni] Deutschland
get [get] 1. bekommen; 2. besorgen, holen; 3. werden; 4. kommen, gelangen; **get to** kommen zu; **get off the train/bus/...** aus dem Zug/Bus/... aussteigen; **get on** aufsteigen, einsteigen; **get out of the car/taxi** aus dem Auto/Taxi aussteigen; **get rid of** wegwerfen, loswerden; **get up** aufstehen; **get used to** sich gewöhnen an; **he gets on their nerves** er geht ihnen auf die Nerven
ghost [gəʊst] Gespenst, Geist; **ghost train** ['gəʊstreɪn] Geisterbahn
girl [gɜːl] Mädchen
girlfriend ['gɜːlfrend] (feste) Freundin
give [gɪv] geben; schenken; spenden
given ['gɪvn]: **I've given** ich habe gegeben (usw.)
glass [glɑːs] Glas, Trinkglas
go [gəʊ] gehen, fahren; **go out (together)** ausgehen, weggehen; miteinander gehen; **go for a walk** spazieren gehen; **go home** nach Hause gehen; **go pot-holing** auf Höhlenforschungstour gehen; **go to bed** ins Bett gehen; **go to Dave's house** zu Dave (nach Hause) gehen; **go to school** zur Schule gehen; **go to the shops** einkaufen gehen; **go to town** in die Stadt gehen; **go to work** arbeiten gehen; **go window-shopping** einen Schaufensterbummel machen
going to ['gəʊɪŋtu, 'gəʊɪŋtə]: **I'm going to win** ich werde gewinnen / ich gewinne
gold [gəʊld] Gold
gone [gɒn]: **I've gone** ich bin gegangen, gefahren
good [gʊd] gut; **good at** gut in, geschickt in; **Good afternoon.** Guten Tag. (nachmittags); **Good evening.** Guten Abend. **Good morning.** Guten Morgen. **Good night.** Gute Nacht. **Goodbye.** [gʊd'baɪ] Auf Wiedersehen.

got [gɒt]: **I got** ich bekam / ich habe bekommen (usw.); **I've got** ich habe bekommen (usw.)
government ['gʌvənmənt] Regierung
gram [græm] Gramm
grandfather ['grænfɑːðə] Großvater
grandma ['grænmɑː] Oma, Großmutter
grandmother ['grænmʌðə] Großmutter
grandparents ['grænpeərənts] Großeltern
grass [grɑːs] Gras; Rasen
great [greɪt] toll, großartig
Greek [griːk] griechisch; Griechisch; Grieche/Griechin
green [griːn] grün
greetings ['griːtɪŋz] Grüße
grew [gruː]: **I grew** ich pflanzte an / ich habe angepflanzt (usw.)
grey [greɪ] grau
group [gruːp] Gruppe
grow [grəʊ] anpflanzen, heranziehen
grown [grəʊn]: **I've grown** ich habe angepflanzt (usw.)
grumpy ['grʌmpi] schlecht gelaunt, mürrisch
guest-house ['gesthaʊs] Pension
guide [gaɪd] Führer, Plan; **guide dog** Blindenhund
guitar [gɪ'tɑː] Gitarre; **play the guitar** Gitarre spielen

H

had [hæd]: **I had** ich hatte / ich habe gehabt; **I've had** ich habe gehabt
hair [heə] Haar, Haare
hair-drier ['heədraɪə] Föhn
hairdresser ['heədresə] Friseur/Friseurin
hairstyle ['heəstaɪl] Frisur
half [hɑːf]: **half past two** halb drei
hall [hɔːl] Halle, Saal; **church hall** Gemeindesaal der Kirche; **sports hall** Sporthalle; **town hall** Rathaus
Hallo. [hə'ləʊ] Hallo. Guten Tag.
hamburger ['hæmbɜːgə] Hamburger
hamster ['hæmstə] Hamster
hand [hænd] Hand
handball ['hændbɔːl] Handball
happen ['hæpən] passieren, geschehen

happy ['hæpi] glücklich, froh; zufrieden; **Happy birthday (to you)!** Herzlichen Glückwunsch zum Geburtstag!
hard [hɑːd] hart; schwer
hat [hæt] Hut
hate [heɪt] hassen; **hate to wait** sehr ungern warten; **hate working** sehr ungern arbeiten
have [hæv] haben; **have a wash** sich waschen; **have breakfast** frühstücken; **have lunch** zu Mittag essen; **have sandwiches / have a cola** Sandwiches essen / eine Cola trinken
have to ['hævtu, 'hævtə] müssen
Hawaii [hə'waɪi] Hawaii
he [hiː] er
headache ['hedeɪk] Kopfschmerzen
hear [hɪə] hören
heard [hɜːd]: **I heard** ich hörte / ich habe gehört; **I've heard** ich habe gehört
hearing dog „hörender Hund" (Hund für Gehörlose)
heart [hɑːt] Herz
heavy ['hevi] schwer
held [held]: **I held** ich hielt / ich habe gehalten; **I've held** ich habe gehalten
help [help] 1. helfen; 2. Hilfe; **He helps himself to coffee.** Er nimmt sich (selbst) Kaffee.
helper ['helpə] Helfer/Helferin
helpful ['helpfl] hilfreich
her [hɜː] 1. ihr/ihre; 2. ihr/sie
here [hɪə] hier; hierhin/hierher; **Here you are.** Hier, bitte.
hers [hɜːz] ihre/ihrer/ihres
herself [hɜː'self] sich (selbst)
Hi. [haɪ] Hallo.
high [haɪ] hoch
hiking ['haɪkɪŋ] Wandern
hill [hɪl] Hügel, (kleiner) Berg
him [hɪm] ihm/ihn
himself [hɪm'self] sich (selbst)
his [hɪz] 1. sein/seine; 2. seine/seiner/seines
history ['hɪstri] Geschichte
hit [hɪt] schlagen; **I hit** ich schlug / ich habe geschlagen; **I've hit** ich habe geschlagen
hobby ['hɒbi] Hobby
hockey ['hɒki] Hockey
hold [həʊld] halten

holiday ['hɒlədeɪ] Feiertag; Ferien, Urlaub; **on holiday** in/im Urlaub
Holland ['hɒlənd] Holland
home [həʊm] 1. Heim, Zuhause; 2. nach Hause, heim; **at home** zu Hause, daheim
homeless ['həʊmləs] heimatlos; obdachlos
homework ['həʊmwɜːk] Hausaufgaben, Schularbeiten
hope [həʊp] hoffen
hospital ['hɒspɪtl] Krankenhaus
hostel ['hɒstl] Wohnheim; Obdachlosenheim
hot [hɒt] heiß; warm
hotel [həʊ'tel] Hotel
hour ['aʊə] Stunde; **(working) hours** Arbeitszeit
house [haʊs] Haus; **Come to my house.** Komm zu mir (nach Hause).
housework ['haʊswɜːk] Hausarbeit
how [haʊ] wie; **How are you?** Wie geht es dir? / Wie geht es Ihnen? **How long …?** Wie lange …? Wie lang …? **How many?** Wie viele? **How much?** Wie viel? **How much is/are …?** Was kostet/kosten …? **How old are you?** Wie alt bist du? / Wie alt sind Sie?
humour ['hjuːmə]: **(a) sense of humour** (Sinn für) Humor
hungry ['hʌŋgri] hungrig; **I'm hungry.** Ich habe Hunger.
hurry ['hʌri] sich beeilen; schnell gehen
hurt [hɜːt] verletzen; **I hurt** ich verletzte / ich habe verletzt; **I've hurt** ich habe verletzt
husband ['hʌzbənd] Ehemann

I

I [aɪ] ich; **I'm OK.** Mir gehts gut. **I'd** [aɪd] (= I would): **I'd like …** Ich möchte … / Ich hätte gern …; **I'd like to go.** Ich möchte gehen.
ice [aɪs] Eis (gefrorenes Wasser)
ice-cream [aɪs'kriːm] (Speise-)Eis
ice-skating ['aɪsskeɪtɪŋ] Schlittschuhlaufen
idea [aɪ'dɪə] Idee, Einfall; Meinung, Einstellung

if [ɪf] 1. wenn, falls; 2. ob
ill [ɪl] krank
illegal [ɪ'liːgl] ungesetzlich, illegal
important [ɪm'pɔːtnt] wichtig
in [ɪn] in; **in a butcher's** in einer Fleischerei; **in 1850** (im Jahre) 1850; **in English** auf Englisch; **in front of** vor; **in my photo** auf meinem Foto; **in October** im Oktober; **in the country** auf dem Land; **in the end** schließlich; **in the morning(s)/afternoon(s)/ evening(s)** morgens/nachmittags/abends; am Morgen/Nachmittag/Abend; **in the world** auf der (ganzen) Welt; **in time** rechtzeitig; **in town** in der (Innen-)Stadt
including [ɪn'kluːdɪŋ] einschließlich
increase [ɪn'kriːs] ansteigen, zunehmen
independent [ɪndɪ'pendənt] unabhängig
indoor ['ɪndɔː]: Innen-, Hallen-; **indoor football** Hallenfußball; **indoor tennis** Tennis in der Halle
industry ['ɪndəstri] Industrie
information [ɪnfə'meɪʃn] Informationen, Auskunft
inherit [ɪn'herɪt] erben
inline-skates ['ɪnlaɪnskeɪts] Inline Skates; **inline-skating** Inline-Skating
inner city ['ɪnə'sɪti] Innenstadt
inside ['ɪnsaɪd] innerhalb (von); (nach) drinnen
instant ['ɪnstənt]: **instant communication** unverzügliche Verständigung
instead [ɪn'sted] stattdessen
instructor [ɪn'strʌktə] Lehrer/Lehrerin, Betreuer/Betreuerin
instrument ['ɪnstrəmənt] Instrument
interest ['ɪntrəst] Interesse
interested ['ɪntrəstɪd] interessiert; **interested in** interessiert an
interesting ['ɪntrəstɪŋ] interessant
interrupt [ɪntə'rʌpt] unterbrechen
interview ['ɪntəvjuː] 1. Interview; 2. interviewen, befragen
into ['ɪntu, 'ɪntə] in (… hinein/herein)
invention [ɪn'venʃn] Erfindung
Ireland ['aɪələnd] Irland
Irish ['aɪrɪʃ] irisch; Irisch; Ire/Irin
is [ɪz]: **he/she/it is** er/sie/es ist

isolated ['aɪsəleɪtɪd] abgelegen, (von der Umwelt) abgeschnitten
it [ɪt] es (er/sie; *nicht bei Personen*)
its [ɪts] sein/seine; ihr/ihre

J

Jamaica [dʒə'meɪkə] Jamaika
January ['dʒænjuəri] Januar
Japanese [dʒæpə'niːz] japanisch; Japanisch; Japaner/Japanerin
jazz [dʒæz] Jazz(musik)
jeans [dʒiːnz] Jeans
jelly ['dʒeli] „Wackelpudding", Grütze
job [dʒɒb] Arbeit, Beruf; Arbeitsstelle; Aufgabe; **nine-to-five job** geregelter Achtstundentag
jogger ['dʒɒgə] Jogger/Joggerin
join [dʒɔɪn] beitreten, Mitglied werden; **joining a club** einem Club beitreten
joiner ['dʒɔɪnə] Tischler/Tischlerin, Schreiner/Schreinerin
joke [dʒəʊk] Witz, Scherz; **practical joke** Streich
joking ['dʒəʊkɪŋ]: **You must be joking!** Du machst wohl Witze!
journey ['dʒɜːni] Fahrt, Weg, Reise
joyrider ['dʒɔɪraɪdə] Person, die ein Auto für eine (Vergnügungs-)Fahrt stiehlt
joyriding ['dʒɔɪraɪdɪŋ] (Vergnügungs-)Fahrt in einem gestohlenen Auto
judo ['dʒuːdəʊ] Judo
juggle ['dʒʌgl] jonglieren
juice [dʒuːs] Saft
July [dʒu'laɪ] Juli
jump [dʒʌmp] springen; **jump at** anspringen
June [dʒuːn] Juni
just [dʒʌst] 1. gerade, soeben; 2. einfach

K

keep [kiːp] halten, behalten
kept [kept]: **I kept** ich (be)hielt / ich habe behalten, gehalten
ketchup ['ketʃəp] Ketchup
key [kiː] Schlüssel; **key phrase** Hauptaussage

kilometre ['kɪləmiːtə] Kilometer
kilt [kɪlt] Kilt *(Schottenrock)*
kind [kaɪnd] liebevoll, freundlich
king [kɪŋ] König
kiss [kɪs] 1. Kuss; 2. küssen
kitchen ['kɪtʃɪn] Küche
knee [niː] Knie
knew [njuː]: **I knew** ich wusste, kannte / ich habe gewusst, gekannt
know [nəʊ] wissen; kennen

L

lake [leɪk] (Binnen-)See
land [lænd] Land, Boden
language ['læŋgwɪdʒ] Sprache
large [lɑːdʒ] groß
lasagne [lə'zænjə] Lasagne
last [lɑːst] letzte/letzter/letztes
late [leɪt] spät; zu spät, verspätet; **I'm late.** Ich bin spät dran; Ich habe mich verspätet. **I'm late for school.** Ich komme zu spät zur Schule.
laugh [lɑːf] lachen; **laugh at** lachen über
law [lɔː] Gesetz
lay [leɪ]: **I lay** ich lag / ich habe gelegen
layout ['leɪaʊt] Layout *(Gestaltungsskizze)*
leader ['liːdə] Leiter/Leiterin
leaf, leaves [liːf, liːvz] Blatt, Blätter
learn [lɜːn] lernen
leave [liːv] (liegen/stehen) lassen; verlassen, weggehen von, abfahren; **leave behind** zurücklassen, hinter sich lassen
left [left]: **I left** ich ließ / ich habe gelassen (usw.); **I've left** ich habe gelassen (usw.)
left [left] linke/linker/linkes; (nach) links; **on the left** links, auf der linken Seite
leg [leg] Bein
legal ['liːgl] gesetzlich, legal
lemonade [lemə'neɪd] Limonade
lend [lend] leihen, verleihen
less [les] weniger
lesson ['lesn] (Unterrichts-)Stunde
let [let]: **Let's go!** Lass/Lasst uns gehen. / Gehen wir!
letter ['letə] 1. Brief; 2. Buchstabe
library ['laɪbrəri] Bücherei

lie [laɪ] liegen
life, lives [laɪf, laɪvz] Leben
lifestyle ['laɪfstaɪl] Lebensstil
light [laɪt] Licht, Lampe; **light show** Lichtershow
like [laɪk] 1. mögen, gern haben; **like to swim** gern schwimmen; **like playing** gern spielen; **I'd like …** Ich möchte … / Ich hätte gern …; **I'd like to go.** Ich möchte gehen. **Would you like …?** Möchtest du / Möchten Sie …?
like [laɪk] (ähnlich) wie; **like this** so, auf diese Weise; **What's it like?** Wie ist es?
line [laɪn] 1. Linie; 2. Zeile
list [lɪst] Liste
listen ['lɪsn] zuhören; **listen to** hören, sich anhören
little ['lɪtl]: **a little** ein wenig
live [lɪv] wohnen, leben
live music [laɪv'mju:zɪk] Livemusik
living-room ['lɪvɪŋru:m] Wohnzimmer
local ['ləʊkl]: **local council** Gemeindeverwaltung; **local newspaper** Lokalzeitung
lonely ['ləʊnli] einsam
long [lɒŋ] lang; **How long …?** Wie lang …? Wie lange …?
look [lʊk] 1. schauen, sehen; 2. aussehen; **look after** sich kümmern um, aufpassen auf; **look at** (sich) ansehen; **look for** suchen; **look forward to** sich freuen auf; **look the same** gleich aussehen
lorry ['lɒri] Lastwagen
lose [lu:z] verlieren
lost [lɒst]: **I'm lost** ich habe mich verlaufen, verirrt; **I lost** ich verlor / ich habe verloren; **I've lost** ich habe verloren
lot [lɒt]: **a lot (of) / lots (of)** viele; viel
loud [laʊd] laut
love [lʌv] lieben, sehr mögen; **love to sing** sehr gern singen; **love skiing** sehr gern Ski fahren
luck [lʌk] Glück
lucky ['lʌki]: **you're lucky** du hast Glück / ihr habt Glück
lunch [lʌntʃ] Mittagessen; **for lunch** zum Mittagessen; **have lunch** zu Mittag essen; **lunch break** Mittagspause
luxury ['lʌkʃəri] Luxus

M

machine [mə'ʃi:n] Maschine, Gerät
Madam ['mædəm]: **Dear Sir or Madam, …** Sehr geehrte Damen und Herren, …
made [meɪd]: **I made** ich machte / ich habe gemacht; **I've made** ich habe gemacht; **made of plastic** aus Plastik
magazine [mægə'zi:n] Zeitschrift
mailbox ['meɪlbɒks] „Mailbox" (eine Art Computerbriefkasten)
make [meɪk] machen, herstellen; **make a date** sich verabreden; **make friends** Freundschaft(en) schließen
man, men [mæn, men] Mann, Männer
manager ['mænɪdʒə] Manager/Managerin
many ['meni] viele; **How many?** Wie viele?
map [mæp] Stadtplan, Landkarte
March [mɑ:tʃ] März
market ['mɑ:kɪt] Markt
match [mætʃ] Spiel, Wettkampf
mate [meɪt]: **school mate** Schulfreund/Schulfreundin
maths [mæθs] Mathe(matik)
matter ['mætə]: **What's the matter?** Was ist los?
May [meɪ] Mai
mayonnaise [meɪə'neɪz] Majonäse
me [mi:] mir/mich
meal [mi:l] Mahlzeit, Speise, (zubereitetes) Essen; **Meals on Wheels** Essen auf Rädern
mean [mi:n] bedeuten; meinen
meant [ment]: **I meant** ich meinte / ich habe gemeint; **I've meant** ich habe gemeint
meat [mi:t] Fleisch
mechanic [mə'kænɪk] Mechaniker/Mechanikerin
medal ['medl] Medaille
medium ['mi:dɪəm] mittel(groß)
meet [mi:t] (sich) treffen (mit); kennen lernen; **meeting place** Treffpunkt
megaphone ['megəfəʊn] Megaphon
member ['membə] Mitglied
membership ['membəʃɪp] Mitgliedschaft
menu ['menju:] Speisekarte

message ['mesɪdʒ] Mitteilung
messy ['mesi] schmutzig, dreckig; unordentlich
met [met]: **I met** ich traf / ich habe getroffen (usw.); **I've met** ich habe getroffen (usw.)
metal ['metl] Metall
metre ['mi:tə] Meter
Mexican ['meksɪkən] mexikanisch; Mexikaner/Mexikanerin
microwave ['maɪkrəweɪv] Mikrowelle
milk [mɪlk] Milch
million ['mɪljən] Million
mind [maɪnd]: **I've changed my mind** ich habe meine Meinung geändert
mine [maɪn] meine/meiner/meines
minibus ['mɪnɪbʌs] Kleinbus
minute ['mɪnɪt] Minute
mirror ['mɪrə] Spiegel
miss [mɪs] vermissen; versäumen, verpassen; **missing** fehlend
mistake [mɪ'steɪk] Fehler
mobile ['məʊbaɪl]: **mobile job** Arbeit, bei der man viel unterwegs ist; **mobile phone** Mobiltelefon, Handy
model ['mɒdl] Modell; Nachbildung
modem ['məʊdem] Modem
modern ['mɒdən] modern
moment ['məʊmənt]: **at the moment** zurzeit, im Augenblick
Monday ['mʌndeɪ, 'mʌndi] Montag; **on Monday** am Montag; montags
money ['mʌni] Geld
monster ['mɒnstə] Monster
month [mʌnθ] Monat
monument ['mɒnjumənt] Denkmal
more [mɔ:] mehr, weitere; **one more** noch ein/eine; **more expensive** teurer
morning ['mɔ:nɪŋ] Morgen, Vormittag; **Good morning.** Guten Morgen. **in the morning(s)** morgens, vormittags; am Morgen; **Sunday morning** Sonntagmorgen; **this morning** heute Morgen
mosque [mɒsk] Moschee
most [məʊst] der/die/das meiste, die meisten; **most dangerous** gefährlichste/gefährlichster/gefährlichstes, am gefährlichsten
mother ['mʌðə] Mutter
motorway ['məʊtəweɪ] Autobahn

mountain ['maontən] Berg; **mountain bike** Mountainbike; **mountain biking** Mountainbikefahren; **mountain climbing** Bergsteigen
mouse, mice [maos, mais] Maus, Mäuse
move [muːv] 1. Umzug; 2. (sich) bewegen; **move (to)** (um)ziehen (nach)
Mr ['mistə] Herr *(vor Namen)*
Mrs ['misiz] Frau *(vor Namen bei verheirateten Frauen)*
Ms [məz] Frau *(vor Namen bei unverheirateten oder verheirateten Frauen)*
much [mʌtʃ] viel; **(like) very much** sehr (gern mögen); **How much?** Wie viel? **How much is/are …?** Was kostet/kosten …?
multiscreen cinema ['mʌltɪskriːn] Multiplex-Kino, Kinocenter
mum [mʌm] Mama, Mutti
museum [mju'ziːəm] Museum
music ['mjuːzɪk] Musik; **music charts** Musikhitparade
musical ['mjuːzɪkl] musikalisch; **musical instrument** Musikinstrument
musician [mjuː'zɪʃən] Musiker/Musikerin
must [mʌst] müssen; **mustn't** ['mʌsnt] nicht dürfen
my [mai] mein/meine
myself [mai'self] mir/mich (selbst)

N

name [neɪm] Name; **first name** Vorname
national ['næʃnəl] national, National-; **National Park** Nationalpark
nationality [næʃə'næləti] Staatsangehörigkeit, Nationalität
near [nɪə] in der Nähe (von); nah; **nearest** ['nɪərɪst] nächste/nächster/nächstes
need [niːd] brauchen; **needn't** nicht brauchen, nicht müssen
neighbour ['neɪbə] Nachbar/Nachbarin
nerves [nɜːvz]: **they get on his nerves** sie gehen ihm auf die Nerven
nervous ['nɜːvəs] nervös
never ['nevə] nie, niemals
new [njuː] neu
news [njuːz] Nachricht(en), Neuigkeit(en)
newspaper ['njuːspeɪpə] Zeitung
next [nekst] nächste/nächster/nächstes
next to ['nekstu, 'nekstə] neben
nice [nais] nett; schön
night [naɪt] Nacht, (später) Abend; **at night** nachts, in der Nacht; **Good night.** Gute Nacht.
nine-to-five job geregelter Achtstundentag
no [nəʊ] 1. nein; 2. kein/keine
nobody ['nəʊbədi] niemand
noise [nɔɪz] Lärm; Geräusch
north [nɔːθ] Nord-; (nach) Norden; nördlich
North Sea [nɔːθ'siː] Nordsee
Northern Ireland ['nɔːðən'aɪələnd] Nordirland
Northern Irish ['nɔːðən'aɪrɪʃ] nordirisch; Nordire/Nordirin
nose [nəʊz] Nase
not [nɒt] nicht; **not … yet** noch nicht
note [nəʊt] Notiz, Briefchen
nothing ['nʌθɪŋ] nichts
November [nəʊ'vembə] November
now [naʊ] nun, jetzt
number ['nʌmbə] Nummer; Zahl; Ziffer
nurse [nɜːs] Krankenpfleger/Krankenschwester

O

o'clock [ə'klɒk]: **at 6 o'clock** um 6 Uhr / 18 Uhr
October [ɒk'təʊbə] Oktober
of [ɒv, əv] von; **a cup of tea** eine Tasse Tee; **of course** [əv'kɔːs] natürlich, selbstverständlich
off [ɒf]: **get off the train/bus/…** aus dem Zug/Bus/… aussteigen; **show off** angeben
offer ['ɒfə] anbieten
office ['ɒfɪs] Büro; **office clerk** Büroangestellte/Büroangestellter, kaufmännische/r Angestellte/r; **office worker** Büroangestellte/Büroangestellter
officer ['ɒfɪsə]: **environment officer** Umweltbeauftragte/Umweltbeauftragter; **(police) officer** (Polizei-)Beamter/Beamtin, Polizist/Polizistin
often ['ɒfn] oft
oil [ɔɪl] Öl
OK [əʊ'keɪ] okay, (schon) gut, in Ordnung; **I'm OK.** Mir gehts gut.
old [əʊld] alt; **old people's home** Altersheim
Olympic Games [ə'lɪmpɪk'geɪmz] Olympische Spiele
on [ɒn] 1. auf; 2. an, eingeschaltet; **on March 20th** am 20. März; **on Monday** am Montag; montags; **on Tuesdays** dienstags; **on foot** zu Fuß; **on holiday** in/im Urlaub; **on TV / on the radio** im Fernsehen / im Radio; **on the bus/train/plane** im Bus/Zug/Flugzeug; **on the left/right** links/rechts, auf der linken/rechten Seite; **on the phone** am Telefon; **on the stall** am Stand
one [wʌn]: **the black one** der/die/das schwarze; **one day** eines Tages; **one in three** jede/jeder/jedes dritte
only ['əʊnli] nur, bloß; erst
onto ['ɒntʊ, 'ɒntə] auf (… hinauf/herauf)
open ['əʊpən] 1. offen, geöffnet; 2. (sich) öffnen, aufmachen; **open day** Tag der offenen Tür; **opening times** Öffnungszeiten
opinion [ə'pɪnjən] Meinung; **in your opinion** deiner Meinung nach
opposite ['ɒpəzɪt] 1. gegenüber (von); 2. Gegenteil
or [ɔː] oder
orange ['ɒrɪndʒ] Orange, Apfelsine
order ['ɔːdə] Reihenfolge
organic [ɔː'gænɪk] biodynamisch *(nur mit natürlichen Düngemitteln angebaut)*
organise ['ɔːgənaɪz] organisieren, veranstalten
orienteering course [ɔːrɪən'tɪərɪŋkɔːs] Orientierungslauf
other ['ʌðə] andere, weitere
our ['aʊə] unser/unsere
ours ['aʊəz] unsere/unserer/unseres
ourselves [aʊə'selvz] uns (selbst)
out [aʊt] hinaus/heraus, aus; **out of** aus (… heraus/hinaus); **day out** Ausflug; **eat out** zum Essen ausgehen

out of work [aʊtəv'wɜːk] arbeitslos
outdoor ['aʊtdɔː]: **outdoor centre** Erlebnisurlaub *(für Jugendliche)*, Ferienlager; **outdoor sports** Sport im Freien; **outdoor swimming-pool** Freibad
outside [aʊt'saɪd] außerhalb (von); (nach) draußen
over ['əʊvə] 1. vorbei, zu Ende; 2. über; **over there** da drüben, dort drüben
own [əʊn] 1. besitzen; 2. eigene/eigener/eigenes
owner ['əʊnə] Besitzer/Besitzerin

P

paddle ['pædl] Paddel
page [peɪdʒ] Seite
Pakistan [pɑːkɪ'stɑːn] Pakistan
paper ['peɪpə] Papier; **paper bank** Altpapiercontainer
parent, parents ['peərənt, 'peərənts] Elternteil, Eltern
park [pɑːk] 1. parken; 2. Park; **car park** (großer) Parkplatz
part [pɑːt] Teil
part-time job ['pɑːttaɪm'dʒɒb] Teilzeitarbeitsstelle
partner ['pɑːtnə] Partner/Partnerin
party ['pɑːti] 1. Party, Fest, Feier; 2. Partei
passenger ['pæsɪndʒə] Fahrgast, Passagier/Passagierin
passive form ['pæsɪvfɔːm] Passivform
past [pɑːst] nach; **half past two** halb drei; **quarter past** Viertel nach
past [pɑːst]: **past the house** am Haus vorbei
path [pɑːθ] Weg, Pfad
pay [peɪ] zahlen, bezahlen; **The job pays well.** Die Arbeit wird gut bezahlt.
PE ['piː'iː] (= Physical Education ['fɪzɪkledʒu'keɪʃn]) Turnen, Turnunterricht
pea [piː] Erbse
pen [pen] Füller
pence (p) [pens, piː] Pence *(brit. Geld)*
pencil ['pensl] Bleistift

pencil-case ['penslkeɪs] Federmäppchen, Schreibetui
people ['piːpl] Leute, Menschen
per [pɜː] pro
per cent [pə'sent] Prozent
perfect ['pɜːfɪkt] vollkommen, perfekt
perhaps [pə'hæps] vielleicht
person ['pɜːsn] Person, Mensch
pet [pet] zahmes Tier, Haustier; **pet shop** Kleintierhandlung, Zoohandlung
phone [fəʊn] 1. anrufen, telefonieren; 2. Telefon; **on the phone** am Telefon; **phone card** Telefonkarte
photo ['fəʊtəʊ] Foto; **in my photo** auf meinem Foto; **take photos** Fotos machen, fotografieren
photography [fə'tɒgrəfi] Fotografie
phrase [freɪz] Redewendung, Ausdruck; **key phrase** Hauptaussage
physics ['fɪzɪks] Physik
pick [pɪk] wählen, aussuchen
picture ['pɪktʃə] Bild, Foto
pig [pɪg] Schwein
pink [pɪŋk] rosa, pink
pipe [paɪp] Rohr
pity ['pɪti]: **That's a pity.** Das ist schade.
pizza ['piːtsə] Pizza
place [pleɪs] Ort, Platz, Stelle; **place of birth** Geburtsort
plan [plæn] 1. planen, vorhaben; 2. Plan
plane [pleɪn] Flugzeug
plant [plɑːnt] 1. (an)pflanzen; 2. Pflanze
plastic ['plæstɪk] Plastik
plate [pleɪt] Teller
platform ['plætfɔːm] Bahnsteig, Gleis
play [pleɪ] spielen; **play the guitar** Gitarre spielen
please [pliːz] bitte
plumber ['plʌmə] Installateur/Installateurin, Klempner/Klempnerin
plural ['plʊərəl] Plural, Mehrzahl
pm ['piː'em] nachmittags, abends
pocket-money ['pɒkɪt'mʌni] Taschengeld
police [pə'liːs] Polizei; **police drama** Krimi; **(police) officer** (Polizei-)Beamter/Beamtin, Polizist/Polizistin; **police station** Polizeiwache
polite [pə'laɪt] höflich

pollution [pə'luːʃn] (Umwelt-)Verschmutzung
pony-trekking ['pəʊnitrekɪŋ] Ponyreiten *(übers Land)*
pop [pɒp] Pop(musik)
popular ['pɒpjələ] beliebt
port [pɔːt] Hafen, Hafenstadt
possible ['pɒsəbl] möglich
post [pəʊst] Post; **post office** Post(amt)
postcard ['pəʊstkɑːd] Postkarte, Ansichtskarte
postcode ['pəʊstkəʊd] Postleitzahl
poster ['pəʊstə] Poster
postman ['pəʊstmən] Briefträger, Postbote
potholing ['pɒthəʊlɪŋ] Höhlenforschung; **go potholing** auf Höhlenforschungstour gehen
potato, potatoes [pə'teɪtəʊ, pə'teɪtəʊz] Kartoffel, Kartoffeln
pound (£) [paʊnd] Pfund *(brit. Geld)*
practical ['præktɪkl]: **practical joke** Streich
practise ['præktɪs] üben, trainieren
prefer [prɪ'fɜː]: **prefer to watch TV** lieber fernsehen
present ['preznt] Geschenk
price [praɪs] (Kauf-)Preis
print [prɪnt] drucken
prison ['prɪzn] Gefängnis
prize [praɪz] Preis, Gewinn
problem ['prɒbləm] Problem
product ['prɒdʌkt] Produkt, Erzeugnis
programme ['prəʊgræm] (Radio-, Fernseh-)Sendung
project ['prɒdʒekt] Projekt, Projektarbeit
promise ['prɒmɪs] Versprechen
protest [prə'test] protestieren
Protestant ['prɒtɪstənt] Protestant/Protestantin
proud [praʊd] stolz; **proud to be Scottish** stolz, Schotte/Schottin zu sein
PS ['piː'es] PS *(Nachtrag zu einem Brief)*
pub [pʌb] Kneipe, Lokal
public ['pʌblɪk] öffentlich
pudding ['pʊdɪŋ] Nachtisch
pull [pʊl] ziehen; **pull down** abreißen, niederreißen
pullover ['pʊləʊvə] Pullover
punctual ['pʌŋktʃʊəl] pünktlich

punish ['pʌnɪʃ] bestrafen
pupil ['pju:pl] Schüler/Schülerin
puppet ['pʌpɪt] (Hand-)Puppe, Kasperlepuppe; **puppet show** Puppentheater
push [pʊʃ] schieben; stoßen
put [pʊt] stellen; legen; *(an einen Platz)* tun; **I put** ich stellte / ich habe gestellt (usw.); **I've put** ich habe gestellt (usw.); **put in** einfügen, hinzufügen; **put on** aufführen *(Theaterstück, Show);* **Put your hands up.** Hebt eure / Hebe deine Hände hoch.

Q

quality ['kwɒlɪti] Eigenschaft
quarter ['kwɔ:tə] Viertel; **quarter past** Viertel nach; **quarter to** Viertel vor
question ['kwestʃən] Frage; **ask a question** eine Frage stellen
queue [kju:] (Warte-)Schlange
quick [kwɪk] schnell
quiet ['kwaɪət] still, ruhig, leise
quiz [kwɪz] Quiz

R

rabbit ['ræbɪt] Kaninchen
race [reɪs] Rennen, (Wett-)Lauf
radio ['reɪdiəʊ] Radio
railway ['reɪlweɪ] Eisenbahn
rain [reɪn] regnen
rainy ['reɪni] regnerisch
ran [ræn]: **I ran** ich rannte / ich bin gerannt
rang [ræŋ]: **I rang** ich klingelte / ich habe geklingelt (usw.)
rap [ræp] Rap(musik)
RE ['ɑ:'ri:] **(Religious Education** [rɪ'lɪdʒəsedʒu'keɪʃn]**)** Religionsunterricht
read [ri:d] lesen, vorlesen
read [red]: **I read** ich las / ich habe gelesen
reader ['ri:də] Leser/Leserin
really ['ri:əli] wirklich, eigentlich
receive [rɪ'si:v] erhalten, bekommen
recognize ['rekəgnaɪz] erkennen

record [rɪ'kɔ:d] aufnehmen, aufzeichnen
recycle [ri:'saɪkl] recyceln, wieder verwerten; **recycling container** Recyclingcontainer, Recyclingbehälter
red [red] rot
Reggae ['regeɪ] Reggae(musik)
regular ['regjələ] regelmäßig
relation [rɪ'leɪʃn] Verwandte/Verwandter
relax [rɪ'læks] „relaxen", entspannen
reliable [rɪ'laɪəbl] zuverlässig
remember [rɪ'membə] sich erinnern (an)
rent [rent] Miete
repair [rɪ'peə] reparieren
report [rɪ'pɔ:t] Bericht
reporter [rɪ'pɔ:tə] Reporter/Reporterin
republic [rɪ'pʌblɪk] Republik
rescue ['reskju:] retten
respect [rɪ'spekt] respektieren
restaurant ['restərɒnt] Restaurant
return [rɪ'tɜ:n] Rückfahrkarte; **day return** ['deɪrɪ'tɜ:n] Tagesrückfahrkarte
rhyme [raɪm] (sich) reimen
rid [rɪd]: **get rid of** wegwerfen, loswerden
ride [raɪd]: **ride a bike** Rad fahren
right [raɪt] 1. richtig. **You're right.** Du hast / Sie haben Recht. 2. rechte/rechter/rechtes; (nach) rechts; **on the right** rechts, auf der rechten Seite
ring [rɪŋ] klingeln, läuten
river ['rɪvə] Fluss
road [rəʊd] Straße
robot ['rəʊbɒt] Roboter
rock [rɒk] Rock(musik)
rock [rɒk] (großer) Stein, Fels
role-card ['rəʊlkɑ:d] Rollenspielkarte
roll [rəʊl] Brötchen
room [ru:m] 1. Zimmer, Raum; 2. Platz
rope [rəʊp] Seil
Rottweiler ['rɒtwaɪlə] Rottweiler *(Hunderasse)*
rough [rʌf]: **sleep rough** im Freien übernachten
rubber ['rʌbə] Radiergummi
rubbish ['rʌbɪʃ] Abfall, Müll
rugby ['rʌgbi] Rugby
rule [ru:l] Regel, Vorschrift

ruler ['ru:lə] Lineal
run [rʌn] rennen, laufen; **I've run** ich bin gerannt
rung [rʌŋ]: **I've rung** ich habe geklingelt (usw.)

S

sad [sæd] traurig
safe [seɪf] sicher, in Sicherheit
said [sed]: **I said** ich sagte / ich habe gesagt
sailing ['seɪlɪŋ] Segeln
salad ['sæləd] Salat
salespeople ['seɪlz'pi:pl]: **travelling salespeople** Handelsreisende, Vertreter/Vertreterinnen
same [seɪm]: **the same** derselbe/dieselbe/dasselbe; der/die/das gleiche; **look the same** gleich aussehen
sandwich ['sænwɪtʃ] Sandwich *(belegtes Brot);* **sandwich bar** „Sandwichladen", Stehcafé
sat [sæt]: **I sat** ich setzte mich / ich habe mich gesetzt
satellite ['sætəlaɪt]: **satellite dish** Satellitenschüssel
Saturday ['sætədeɪ, 'sætədi] Samstag, Sonnabend
sausage ['sɒsɪdʒ] Wurst, Würstchen
save [seɪv] sparen
saw [sɔ:]: **I saw** ich sah / ich habe gesehen (usw.)
say [seɪ] sagen
school [sku:l] Schule; **after school** nach der Schule; **at school** in der Schule; **go to school** zur Schule gehen; **school mate** Schulfreund/Schulfreundin
science ['saɪəns] Naturwissenschaft
scientist ['saɪəntɪst] (Natur-)Wissenschaftler/Wissenschaftlerin
Scotland ['skɒtlənd] Schottland
Scottish ['skɒtɪʃ] schottisch; Schotte/Schottin
scream [skri:m] schreien
seaside ['si:saɪd] Küste
season ['si:zn] Jahreszeit
second-hand shop [sekənd'hændʃɒp] Secondhandshop *(Laden, in dem gebrauchte Sachen verkauft werden)*

secret ['siːkrət] 1. heimlich, geheim; 2. Geheimnis
secretary ['sekrətri] Sekretär/Sekretärin
section ['sekʃən] Abteilung
see [siː] sehen; sich ansehen, besichtigen; **See you.** Bis dann.
seen [siːn]: **I've seen** ich habe gesehen (usw.)
sell [sel] verkaufen
send [send] schicken, senden
sense [sens]: **a sense of humour** (Sinn für) Humor
sent [sent]: **I sent** ich schickte / ich habe geschickt; **I've sent** ich habe geschickt
sentence ['sentəns] Satz
September [sep'tembə] September
serve [sɜːv] servieren, bedienen
service ['sɜːvɪs] Service
session ['seʃn] Treffen; Sitzung
settle ['setl] sich niederlassen; sich einleben
share [ʃeə] teilen
she [ʃiː] sie
sheep [ʃiːp] Schaf, Schafe
shelf, shelves [ʃelf, ʃelvz] Regal, Regale
ship [ʃɪp] Schiff
shirt [ʃɜːt] Hemd
shoe [ʃuː] Schuh
shop [ʃɒp] Laden, Geschäft; **go to the shops** einkaufen gehen; **shop assistant** Verkäufer/Verkäuferin; **shopping** Einkaufen; **do the shopping** Einkäufe machen; **shopping centre** Shoppingcenter, Einkaufszentrum; **shopping street** Einkaufsstraße
short [ʃɔːt] kurz; klein
should [ʃʊd, ʃəd]: **he should** er soll/sollte
shout (at) [ʃaʊt] (an)schreien, laut rufen; **the shouting** das (laute) Rufen
show [ʃəʊ] 1. zeigen, vorzeigen; 2. Schau, Show, Vorführung, Aufführung; **show off** angeben
shown [ʃəʊn]: **I've shown** ich habe gezeigt (usw.)
side [saɪd] Seite; **side of the lake** Seeufer; **side of the road** Straßenrand
sight [saɪt] Sehenswürdigkeit
sign [saɪn] Schild; Zeichen

silly ['sɪli] dumm, albern
sing [sɪŋ] singen
single ['sɪŋgl] einfache Fahrkarte
Sir [sɜː]: **Dear Sir or Madam, …** Sehr geehrte Damen und Herren, …
sister ['sɪstə] Schwester
sit [sɪt] sitzen; sich setzen
ski [skiː] Ski fahren
ski-lift ['skiːlɪft] Skilift
sleep [sliːp] schlafen; **sleep rough** im Freien übernachten
slept [slept]: **I slept** ich schlief / ich habe geschlafen; **I've slept** ich habe geschlafen
slogan ['sləʊgən] Slogan
slope [sləʊp] Abhang, Piste
slow [sləʊ] langsam
small [smɔːl] klein
smile [smaɪl] lächeln
snack [snæk] Imbiss, Snack
snooker ['snuːkə] *(eine Art)* Billard
snow [snəʊ] Schnee
snowboard ['snəʊbɔːd] Snowboard; **snowboarding** Snowboarding
snowy ['snəʊi]: **it's snowy** es schneit viel
so [səʊ] also, daher; so
soap [səʊp] Seifenoper, Unterhaltungsserie
social ['səʊʃl] sozial, Sozial-
sock [sɒk] Socke, Strumpf
soft [sɒft] weich; weichherzig, verweichlicht
sold [səʊld]: **I sold** ich verkaufte / ich habe verkauft; **I've sold** ich habe verkauft
some [sʌm] 1. einige, ein paar; 2. etwas
somebody ['sʌmbədi] jemand
something ['sʌmθɪŋ] etwas
sometimes ['sʌmtaɪmz] manchmal
son [sʌn] Sohn
song [sɒŋ] Lied
soon [suːn] bald
sore throat ['sɔːˈθrəʊt] Halsschmerzen
sorry ['sɒri]: **I'm sorry. / Sorry.** Tut mir Leid.
sort [sɔːt]: **What sort of …?** Was für …? **all sorts of people** alle möglichen Leute
Soul [səʊl] Soul(musik)
south [saʊθ] Süd-; (nach) Süden; südlich

souvenir [suːvə'nɪə] Souvenir, Andenken
spaghetti [spə'geti] Spaghetti
speak [spiːk] sprechen
special ['speʃl] besondere/besonderer/besonderes
spend [spend] *(Zeit)* verbringen
spent [spent]: **I spent** ich verbrachte / ich habe verbracht; **I've spent** ich habe verbracht
spoke [spəʊk]: **I spoke** ich sprach / ich habe gesprochen
spoken ['spəʊkən]: **I've spoken** ich habe gesprochen
sport [spɔːt] Sport, Sportart; **sports centre** Sportzentrum; **sports hall** Sporthalle
spray [spreɪ] (be)sprühen, sprayen
spring [sprɪŋ] Frühling
stadium ['steɪdiəm] Stadion
stall [stɔːl] (Verkaufs-)Stand
stamp [stæmp] Briefmarke
stand [stænd] stehen; **I can't stand soaps.** Ich kann Seifenopern nicht ausstehen.
star [stɑː] Star *(berühmte Persönlichkeit)*
start [stɑːt] 1. anfangen, beginnen (mit); **Start here.** Fang/Fangt hier an. 2. Anfang
station ['steɪʃn] Bahnhof; **police station** Polizeiwache
stay [steɪ] 1. bleiben; 2. übernachten; **stay up** aufbleiben
steal [stiːl] stehlen
steel [stiːl] Stahl
steep [stiːp] steil
stepfather ['stepfɑːðə] Stiefvater
stereo ['steriəʊ] Stereo
still [stɪl] 1. immer noch; 2. trotzdem
stole [stəʊl]: **I stole** ich stahl / ich habe gestohlen
stood [stʊd]: **I stood** ich stand / ich habe gestanden; **I've stood** ich habe gestanden
stop [stɒp] aufhören; anhalten, stoppen
story ['stɔːri] Geschichte, Erzählung
street [striːt] Straße
strict [strɪkt] streng
student ['stjuːdnt] Schüler/Schülerin; Student/Studentin
studio ['stjuːdiəʊ] Studio
style [staɪl]: **style of music** Musikrichtung

subject [ˈsʌbdʒɪkt] (Schul-)Fach
success [səkˈses] Erfolg
suddenly [ˈsʌdnli] plötzlich
sugar [ˈʃʊgə] Zucker
suggestion [səˈdʒestʃən] Vorschlag
summer [ˈsʌmə] Sommer
Sunday [ˈsʌndeɪ, ˈsʌndi] Sonntag
sunny [ˈsʌni] sonnig
super [ˈsuːpə] super, toll
supermarket [ˈsuːpəmɑːkɪt] Supermarkt
support [səˈpɔːt] unterstützen
supporter [səˈpɔːtə] Unterstützer/Unterstützerin
sure [ʃʊə] sicher
surf [sɜːf]: **surf the Internet** „im Internet surfen" *(sich im weltweiten Computerdatennetz umschauen)*
surprise [səˈpraɪz] Überraschung; Überraschungs-
surprised [səˈpraɪzd] überrascht
surprisingly [səˈpraɪzɪŋli] überraschenderweise
survey [ˈsɜːveɪ] Umfrage; Untersuchung
swam [swæm]: **I swam** ich schwamm / ich bin geschwommen
sweatshirt [ˈswetʃɜːt] Sweatshirt
sweet [swiːt] Süßigkeit, Bonbon
swim [swɪm] schwimmen
swimmer [ˈswɪmə] Schwimmer/Schwimmerin
Swimming Club [ˈswɪmɪŋklʌb] Schwimmverein
swimming-pool [ˈswɪmɪŋpuːl] Schwimmbad
swum [swʌm]: **I've swum** ich bin geschwommen

T

T-shirt [ˈtiːʃɜːt] T-Shirt
table [ˈteɪbl] Tisch
table-tennis [ˈteɪbltenɪs] Tischtennis
take [teɪk] 1. nehmen, mitnehmen; bringen; 2. dauern; **take photos** Fotos machen, fotografieren; **take the dog for a walk** mit dem Hund rausgehen, mit dem Hund spazieren gehen
taken [ˈteɪkən]: **I've taken** ich habe (mit)genommen (usw.)

talk [tɔːk] reden, sprechen, sich unterhalten; **talk to** sprechen mit, reden mit; **talk show** Talkshow
tall [tɔːl] lang, groß
taught [tɔːt]: **I taught** ich brachte bei, ich unterrichtete / ich habe beigebracht, ich habe unterrichtet; **I've taught** ich habe beigebracht, ich habe unterrichtet
taxi [ˈtæksi] Taxi
tea [tiː] Tee; **(afternoon) tea** Tee *(Nachmittagsmahlzeit, frühes Abendbrot)*
teach [tiːtʃ] beibringen, unterrichten
teacher [ˈtiːtʃə] Lehrer/Lehrerin
team [tiːm] Team, Mannschaft
technology [tekˈnɒlədʒi] Technik, Technologie; **design and technology** künstlerisches Gestalten und Werken
teenager [ˈtiːneɪdʒə] Teenager
tooth, teeth [tuːθ, tiːθ] Zahn, Zähne
telephone [ˈtelɪfəʊn] Telefon
tell [tel] erzählen; sagen; angeben
tenpin bowling [tenpɪnˈbəʊlɪŋ] Bowling
tennis [ˈtenɪs] Tennis
tent [tent] Zelt
terrible [ˈterəbl] schrecklich, fürchterlich
terrorism [ˈterərɪzəm] Terrorismus
test [test] 1. testen, prüfen; 2. Test, Prüfung
than [ðæn]: **nicer than** schöner als
thank [θæŋk]: **Thank you.** Danke (schön). **Thanks.** [θæŋks] Danke.
that [ðæt] 1. das; der/die/das (da); 2. dass; 3. der/die/das *(in Relativsätzen)*; **that's why** deshalb, darum; **That's £8.45.** Das macht 8 Pfund 45. **That's what friends are for.** Dazu sind Freunde da.
the [ðə, ði] der/die/das
their [ðeə] ihr/ihre
theirs [ðeəz] ihre/ihrer/ihres
them [ðem, ðəm] ihnen/sie
themselves [ðəmˈselvz] sich (selbst)
then [ðen] dann
there [ðeə] da, dort; dahin, dorthin; **there are** da sind, es gibt, es sind; **there's (= there is)** da ist, es gibt, es ist
these [ðiːz] diese, die (hier); **these days** heutzutage

they [ðeɪ] sie
thief, thieves [θiːf, θiːvz] Dieb/Diebin, Diebe/Diebinnen
thin [θɪn] dünn
thing [θɪŋ] Ding, Sache
think [θɪŋk] finden, meinen; glauben; (nach)denken; **think of** denken an; **I think so, too.** Das finde ich auch. **I don't think so.** Das finde ich nicht.
thirsty [ˈθɜːsti] durstig; **I'm thirsty.** Ich habe Durst.
this [ðɪs] dies/das (hier); diese/dieser/dieses; **this morning/afternoon/evening** heute Morgen/Nachmittag/Abend
those [ðəʊz] diese, jene, die (da)
thought [θɔːt]: **I thought** ich dachte / ich habe gedacht (usw.); **I've thought** ich habe gedacht (usw.)
threw [θruː]: **I threw** ich warf / ich habe geworfen
through [θruː] durch, hindurch
throw [θrəʊ] werfen
thrown [θrəʊn]: **I've thrown** ich habe geworfen
Thursday [ˈθɜːzdeɪ, ˈθɜːzdi] Donnerstag
ticket [ˈtɪkɪt] Fahrkarte; Eintrittskarte
tidy [ˈtaɪdi] 1. aufräumen; 2. ordentlich, aufgeräumt
tiger [ˈtaɪgə] Tiger
till [tɪl] bis
time [taɪm] Zeit; Uhrzeit; **What time is it?** Wie spät ist es? **at any time** jederzeit; **in time** rechtzeitig; **this time** diesmal; **a waste of time** Zeitverschwendung
timetable [ˈtaɪmteɪbl] Stundenplan; Fahrplan
tip [tɪp] Tipp, Hinweis
tired [ˈtaɪəd] müde
to [tuː, tu, tə] 1. zu, nach, an; 2. vor; 3. bis; 4. um … zu; **start to run** beginnen zu rennen; **I've been to …** Ich bin in/bei … gewesen. **quarter to** Viertel vor
toast [təʊst] 1. toasten *(Brot rösten)*; 2. Toast(brot)
toaster [ˈtəʊstə] Toaster
today [təˈdeɪ] heute
together [təˈgeðə] zusammen
toilet [ˈtɔɪlət] Toilette

told [təʊld]: **I told** ich erzählte / ich habe erzählt
tolerate ['tɒləreɪt] tolerieren, dulden; sich gefallen lassen
tomorrow [tə'mɒrəʊ] morgen
tonight [tə'naɪt] heute Abend; heute Nacht
too [tu:] 1. auch; 2. **too late** zu spät
took [tʊk]: **I took** ich nahm (mit) / ich habe (mit)genommen (usw.)
tool [tu:l] Werkzeug
toothache ['tu:θeɪk] Zahnschmerzen
top [tɒp]: **at the top** auf der Spitze; **top ten** die Top 10, die wichtigsten 10
torch [tɔ:tʃ] Taschenlampe
touch [tʌtʃ] berühren, anfassen
tough [tʌf] hart, schwer
tour [tʊə] Tour, Reise; Rundgang
tourist ['tʊərɪst] Tourist/Touristin; **tourist office** Touristeninformation, Fremdenverkehrsbüro
towards [tə'wɔ:dz]: auf ... zu, in Richtung
town [taʊn] Stadt; **go to town** in die Stadt gehen; **in town** in der (Innen-)Stadt; **town hall** Rathaus
toy [tɔɪ] Spielzeug
track [træk] Rennstrecke
traffic ['træfɪk] Verkehr
train [treɪn] Zug, Eisenbahn
train [treɪn] dressieren, abrichten; **train as** ausgebildet werden zum/zur
trainer ['treɪnə] Sportschuh
trainer ['treɪnə]: **fitness trainer** Fitnesstrainer/Fitnesstrainerin
tram [træm] Straßenbahn
travel ['trævl] reisen, fahren; **travel agency** Reisebüro; **travel around the city** durch die Stadt fahren; **travelling salespeople** Handelsreisende, Vertreter/Vertreterinnen
tree [tri:] Baum
trick [trɪk] Trick
trifle ['traɪfl] Trifle *(brit. Süßspeise)*
trip [trɪp] Ausflug, Reise
trust [trʌst] vertrauen
try [traɪ] versuchen, probieren; **try on** anprobieren
Tuesday ['tju:zdeɪ, 'tju:zdi] Dienstag
tunnel ['tʌnl] Tunnel

turn [tɜ:n] abbiegen, einbiegen; **turn left/right (into)** nach links/rechts abbiegen (in); **turn back** umkehren, zurückgehen
TV ['ti:'vi:] Fernsehen; Fernsehgerät; **TV programme** Fernsehsendung; **on TV** im Fernsehen; **watch TV** fernsehen
twice [twaɪs] zweimal

U

uncle ['ʌŋkl] Onkel
uncomfortable [ʌn'kʌmftəbl] unbequem
under ['ʌndə] unter
underground ['ʌndəgraʊnd] U-Bahn
understand [ʌndə'stænd] verstehen
understood [ʌndə'stʊd]: **I understood** ich verstand / ich habe verstanden
unemployed [ʌnɪm'plɔɪd] arbeitslos
unfriendly [ʌn'frendli] unfreundlich
unhappy [ʌn'hæpi] unglücklich
United Kingdom [ju:'naɪtɪd'kɪŋdəm] Vereinigtes Königreich
unlucky [ʌn'lʌki]: **we were unlucky** wir hatten Pech
unpack [ʌn'pæk] auspacken
untidy [ʌn'taɪdi] unordentlich, unaufgeräumt
up [ʌp] hinauf/herauf
upset stomach ['ʌpset'stʌmək] Magenverstimmung
upside down [ʌpsaɪd'daʊn] mit dem Kopf nach unten; verkehrt herum
upstairs [ʌp'steəz] oben (im Haus); nach oben
Urdu ['ʊədu:] Urdu
us [ʌs] uns
use [ju:z] benutzen, verwenden
used [ju:zt, ju:zd]: **get used to** sich gewöhnen an; **it's used for sending ...** es wird benutzt, um ... zu schicken
useful ['ju:sfʊl] nützlich
user ['ju:zə] Benutzer/Benutzerin
usually ['ju:ʒʊəli] meistens, normalerweise, gewöhnlich

V

Valentine's Day ['væləntaɪnzdeɪ] Valentinstag
van [væn] Lieferwagen, Kleinbus
vanilla [və'nɪlə] Vanille
vegetable ['vedʒtəbl] Gemüse
vegetarian [vedʒə'teəriən] Vegetarier/Vegetarierin
verb [vɜ:b] Verb, Zeitwort
very ['veri] sehr; **(like) very much** sehr (gern mögen)
video ['vɪdiəʊ] Videofilm, Video
video-recorder ['vɪdiəʊrɪ'kɔ:də] Videorecorder
village ['vɪlɪdʒ] Dorf
vinegar ['vɪnɪgə] Essig
visit ['vɪzɪt] 1. besuchen; besichtigen; 2. Besuch, Aufenthalt
voice [vɔɪs] Stimme

W

wait [weɪt] warten; **wait for** warten auf
waiter ['weɪtə] Kellner, Ober
waitress ['weɪtrəs] Kellnerin
wake [weɪk] wecken, aufwecken
Wales [weɪlz] Wales
walk [wɔ:k] (zu Fuß) gehen, laufen; wandern; **go for a walk** spazieren gehen; **take the dog for a walk** mit dem Hund rausgehen, spazieren gehen
walkman ['wɔ:kmən] Walkman
wall [wɔ:l] Wand, Mauer
want [wɒnt] wollen; **want to go** gehen wollen
warden ['wɔ:dn] 1. Herbergsmutter/Herbergsvater; 2. Heimleiter/Heimleiterin
warm [wɔ:m] warm
was [wɒz, wəz]: **I was** ich war
wash [wɒʃ]: **have a wash** sich waschen; **wash the dishes** (Geschirr) spülen; **wash up** abwaschen, spülen
washing-machine ['wɒʃɪŋmə'ʃi:n] Waschmaschine
waste [weɪst]: **a waste of time** Zeitverschwendung

watch [wɒtʃ] zusehen, sich anschauen, beobachten; **watch TV** Fernsehen
water ['wɔːtə] Wasser; **water chute** Wasserrutsche
way [weɪ] Weg; **a long way from** weit entfernt von
we [wiː] wir
wear [weə] tragen, anziehen
weather ['weðə] Wetter
web [web]: **word web** „Wortnetz"
Wednesday ['wenzdeɪ, 'wenzdi] Mittwoch
week [wiːk] Woche
weekday ['wiːkdeɪ] Wochentag
weekend [ˌwiːk'end] Wochenende; **at the weekend** am Wochenende
welcome ['welkəm] begrüßen; willkommen heißen; **Welcome to …** Willkommen in/im/bei …
well [wel] gut
Well, … [wel] Nun, …
Welsh [welʃ] walisisch; Walisisch; Waliser/Waliserin
went [went]: **I went** ich ging, fuhr / ich bin gegangen, gefahren
were [wɜː]: **you were** du warst; ihr wart; Sie waren
west [west] West-; (nach) Westen; westlich
wet [wet] nass, feucht
what [wɒt] 1. was; 2. welche/welcher/welches; **What a …!** Was für ein/eine …! **What about …?** Wie wäre es mit …? Was ist mit …? **What colour is …?** Welche Farbe hat …? **What ... for?** Wofür …? **What sort of…?** Was für …? **What time is it?** Wie spät ist es? **What's it like?** Wie ist es? **What's the matter?** Was ist los? **What's this/… in English?** Was heißt dies/… auf Englisch? **What's wrong with you?** Was hast du? Was ist los mit dir? **What's your name?** Wie heißt du? / Wie heißen Sie?
wheel [wiːl] Rad; **Meals on Wheels** Essen auf Rädern
when [wen] 1. wann; 2. wenn; 3. als; **When's the next train to Chester?** Wann fährt der nächste Zug nach Chester?
where [weə] wo; wohin; **Where are you from?** Wo kommst du her? / Wo kommen Sie her?
which [wɪtʃ] welche/welcher/welches
while [waɪl] während
whisky ['wɪski] Whisky
white [waɪt] weiß
who [huː] 1. wer; 2. der/die/das *(in Relativsätzen)*
whole [həʊl] ganz
why [waɪ] warum, weshalb; **that's why** deshalb, darum
wife, wives [waɪf, waɪvz] Ehefrau, Ehefrauen
will [wɪl]: **I will** (= **I'll** [aɪl]) ich werde
win [wɪn] gewinnen
window ['wɪndəʊ] Fenster, Schaufenster
windsurfing ['wɪndsɜːfɪŋ] Windsurfen
windy ['wɪndi] windig
winter ['wɪntə] Winter
with [wɪð] mit; bei
without [wɪð'aʊt] ohne
woke [wəʊk]: **I woke her** ich weckte sie (auf) / ich habe sie (auf)geweckt
woken ['wəʊkən]: **I've woken her** ich habe sie (auf)geweckt
woman, women ['wʊmən, 'wɪmɪn] Frau, Frauen
won [wʌn]: **I won** ich gewann / ich habe gewonnen
won't [wəʊnt] (= **will not**): **I won't** ich werde nicht
wood [wʊd] 1. Holz; 2. Wald
word [wɜːd] Wort; **word web** „Wortnetz"
wore [wɔː]: **I wore** ich trug, zog an / ich habe getragen, angezogen
work [wɜːk] 1. arbeiten; funktionieren; 2. Arbeit; **at work** bei der Arbeit; **go to work** arbeiten gehen; **out of work** arbeitslos
work experience ['wɜːk ɪkˈspɪəriəns] Berufspraktikum
worker ['wɜːkə] Arbeiter/Arbeiterin
working dog ['wɜːkɪŋdɒg] „arbeitender Hund" *(für eine bestimmte Arbeit abgerichteter Hund)*
working hours ['wɜːkɪŋˈaʊəz] Arbeitszeit
world [wɜːld] Welt; **in the world** auf der (ganzen) Welt
worn [wɔːn]: **I've worn** ich habe getragen, angezogen
worry ['wʌri] sich Sorgen machen, beunruhigt sein; **Don't worry.** Mach dir keine Sorgen.
would [wʊd]: **Would you like …?** Möchtest du / Möchten Sie …? **I'd like** [aɪd'laɪk] (= **I would like**) … Ich möchte … / Ich hätte gern … **I'd like to go.** Ich möchte gehen.
write [raɪt] schreiben
written ['rɪtn]: **I've written** ich habe geschrieben
wrong [rɒŋ] falsch; **What's wrong with you?** Was hast du? Was ist los mit dir? **You're wrong.** Du hast / Sie haben Unrecht.
wrote [rəʊt]: **I wrote** ich schrieb / ich habe geschrieben

Y

year [jɪə] Jahr; Jahrgang
yellow ['jeləʊ] gelb
yes [jes] ja
yesterday ['jestədeɪ, 'jestədi] gestern
yet [jet]: **not … yet** noch nicht
yoghurt ['jɒgət] Joghurt
you [juː] 1. du; ihr; Sie 2. man
young [jʌŋ] jung
your [jɔː] dein/deine; euer/eure; Ihr/Ihre
yours [jɔːz] deine(r, s); Ihre(r, s); eure(r, s); **Yours faithfully, …** Mit freundlichen Grüßen …
yourself [jɔː'self] dir/dich (selbst)
yourselves [jɔː'selvz] euch (selbst); sich (selbst)
youth club ['juːθklʌb] Jugendclub
youth hostel ['juːθhɒstl] Jugendherberge; **youth hostel card** Jugendherbergsausweis
youth worker ['juːθwɜːkə] Jugendpfleger/Jugendpflegerin

Z

zoo [zuː] Zoo

List of names

■ PLACES

Abbeydale [ˈæbideɪl]
Alton Towers [ˈɔːltənˈtaʊəz]
Bahamas [bəˈhɑːməz]
Bangalore [bæŋgəˈlɔː]
Barbados [bɑːˈbeɪdɒs]
Bessemer Close [ˈbesɪməkləʊs]
Bombay/Mumbai [bɒmˈbeɪ/ˈmumbaɪ]
Bradford [ˈbrædfəd]
Calais [ˈkæleɪ]
Chennai/Madras [ˈtʃənaɪ/məˈdrɑːs]
Crewe [kruː]
Darnall [ˈdɑːnəl]
Derbyshire [ˈdɑːbɪʃə]
Endcliffe Park [ˈendklɪfˈpɑːk]
Grindleford [ˈgrɪndlfəd]
Highgate [ˈhaɪgeɪt]
Jamaica [dʒəˈmeɪkə]
Kingston [ˈkɪŋstən]
Leopold Street [ˈliːəpəʊldstriːt]
North America [nɔːθəˈmerɪkə]
Paris [ˈpærɪs]
Peace Gardens [ˈpiːsgɑːdnz]
Peak District [ˈpiːkˈdɪstrɪkt]
Perth [pɜːθ]
Pinstone Street [ˈpɪnstəʊnstriːt]
Quebec [kwɪˈbek]
Sharrow [ˈʃærəʊ]
Sheffield [ˈʃefiːld]
Sheffield Arena [ˈʃefiːldəˈriːnə]
Sligo [ˈslaɪgəʊ]
South America [saʊθəˈmerɪkə]
Sydney [ˈsɪdni]
Tobago [təˈbeɪgəʊ]
Trinidad [ˈtrɪnɪdæd]
Tudor Square [ˈtjuːdəˈskweə]

■ OTHER NAMES

Bookworm [ˈbʊkwɜːm]
Brightways [ˈbraɪtweɪz]
Coffee Pot [ˈkɒfipɒt]
Coronation Street [kɒrəˈneɪʃnstriːt]
Daisy [ˈdeɪzi]
Eastenders [iːstˈendəz]
Flash [flæʃ]
Inuit [ˈɪnuɪt]
Jess [dʒes]
Joseph Parry [ˈdʒəʊzɪfˈpæri]
Marathon [ˈmærəθən]
Meadowhall [ˈmedəʊhɔːl]
Midlands College [ˈmɪdləndzˈkɒlɪdʒ]
Oasis [əʊˈeɪsɪs]
Ralph Waldo Emerson [ˈrælfˈwɔːldəʊˈeməsən]
Rover [ˈrəʊvə]
Samaritans [səˈmærɪtənz]
Sammy [ˈsæmi]
Sat 1 [sætˈwʌn]
Sharks! [ʃɑːks]
Sky [skaɪ]
Sparkbrook [ˈspɑːkbrʊk]
Supertram [ˈsuːpətræm]
The Big Issue [ðəbɪgˈɪʃuː]
The Queen [ðəˈkwiːn]
Trend [trend]
Tunnel of Love [ˈtʌnləvˈlʌv]
Unplugged [ʌnˈplʌgd]
Voyager [ˈvɔɪɪdʒə]
Wheels [wiːlz]

■ GIRLS/WOMEN

Beth [beθ]
Clare [kleə]
Donna ['dɒnə]
Fatima ['fɑːtɪmə]
Geeta [giːtɑː]
Gemma ['dʒemə]
Jade [dʒeɪd]
Joanna [dʒəʊ'ænə]
Jody ['dʒəʊdi]
Katy ['keɪti]
Kristy ['krɪsti]
Lara ['lɑːrə]
Marian ['mæriən]
Natalie ['nætəli]
Rebecca [rɪ'bekə]
Shellina [ʃeliːnə]
Sophie ['səʊfi]
Susan ['suːzn]
Tanya ['tɑːniə]
Tess [tes]

■ BOYS/MEN

Alex [ælɪg'z]
Alexander [ælɪg'zɑːndə]
Ali ['ɑːli]
Andy ['ændi]
Brian ['braɪən]
Daniel ['dænjəl]
Darren ['dærən]
David ['deɪvɪd]
Gerald ['dʒerəld]
Ian ['iːən]
Imran ['ɪmrɑːn]
Jack [dʒæk]
Linford ['lɪnfɔːd]
Mirza ['mɪəzɑː]
Mohammed [məʊ'hæmɪd]
Neville ['nevl]
Phil [fɪl]
Ras [ræs]
Ray [reɪ]
Rob [rɒb]
Rod [rɒd]
Ross [rɒs]
Stephen ['stiːvn]
Thomas ['tɒməs]
Trevor ['trevə]
Wayne [weɪn]

■ FAMILIES

Akbar ['ækbɑː]
Barker ['bɑːkə]
Barnes [bɑːnz]
Bolt [bəʊlt]
Canfield ['kænfiːld]
Chandler ['tʃɑːndlə]
Christie ['krɪsti]
Collins ['kɒlɪnz]
Cox [kɒks]
Homan ['həʊmən]
Hudson ['hʌdsn]
Kennedy ['kenədi]
Langley ['læŋli]
Longhurst ['lɒŋhɜːst]
Morris ['mɒrɪs]
Mushtaq ['mʊʃtək]
Palmer ['pɑːmə]
Proudfoot ['praʊdfʊt]
Rogers ['rɒdʒəz]
Saunders ['sɔːndəz]
Skelton ['skeltən]
Stokes [stəʊks]
Toft [tɒft]

Irregular verbs

INFINITIVE FORM
(Grundform)

SIMPLE PAST FORM
(Einfache Vergangenheit)

PRESENT PERFECT FORM
(Vollendete Gegenwart)

be	I was, you were, she was	I've been	sein
have	I had	I've had	haben
do	I did	I've done [dʌn]	tun, machen
become	I became	I've become	werden
bet	I bet	I've bet	wetten
bite	I bit	I've bitten	beißen
break	I broke	I've broken	brechen, zerbrechen
bring	I brought	I've brought	bringen, mitbringen
build	I built	I've built	bauen
buy	I bought	I've bought	kaufen
choose	I chose	I've chosen	(aus)wählen, aussuchen
come	I came	I've come	kommen
cost	it cost	it has cost	kosten
draw	I drew	I've drawn	zeichnen
drink	I drank	I've drunk	trinken
drive	I drove	I've driven ['drɪvn]	fahren
eat	I ate [et]	I've eaten	essen
fall	I fell	I've fallen	fallen
feed	I fed	I've fed	füttern
feel	I felt	I've felt	(sich) fühlen
find	I found	I've found	finden
forget	I forgot	I've forgotten	vergessen
get	I got	I've got	bekommen; besorgen
give	I gave	I've given	geben; schenken
go	I went	I've gone [gɒn]	gehen, fahren
grow	I grew	I've grown	anpflanzen, heranziehen
hear	I heard [hɜːd]	I've heard [hɜːd]	hören
hit	I hit	I've hit	schlagen
hold	I held	I've held	halten
hurt	I hurt	I've hurt	verletzen
keep	I kept	I've kept	halten, behalten
know	I knew	I've known	wissen; kennen
leave	I left	I've left	lassen; verlassen
lie	I lay	I've lain	liegen
lose	I lost	I've lost	verlieren
make	I made	I've made	machen
mean	I meant [ment]	I've meant [ment]	bedeuten; meinen
meet	I met	I've met	treffen; kennenlernen
pay	I paid	I've paid	zahlen, bezahlen
put	I put	I've put	stellen; legen
read	I read [red]	I've read [red]	lesen, vorlesen
ride	I rode	I've ridden	(rad)fahren

INFINITIVE FORM (Grundform)	**SIMPLE PAST FORM** (Einfache Vergangenheit)	**PRESENT PERFECT FORM** (Vollendete Gegenwart)	
ring	I rang	I've rung	klingeln, läuten
run	I ran	I've run	rennen, laufen
say	I said [sed]	I've said [sed]	sagen
see	I saw	I've seen	sehen; besichtigen
sell	I sold	I've sold	verkaufen
send	I sent	I've sent	senden, schicken
show	I showed	I've shown	zeigen
sing	I sang	I've sung	singen
sit	I sat	I've sat	sitzen; sich setzen
sleep	I slept	I've slept	schlafen
speak	I spoke	I've spoken	sprechen
spend	I spent	I've spent	*(Zeit)* verbringen
stand	I stood	I've stood	stehen
steal	I stole	I've stolen	stehlen
swim	I swam	I've swum	schwimmen
take	I took	I've taken	nehmen, mitnehmen
teach	I taught	I've taught	beibringen, unterrichten
tell	I told	I've told	erzählen; sagen
think	I thought	I've thought	finden; glauben; denken
throw	I threw	I've thrown	werfen
understand	I understood	I've understood	verstehen
wake	I woke	I've woken	wecken, aufwecken
wear	I wore	I've worn	tragen, anziehen
win	I won	I've won	gewinnen
write	I wrote	I've written	schreiben

Quellen

BILDQUELLEN

Arakaki/IFA-Bilderteam, Düsseldorf (S. 79 unten rechts); B. Bachmann/Okapia, Frankfurt (S. 42 unten Mitte links); Anna Baker, York (S. 21 Fotos A-D; S. 38 oben rechts; S. 44 oben links; S. 50 oben rechts; S. 51 oben rechts; S. 98 oben links u. Mitte rechts; S. 103 unten Fotos A-D; S. 107 oben rechts; S. 110 oben links; S. 111 Foto 1-5; S. 112 oben rechts; S. 115 oben rechts); Bavaria, Gauting (S. 43 unten links); BBC, London (S. 50 Mitte links u. Mitte Mitte; S. 51 Mitte rechts); Tim Beddow/Tony Stone, Hamburg (S. 96 unten links); Belfast Exposed, Belfast (S. 69 Mitte rechts); Daimler Benz, Untertürkheim (S. 114 Foto C links); Bildarchiv Engelmeier, München (S. 51 Mitte links); John Birdsall, Nottingham (S. 25 oben Mitte u. oben rechts); S. Bongarts Sportfotografie, Hamburg (S. 56 unten rechts); H.R. Bramaz/Bavaria, Gauting (S. 89 oben links Hintergrundbild); Darrin Braybrook/Sportimage, Hamburg (S. 43 Mitte links u. Mitte rechts); British Tourist Authority, Frankfurt a.M. (S. 100 Mitte rechts); Graham Burns/Environmental Images, London (S. 72 Foto 5); Bygott Photos, Oxford (S. 16 Fotos A-G; S. 68 Fotos A-D; S. 70 Foto A, B, C, F, G; S. 88 Foto A, B, E, F, H, I); Carlton Television, London (S. 50 Mitte rechts); J. Allan Cash, London (S. 9 Mitte oben; S. 26 oben links; S. 38 Mitte links); Luis Castaneda/Image Bank, Berlin (S. 17 oben Hintergrund); Cirotteau-Lambolez/Vandystadt/Focus, Hamburg (S. 18 Foto 5); City Treasury, Sheffield (S. 62 oben links; S. 65 oben links); Cornelsen Verlag, Berlin (S. 57 Foto C); Creastock/Bavaria, Düsseldorf (S. 71 oben Hintergrundbild); Cyberimage/Tony Stone Bilderwelten, Hamburg (S. 79 unten links); Destination Sheffield, Sheffield (S. 15 oben rechts; S. 20 Mitte rechts; S. 72 Mitte rechts; S. 99 oben Mitte links u. Mitte rechts); Diaphor/Superbild, Berlin (S. 53 oben Hintergrundbild); Döhrn/PhotoPress, Stockdorf/München (S. 89 unten rechts); David Dore, Guildford (S. 69 Mitte links; S. 92 oben rechts); Tony Duffy/Tony Stone Bilderwelten, Hamburg (S. 79 oben Mitte); Steve Dunwell/Image Bank, Berlin (S. 18 Foto 2); Ermert/Zefa, Hamburg (S. 115 Mitte links); Geoff du Feu/Helga Lade, Berlin (S. 78/79 Hintergrundbild); Fischer/IFA Bilderteam, Düsseldorf (S. 35 Mitte rechts); Mike Ford, Sheffield (S. 6 Mitte links und Fotos 1-4 unten; S. 7 Mitte oben, Mitte und unten rechts; S. 8 Mitte rechts und unten links; S. 10 oben rechts; S. 14 oben rechts und Mitte links; S. 26 Mitte links; S. 28 oben rechts; S. 29 oben Fotos 1-4; S. 32 oben rechts u. unten rechts; S. 33 oben rechts u. Mitte rechts; S. 36 Mitte rechts; S. 39 Fotos A-F; S. 44 unten links; S. 45 oben rechts; S. 62 Mitte links; S. 63 oben rechts; S. 64 oben rechts; S. 65 oben rechts u. Mitte links; S. 75 Foto C; S. 81 unten rechts; S. 82 oben rechts u. Mitte rechts u. unten rechts; S. 83 oben rechts); Franklin/Magnum/Focus, Hamburg (S. 18 Foto 1); Gazidis/Greenpeace, Amsterdam (S. 72 Foto 1); Globe Press/Transglobe Agency, Hamburg (S. 61 oben links); Gottschalk/IFA-Bilderteam, Düsseldorf (S. 42 Mitte links u. Mitte rechts; S. 43 Mitte Mitte); Peter Grumann/Image Bank, Berlin (S. 18 Foto 6); Haigh/IFA-Bilderteam, München (S. 6 oben rechts); Hearing Dogs for the Deaf, Training Centre, Oxford (S. 103 oben links); Herdt/PhotoPress, Stockdorf/München (S. 96 Mitte rechts); J. Heron/IFA Bilderteam, Düsseldorf (S. 35 oben links); Robert Holland/Image Bank, Berlin (S. 18 Foto 4); Hunter/IFA-Bilderteam, Düsseldorf (S. 79 oben rechts); IFA-Bilderteam, Düsseldorf (S. 60 unten links, S. 79 Mitte rechts); IFA-Bilderteam - Fotostock B.V, Düsseldorf (S. 110 Mitte rechts); Impact/Liz Thompson/Tony Stone, Hamburg (S. 42 u. 43 Hintergrundbild); Int. Stock/IFA Bilderteam, Düsseldorf (S. 38 Mitte rechts, S. 78 unten links); B. Jorjorian/Tony Stone Images, Hamburg (S. 35 oben, Hintergrundbild); Barbara Jung, Berlin (S. 57 Foto A u. B; S. 61 Mitte links; S. 70 Foto E); Kai/Environmental Images (S. 72 Foto 3); Pawel Kanicki/Transglobe, Hamburg (S. 114 Foto C rechts); Catherine Karnow/Woodfin Camp/Focus, Hamburg (S. 24 unten rechts); Keetwan/PhotoPress, Stockdorf/München (S. 89 oben rechts Hintergrundbild); Keystone, Hamburg (S. 43 unten rechts); Tom King/Image Bank, Berlin (S. 9 unten links); Kinoarchiv Engelmeier, Hamburg (S. 52 Foto A-F); Klein & Hubert/Bios/Okapia, Frankfurt (S. 42 unten links u. unten rechts); Michael Kunkel/Bongarts Sportpressephoto, Hamburg (S. 56 oben links); Lally, York (S. 86 oben rechts u. Mitte rechts; S. 88 Foto D u. G); Sally Lancaster/Format, London (S. 25 Mitte links); J.-M. Loubat/Vandystadt/Focus, Hamburg (S. 9 Foto D); Meadowhall Centre, Sheffield (S. 20 Fotos oben links und unten links; S.20 Karte oben rechts); Mehta, Dilip/Contact/Focus, Hamburg (S. 61 unten rechts); Michael J. Morgan/Harris Morgan & Son, Bicester (S. 104 oben Mitte); Mitchell/Greenpeace, Amsterdam (S. 72 Foto 4); Nimtsch/Greenpeace, Amsterdam (S. 75 Foto B); Joanne O'Brian/Format, London (S. 88 Foto C); Picture Bank, Kingston (S. 106 oben rechts); Ulrike Preuss/ Format, London (S. 35 oben rechts); Henrik Pohl, Berlin (S. 17 Mitte Mitte und Mitte rechts); Ponds Forge, Sheffield (S. 99 Foto oben links, oben Mitte und oben rechts); The Post Office, London (S. 103 Foto A); Pascal Quittemelle/Transglobe Agency, Hamburg (S. 79 oben links); Hans Reinhard/Okapia, Frankfurt (S. 60/61 Hintergrundbild); Rex Features, London (S. 9 oben rechts und oben links); Richardson/Transglobe, Hamburg (S. 60 oben rechts); Paul Robson, York (S. 70 Foto D; S. 75 Foto D; S. 88 Foto J; S. 114 A links u. rechts, B links, D links u. rechts; S. 117 Foto A-E); Alan Root/Okapia, Frankfurt (S. 42 unten Mitte rechts); Bob Sacha/Focus, Hamburg (S. 24-25 Hintergrund); Safeway Stores, Hayes, Middlesex (S. 114 Foto B rechts); Dorothee Schledz, Berlin (S. 24 oben Mitte; S. 42 oben links; S. 60 oben links; S. 78 unten links); H. Schrempp/Okapia, Frankfurt (S. 102 oben rechts); Flip Schulke/Transglobe, Hamburg (S. 8 oben links); Barbara Schumacher, Berlin (S. 25 oben links u. Mitte rechts u. unten links und rechts); Selma/IFA Bilderteam, Düsseldorf (S. 38 unten rechts); Sheffield City Airport, Sheffield (S. 65 Mitte rechts); Sheffield Ski Village, Sheffield (S. 30 oben); Shout, Northants (S. 104 Mitte rechts; S. 108 oben Hintergrundbild); South Yorkshire Supertram Ltd., Sheffield (S. 72 unten rechts); Martin Stott/Environmental Images, London (S. 72 Foto 2); Oliver Strewe/Tony Stone Bilderwelten, Hamburg (S. 43 oben links; S. 97 unten links); Sports File/Focus, Hamburg (S. 18, Foto 3); Michael Tavorka/Tony Stone Bilderwelten, Hamburg (S. 79 Mitte links); Teubner, Füssen (S. 61 Mitte rechts); The Image Bank, Berlin (S. 35 Mitte links); The Sheffield Colleges, Sheffield (S. 80 Mitte links); David Townsend/Environmental Images, London (S. 75 Foto A); Transglobe Agency, Hamburg (S. 61 oben links und oben rechts); Penny Tweedie/Tony Stone Bilderwelten (S. 43 oben rechts); Jay Ullal/Picture Press, Hamburg (S. 60 oben rechts; S. 61 unten links); R. Valacher/Bios/Okapia, Berlin (S. 78 unten rechts); Walmsley, Guildford (S. 80 oben links; S. 87 Mitte rechts); Welsh/IFA-Bilderteam, Düsseldorf (S. 56 unten links); Wolf/PhotoPress, Stockdorf/München (S. 97 oben rechts); Adam Woolfitt/Woodfin Camp/Focus, Hamburg (S. 24 unten links)

Einband Lupe Cunha Photo Library, London

LIEDQUELLEN

I want to be free (Willcox, Toyah/Bogen, Joel) © Mambo Music Verlags + Produktions GmbH + Co KG (Sony Music Publishing)
Where do the children play? (von Cat Stevens - Text und Musik: Cat Stevens) Copyright © 1970 Cat Music Limited

TEXTQUELLEN

The Language of Friendship ed. by Susan Polis Schutz. © 1977 Edition Athena International